Revolutions and History

D1439993

To my parents, who often listened to me talking of what I planned
to write, but did not live to see the product

Revolutions and History

An Essay in Interpretation

Noel Parker

Polity Press

First published in 1999 by Polity Press
in association with Blackwell Publishers Ltd

Editorial office:
Polity Press
65 Bridge Street
Cambridge CB2 1UR, UK

Marketing and production:
Blackwell Publishers Ltd
108 Cowley Road
Oxford OX4 1JF, UK

Published in the USA by
Blackwell Publishers Inc.
Commerce Place
350 Main Street
Malden, MA 02148, USA

ISBN 0-7456-1135-4
ISBN 0-7456-1136-2 (pbk)

A catalogue record for this book is available from the British Library.

Library of Congress Cataloging-in-Publication Data

Parker, Noel, 1945–
    Revolutions and history : an essay in interpretation / Noel Parker.
        p.   cm.
    Includes bibliographical references (p.   ) and index.
    ISBN 0-7456-1135-4. — ISBN 0-7456-1136-2 (pbk.)
    1. Revolutions—History.   2. History—Philosophy   I. Title.
D16.9.P2654   1999
306.6'4'09—dc21   99-10927
                                                                          CIP

Typeset in 10.5 on 12 pt Times Roman by Ace Filmsetting Ltd, Frome, Somerset
Printed in Great Britain by MPG Books Ltd, Bodmin, Cornwall

This book is printed on acid-free paper.

Contents

Acknowledgements

This book is the outcome of work carried on over a number of years. There are, accordingly, many people who have offered help along the way. The British Open University, in particular its Social Science Faculty, gave me both the initial push to get into the topic and assistance, with facilities and research funding, to develop my ideas over the years from 1990. My colleagues in the Department of Linguistic and International Studies found space for me to pursue my own line of thinking in the European Studies Section, and tolerated my absence in Denmark for the last six months as I brought the project to completion. David Held of Polity Press has maintained faith in my commitment to complete a book that the Press would want to publish. During 1998, I have had the extraordinary good fortune to be a guest at the Center for Cultural Studies of the University of Århus and the Dansk Udenrigspolitisk Institut in Copenhagen. In both institutions, the research facilities and warmth of the welcome extended to me have been vital to me in finalizing my ideas and my text. Members of the European Studies Section of the Center at Århus, and also of the History Seminar of the University of Odense, have listened patiently to my explanations of the ideas contained in the book and asked questions about my historical interpretations which the final text has greatly benefited from. Bill Armstrong, Maurice Hutt, Lloyd Spencer and Grahame Thompson, along with an anonymous reader from Polity Press, have all taken the trouble to labour through the penultimate draft and offer comments which have helped me to amendments that make this a better book than it might otherwise be. The failings that persist are, unhappily, mine. Last, and anything but least, my immediate family – Iben, Lewis and Nick – have, each in their way, shown affection and interest which encouraged me in my labours but kept before me the truth that there are other more important things in life.

Introduction: Meanings of Revolution in Time and Space

This book is an 'essay' in the sense that it reflects on something: it considers a topic from a number of different points of view so as to offer insights for our understanding. But such reflections tend to be open-ended, or (if the reader is ill-disposed to them) inconclusive: so, it is also an essay in the sense of an attempt. The object of the reflections here is a phenomenon *and* an idea: revolution. From my perspective, the topic of revolution is very much a European/Western story. That is not to say that revolutions have occurred more often in Europe than elsewhere: indeed, the reverse is more likely true. Rather, revolution is 'European' in the sense that it has to be seen in the context of 'history', which is the other term in my title. And history at a world level must inevitably be traced back to Europe's intrusive relationship with the rest of the world during the modern period. Neither is it saying that revolution *remains* European, any more than the other outcomes of Europe's formative role in world history remain confined to Europe or reach their fullest development in Europe. Rather, like the state, the capitalist market, development, natural law and so on – in short, that is to say like 'modernity' itself – revolution has to be traced back to the spreading impact (for good and ill) of Europe and its 'modernizing' effects.[1]

But then we have a problem about revolution, which (as I shall try to explain over the length of the book) has to do precisely with the evolution of modernity at the world level. When, in 1972, John Dunn published the first edition of his classic *Modern Revolutions: An Introduction to the Analysis of a Political Phenomenon*, the subject was clear enough from the title. 'Modern' revolutions were a clearly identifiable group of socio-political events. Likewise, when Krishan Kumar published a selection of texts in 1971 under the title *Revolution: The Theory and Practice of a European Idea*, the range of texts could be predicted with confidence from the title. The impact, progressive rhetoric and socialist aspirations of revolutions could be taken for granted. The questions at issue followed from that: Why did revolutions happen when they did, in that sequence, and in what relation to particular circumstances? What was the strength of the revolutionary tradition? How did the individual case differ from, or modify, what the tradition envisaged? At the time Dunn and Kumar wrote their books, revolutions, in particular socialist revolutions, were – like it or not – an ongoing historical reality. Kumar followed a single sequence of texts; Dunn could pursue issues of explanation, political theory and the philosophy of action posed by a common sequence of events.[2]

But, increasingly since roughly the mid-1970s, the picture has changed. Revolutions now appear in too many modes for easy comprehension: as instant coups and as great upsurges, transcending or modifying the given boundaries of states, which then evaporate or change direction. The very expression 'revolution' may now be thought to embrace either a small number of cases, selected on apparently arbitrary grounds, or a vast range of political resistance, change or insurgency (Foran 1997, Tilly 1993). Revolutions are directed at outcomes as diverse as the rule of the Ayatollah or the approbation of the international financial community. Though frequent as ever, revolutions in the later decades of the twentieth century no longer appear to partake in any single historical process: their meaning and their historical role have become mysterious.

No definition will tell us authoritatively which particular events count as revolutions or not. That is tellingly illustrated by the designation of the *same* events by apparently opposite terms, such as 'restoration' or 'counter-revolution'. We manage to remain relatively confident about certain paradigm cases of revolution: France in 1789, Russia in 1917 etc. But even they *contain* 'reforms', 'coups', 'counter-revolutions', 'restorations' and so forth. And after them, the definitional picture gets hazier: England in the seventeenth century, or the USA in 1776? Sometimes Yes, sometimes No (I prefer Yes). What of Hungary in 1956, Romania in 1989? Almost certainly not. Part of the problem is that a failed revolution is in some sense a revolution – just as a broken glass *is* a glass, and a missed shot at a goal *is* a shot at goal. When it comes to a revolution, though, how and when do you decide that it has failed – and failed to do what exactly? When asked for his assessment of the French Revolution, the late Chinese prime minister, Chou En Lai, is reported to have replied that it was 'too early to say'. In the 1990s some are calling even the previously classic case of 1917 a failed revolution. (Its ambiguity is now such that, rather than consider 1917 alongside the historical context of its own time, I myself have chosen to defer my main treatment of it to the perspective of the end of the twentieth century – that is, in chapter 4.) In short, we have to delineate the field of revolutions through a definition which enables us to keep a weather eye on a historically changing group of events that epitomize 'revolution' for us.

The mere diversity of forms that revolutions have by now taken calls us to take stock. But that cannot just be a matter of asking again what common features can underpin analysis. This approach has been thoroughly, indeed painstakingly pursued by a number of analysts (DeFronzo 1991, Foran 1997, Goldstone 1986 and 1991, Greene 1974). Despite impressive results, the net effect of these efforts is to suggest that some new *dimension* of analysis is necessary if we are to avoid simply adding to an already long list further aspects of revolution which the theories of others have under-emphasized. Rather than pursuing ever-denser comparisons of common or distinguishing features, I suggest, we can approach revolutions as truly *historical* phenomena: asking not simply what they 'are', but also what connection they have with any kind of historical process. The coherence of the past conception of revolutions lay not only in likening one revolution to another, but also in being able to place them all in a coherent historical framework. It is confusion about the latter that leaves the field of 'revolutions' hard to determine.

I contend that we will not re-establish an understanding of revolution without also taking the measure of history and the understanding we have of history. It will not be possible, that is to say, to re-establish coherence in our understanding of revolutions without also addressing diachronous historical frameworks. Revolutions have always had a big part in the modern world's sense of history; just as broad lines perceived in history have always highlighted certain revolutions as models. Then the revolutions of 1989 brought us up with a shock. They showed how hazy the sense of history had become by the end of the twentieth century. Among commentators, it was recognized that 1989 represented a historic challenge: a seismic shift in the nature of Europe (Kumar 1992), or of revolution itself (Bauman 1994). It appeared, then, that a new historical paradigm for revolution was afoot.

Given those considerations, in this essay I deliberately intermingle *analytical* questions about revolutions with *historical* questions about large historical frameworks. Though one may start with a synchronic definition of revolutions, there is no avoiding the tension between synchronic analysis and diachronic evolution in the character of the world we are considering. The meaning of revolution (like other concepts for whatever has a primarily historical existence) has always quite properly been a matter of paradigm moments, with other more or less similar instances conceptually arranged around them. My initial aim will therefore be to review how revolutions have come to be grouped so as to possess historical significance. Though I offer below an initial, open-ended definition of 'revolution', the chapters following in Part I will fill that in with a discussion of how revolutions have themselves evolved over the course of history. This prompts a number of lines of questioning. Not only how have revolutions happened *in* past history, but also how have they been shaped *by* past history, and even how have they been *understood* in past history? And alongside all those: how have revolutions *shaped* history?

Part I then closes by posing those questions afresh for a different historical moment: how, at the end of the twentieth century, might it be said that history shapes, or is shaped by, revolutions? Given what has by then been established about revolutions over the course of past history, the answer I propose to those questions is sceptical: provocative to some, cheering to others. Revolutions are doomed to be more and more the passive effects of historical forces from outside. Yet it is also an answer charged with possibilities for further interpretation, which are pursued in Part II. For revolutions do not only 'matter' because they 'happen'. Revolutions have *always* been *more or less* passive effects of historical forces from outside. That has not prevented them, all the same, from having a role in past history. Because the *idea* of revolution has meaning. So Part II pursues the question of how that other role can be understood. The phoenix rises, transfigured: critics and supporters change places, perhaps. But before explaining the tenor of Part II, it is necessary to pursue the matter of definition further.

In moments or periods of revolution, deliberate, accelerated change is pursued with some degree of success. Let us say, then, that 'a revolution' consists of a sudden, profound, deliberately provoked crisis about legitimate power over a society, tending to produce an upheaval and change in both the political and the social spheres. There is a quantitative aspect to this definition: less profound, or slower change, or change which did not touch the full breadth of a society's social and political life would be excluded. The other key elements are change itself and some kind of wide-ranging intention to produce change. This definition implies an alteration in the holders and/or the structures of power in a society. In consequence, a revolution will usually involve specifically political change plus the threat of violence, and usually its actual use. Yet crises of legitimacy, political change and political violence all occur in many circumstances without a revolution: individually, therefore, these elements are not *defining* features of revolution. It is their combination with a more or less successful attempt at a profound structural change which makes events into a revolution.

This definition focuses attention on how revolutions overtake the normal capacities of the political and social order to reproduce itself, and break the continuity of a society's history. It points to revolutions as moments of intense historical movement, when processes of change in society go suddenly into top gear. So, the definition enables us to consider processes of social and political change within and without the given revolutions. And that, indeed, is a theme of the book: revolution as a paradigm, exemplary instance of the *modern experience of change*. I take change and the intention to change as key dimensions of revolution. The two have to be kept apart analytically: for many a revolution fails in the sense that it produces no serious change or (more commonly) that it produces largely *unintended* changes contrary to earlier intentions. Hence the caution of my earlier phrase about 'deliberately *provoked* crisis'; to provoke change is not to achieve it. It is more than possible that (as so often with social and historical processes) other forces or others' activities may overtake the purposes of those primarily engaged in the deliberate pursuit of revolutionary change. So I take the deliberate *pursuit* of change, with *some* effect, as a defining feature.

If we place change at the root of our concept of revolution, we will want terms by which to relate revolutions to change. In the circumstances where a revolution occurs, we may expect to be able to identify certain 'forces for change', social groupings or institutional pressures which more or less wittingly promote change: dissident intellectuals, governmental inertia, discontented military elites, articulate lower classes excluded from power and influence, etc. To select this sort of thing as the 'forces' for change is not, however, to identify the 'direction of change' which they foster: the dissident intellectuals, or others, may promote new, competing models of government; the discontented military are likely to have quite a different notion of the way forward from the politically excluded working class. Nor, of course, does the group of internal forces for change embrace the full set of 'conditions for change', which may well include external circumstances such as bad harvests or military intervention from outside. We need to keep these three concepts distinct, for the forces, directions and conditions of change may perfectly well not operate in alignment with one another. That is how we get change that contradicts the directions that appear to have been present beforehand, or confounds the preferences and efforts of some, or all, of the forces for change.

In the modern world, the priority accorded to change has meant that revolutionary change has become an explicit *aim*, or even a *boast* by those claiming to undertake a serious irreversible improvement. 'Revolutionary' leadership will often pronounce a programme and successfully disseminate claims about its achievement, even though they are going (perhaps unwittingly) in an altogether different direction.[3] Conversely, stable established regimes may construct a story of their nation's own 'revolutionary' past, thus claiming to be at least as revolutionary as the dissidents opposed to them. The British state's use of the 'Glorious Revolution' of 1688 (which first saw life as a mere *coup d'état* if ever there was one), or Mexico's oxymoronically named 'Institutional Revolutionary Party' exemplifies this tactic. Our problem is that, when examining revolutions, we have no definitive test of whether we have before us real *or* intended *or* even imagined change. This increases the need to set revolutions in a historical overview in order merely to delineate the field.

One final definitional point. There is a profusion of cognate terms for 'revolution', which need to be distinguished, though they cluster around revolution proper. Once again, we can discover no entirely clear-cut boundary between some of these cognate terms and 'revolution' itself. This is so most particularly with the terms 'rebellion' and 'revolt', two express-ions for violent uprising against existing power. Those often form a part of a revolution, as do what is referred to under a number of other expressions. *Putsch* and *coup d'état*, for example, are rapid, organized takeovers of the centres of power, conducted with military force and organization (though the latter term has now acquired a metaphorical sense which does not require military force). 'Insurgency' and 'guerrilla warfare', on the other hand, refer to longer-drawn-out actions against an established power, mounted away from its main centres – and, implicitly, as yet without success. 'Civil war', which again often occurs in the context of revolution proper, merely indicates warfare conducted *within* what is taken to be a single socio-political entity. It does not require that one side has rebelled against an 'established power' on the other. The parameters to distinguish 'revolution' from these other expressions are to be found in the breadth of the attack that the events mount against an established order. Typically, revolution embraces a bigger range of population, uses wider means of confrontation, and attacks the established power across the range of its manifestations.

I believe that the prospect of irreversible change, which is incorporated at the root of the above definition, is characteristic of modern history. It is this, indeed, which gives the idea of revolution much of its essential importance for the modern world's experience of history, and motivates the reflections in this essay. For *belief* in irreversible change in the socio-political world is a specific feature of the era of modern history. Before the last decade of the eighteenth century, the expression 'revolution' referred rather to *changes* from one state of affairs (power-holder etc.) to another, which could perfectly well be *repeated* from time to time – hence the idea of mere rotation in the etymology of the word. But a central modern belief is that *one-way* change, apparently in some direction or other, is normal, necessary or even good. This is a source of power, interest *and* difficulty for us in the *idea* of revolution. For it follows that there is a history of the *idea* of 'revolution', which takes place alongside history *simpliciter* (in-cluding the history of revolutions *simpliciter*) and has, at least in principle, to be kept analytically distinct. That is why Part II of this book can consider the historical role of the *idea* of 'revolution', separate from the account of historical revolutions in Part I.

Any objective sequence of events in which revolutions appear is inter-fused (like other events) with the *perceptions* that human actors *in* history have about their own places in some historical sequence (or indeed *stasis*). Perceptions double back, as it were, both upon events (actors behave according to where they *believe* events are going) and upon sequences of events. Others have shown how an account straddling revolutions and perceptions of resistance can mediate the theoretical opposition between theories stressing the role of global, structural forces and those more interested in motivation (DeFronzo 1991, Foran 1997). This was also the crucial strength that Kimmel found (1990, ch. 7) in the influential 'Tilly synthesis', in which the historical sociology of the modern state was shown to pose the conditions for revolutionary mobilization. Ideas of resistance and revolution have shown a remarkable capacity to traverse, and interact with, the spatio-historical formation of the modern state – yet not infrequently they have been *mis*applied or inverted in the process (Kimmel 1990, pp. 218–20). In Part II, I pursue that thought with a conception of how the form of the idea of revolution – taken as a historical reality in its own right, on a par with structural forces – moves and doubles back across historical time.

These shifts appear more complex and more interesting as we begin the twenty-first century, because the historical field has changed. The coherence of the field of 'revolutions' in the early 1970s lay not a little in the sense among participants in revolution that they partook in a *single* historical sequence. Indeed, a sense of *some* overall space in which 'historical' events took place was widespread at that time, both among participants in 'historic' events and among non-participants. That historical sense underpinned the coherence of the synchronous analysis of revolutions at the time. The 'classic' revolution of them all, 1789, had *crystallized* a belief in a knowable, overarching space in which history could have a direction (just as it had promoted the 'philosophy of history'). From that point on, thanks to the shared sense of the historical frame in which such events all belonged, events such as revolutions could be analysed together – even if their exact content was disputed. Hence, the taken-for-granted cogency of a field of 'revolutions' which embraced France, Russia and China. The taken-for-granted sequence was, of course, both subject to variation on the margins and historically (not to say politically) generated. Thus, England might be tacked on earlier in the sequence, and anti-colonial revolutions such as Vietnam at the end. The received view was a nineteenth-century, post-French-Revolution speculative sequence taken over – through of course political persuasion as well as rational argument – by twentieth-century communism. By the end of the twentieth century not only is the particular sequence in dispute: the shared sense of a historical frame is weaker than it has been for a long time (Alexander 1995, Baudrillard 1994, Kumar 1996).

This essay cannot then take that common framework for granted. Instead it questions the socio-political analysis of revolutions *alongside* their possible place in a meaningful history. Naturally, such reflection has a historical moment of its own: the end of the twentieth century, which has posed the problem by dissolving the previous, shared historical frame in which certain established revolutions held a definite place. That is to say, this essay avoids a (to my mind) facile response to the collapse of the Eastern Bloc of 'revolutionary' states, which consists of concluding that their existence was merely a temporary aberration, leaving undamaged the historical scheme worked out in the nineteenth century (McCarney 1991). Given that aspiration, the logic of my argument is to move from a historical overview of revolutions; to the historical evolution of perceptions of the place revolutions occupy in history; and then to the evolution of those perceptions of revolutions *within* history. Interweaving events and perceptions in this way of course problematizes both. Yet a revised overview – of history, of revolutions, and of how history and revolutions have historical meaning – then becomes possible. That, in my view, is the extent of the conceptual reorganization necessary to offer renewed scope for the analysis and interpretation of revolutions.

So the final difficulty of delineating my field of inquiry – but also the principal theme of this book – is the way that revolutions have *meaning*. In this they resemble many other phenomena, both social and non-social. They mean something to those who are involved, to those who witness from the side-lines and to those who study them. These meanings are, of course, unlikely to be the same. In that sense, revolution and/or particular revolutions figure in discourses. The idea of revolution (or of a revolution) is a site whose meaning is disputed – just as it is claimed by one political side or another. To put it another way, by virtue of possessing 'meaning' things can appear as items in the exchanges of a discourse: expressions of dreams of freedom, for example, or demands for change, etc. Discourses of legitimation often deploy the idea of revolution (or a particular historical revolution) in this way, as do the discourses of political resistance, and likewise those of war-making (when, for example, they demand commitment to the cause or aim their conquests at proselytization). The idea of revolution appears as well in discourses about historical time. Because of the powerful role of change in the modern world, I stress the role that revolution has in the modern discourse about historical change. This too is a discourse which takes place, of course, both *within* and *outside* actual revolutions or the thinking of revolutionaries.

All in all, over and above revolutions themselves, it is necessary, then, to talk of the form that the idea of revolution takes in discourses of history and change. I give that form the name 'the revolutionary narrative', and it is the running theme of Part II. The 'revolutionary narrative' is the *form* within which the events and actions that constitute one revolution or another are interpreted and acted upon. It consists of ideas that determine and interpret any given revolution, and also its relationship with other historical events. These ideas include such notions as the potential for irreversible change in some definite direction; the possibility of power to initiate or control change; the expectation that there are one or more agents with powers and intentions over the future; and a frame of historical time with normative and predictive indicators for the anticipated future. Of course, this revolutionary narrative could not have a life independently of revolutions themselves. But it does not depend upon events alone. Indeed, I try to demonstrate, in chapter 5, that the revolutionary narrative has a deep, 'phenomenological' force for the modern perception of time and change. It is therefore the setting for a great deal more than the mere reflection of realities in revolutionary events themselves. Hence, for the purpose of analysis, it is necessary to talk separately, as I do, of revolutions and of the *narrative* of revolutions.

Put briefly, my discussion attempts the following with this idea of a 'revolutionary narrative'. First, by expounding how the nineteenth-century 'revolutionary narrative' postulated that the people-nation could together recast their history along lines underwritten by history itself, it explains why certain revolutions have been historical paradigms. Secondly, it considers what this implies for late-twentieth-century revolutions, which (like their pre-eighteenth-century fellows) fit with difficulty into the form of the classic revolutionary narrative. Thus Part II of the book provides a critical account of how the narrative rested on, and promoted, now disputed concepts of the politically autonomous nation determining its fate for itself. Yet, finally, the discussion qualifies its own case, by showing that, historically re-situated, the value of the revolutionary narrative may be rediscovered in a form which – though more modest – squares more satisfactorily with late-twentieth-century experience. The phoenix rises again.

The case I seek to adduce for the argument made over the length of both parts is diverse. To begin with, there is a demonstrable overall trend, both chronological and spatial, in the incidence of revolutions since the fifteenth century. That is because revolutions are a specific kind of reaction to the gradual spread of various forms of European-style 'modernization' (a term which I discuss more fully in chapters 2, 3 and 5, without claiming to give it any single, authoritative meaning). Revolutions are a kind of reaction to modernization, which opens up in a uniquely explicit way the terms on which modernization will happen. Yet, they impinged quite late upon the European core of the global modernization process. For it is more normal for revolutions to occur on the margins of the already modernized core, and subsequently on the margins of global modernization. Moreover, as this core expands, revolutions naturally tend to occur further from its centre. Indeed, in due course the 'core' of modernization itself subdivides, so that revolutions begin to arise in response to different, even competing versions of modernization.

Revolutionary action entails a claim (by no means necessarily valid, of course) to be able to take over and direct social change. Any trend in the incidence of revolutions of the kind described above must have implications for the ideological claims made in, and the historical meanings attributed to, revolutions. We can indeed expect a diminishing tendency for revolutions which are ever further from the global core to threaten or redirect the fundamental character of the historical growth of modernization. Moreover, as the character of the core 'advanced' societies itself diversifies, it will be inherently less obvious what alternative future is to be put forward by a revolutionary challenge. In the latter half of the twentieth century, these inherent tendencies have broken up the classic revolutionary narrative, primarily grounded in the French Revolution and subsequently modified in twentieth-century communist revolutions. Modernization no longer exhibits a single model, upon which a definite set of harmonic variations might be constructed.

On the other hand, none of that entails that margin–core interactions now cease, or that revolutions will simply lose all historical impact or meaning – for example through the impact of the marginal revolutions upon the legitimacy claims sustaining structures at the core. Though the claim that a revolution is *leading the way* loses its force as the incidence of revolution moves away from the core, a broader perception remains valid: that of an interaction between core(s) and periphery(-ies) in which revolutionary narrations take their place. Revolutionary responses on the periphery evoke principles ostensibly enshrined in the core societies from an earlier 'revolutionary' historical moment. For the core societies, revolutions may still represent confirmations, alternatives or calls to return to first principles. Thus they may modify political forms and struggles at both core and periphery. The classic revolutionary narrative encapsulated a notion of a collective agency capable of seizing control of the direction of a society's existence. Such a concept remains embedded within the formation of the social group in the modern world. Even where classic collective agents – such as the people, certain classes or the nation-state – are undermined, an unstable variety of other agents is sought (notably, at the present time, the ethnic 'nation'). These occupy the places in the schema of collective agency where the classic entities have lately lost ground (Dunn 1996, p. 224). Diverse transforms of the revolutionary narrative thus survive the drift which has undermined the classic nineteenth-century version. They remain as effects capable of directing, legitimizing or undermining various forms of politics and of society.

So what, in sum, am I saying over the length of the book? That revolutions in that open sense, of crisis and provocation to change, evolve and develop according to spatio-temporal circumstances – notably the development of the state as a target for contention over society[4] (chapter 1). That the mix of underlying elements in that definition – breakdown, change and agency – varies according to the spatio-historical moment, and that the historical story of revolutions has skewed the perception accordingly: especially away from agency and towards structural breakdown (chapter 2). That the common thread of revolutionary moments is the pressure of spreading and evolving 'modernization' (chapter 3). That by the end of the twentieth century the spread of modernization has so divided them that the form of revolutions themselves has become confused and their impact has been visibly reduced (chapter 4). This is the first part, considering revolutions as events that happen.

But revolutions do not matter only because they happen. So Part II defines a way of thinking about change and power over change, 'the revolutionary narrative', which is contained within revolutionary experiences (chapter 5). Regardless almost of actual revolutionary events, the revolutionary narrative speaks to our condition as people subject to the pressures of modernization, needing to discover whatever shared power we can wield over it. I accordingly trace the revolutionary narrative through various narrations, revolutionary aspirations and reactions in the nineteenth century (chapter 6) and the twentieth century (in the final chapter). By the end of that examination, it is clear how much meaning can be invested in the revolutionary narrative, with consequent political effects, opportunities and illusions. In the changed global environment of the end of the twentieth century, I do not believe that people will, or should, cease to think about society, history and change through the revolutionary narrative. Nor do I suppose for a moment that resistance itself will cease in the many places around the world where oppression can be felt, or that it will cease to adopt and convey the revolutionary narrative. The manifestations of the narrative being so varied and overlaid with meanings, however, I do not attempt to predict how in future 'revolutionary' resistance will adapt the revolutionary narrative. Rather, I end by describing the conditions needed for human groups to assert some conscious control over the structures they must live in, and (in the appendix) supplementing that with the claims of a modest 'philosophy of history' to assist our understanding in that experience.

It will be evident that the case I am making draws on a number of distinct disciplines. Necessarily so, for I wish to adopt the lessons of history and of historical sociology for contemporary discourse and philosophies of time and change. This disciplinary pluralism will be a source of stimulation for some readers, and scepticism for others. A writer who visits the different disciplinary houses of academia in order to steal the silver may well provoke cries of 'thief' from the householders, and will certainly end up using out-of-date goods (Goldthorpe 1996). The literature of history has been raided (pillaged perhaps) in a calculated pursuit of examples. Notwithstanding their differences, the findings of historical sociologists (in which I find a great deal to admire) have been slotted together, so as to construct a spatio-temporal model of change in which to place an account of the *discourse* around revolutions. Developments in the theory of international relations have been bent to the purpose of determining the contemporary movement of the 'revolutionary narrative'. Ideas and techniques of discourse and narrative analysis have spiced the argument at crucial points. Philosophies of time and of action have been employed to account for the historical effectiveness of the revolutionary narrative – in spite of the fact that this tactic lifts them from their philosophical roots and replants them in historical soil, which philosophy usually tries wisely to avoid. In a final impertinence to philosophy, my appendix defends, on socio-historical grounds, a revised version of the discredited philosophy of history. All this syncretism can be a source of strength or weakness, interest or irritation. It is certainly a source of incompleteness, and hence is another sense in which this book has to remain an 'essay'.

Part I

How Revolutions Happen

1

Revolutions in Past History

All the problems of definition and delineation which I explained in the Introduction underpin the interest and importance of revolution as well as the difficulties of reflecting upon it. The experience of 'revolution', of deliberately provoked, irreversible socio-political change, captures and responds to something that belongs to the modern world. The prospect of socio-political change threatens and liberates modern people; and the idea of revolution has constituted an archetype of how to respond to that threat/ liberation. Hence, the need to define it, but also to identify how the thing itself, and its impact, evolve in the movement of history itself. This chapter will try to capture that evolution through a classificatory periodization of the many revolutions of modern history. It is an open classification, as anticipated in the Introduction: identifying paradigm instances around which others more or less similar may be arranged conceptually.

We have seen that the set of revolutions is a loose group of events, with certain manifest instances at its core and many others on the margins. So, one way to confront the difficulty of understanding the group 'revolutions' as a whole is to consider why some particular revolutions have come to belong closer to a core type than others. The question 'why' is applied in two senses: what are the features that prompt us to *say* that revolution X or Y is a 'core' instance; and what objective factors in their situation gave rise to those 'core' features. My belief is that both these aspects of the question of definition – the question why some revolutions are paradigm instances – permit of a historical answer. In other words, when and where putative revolutions have occurred affects not only, of course, their character and outcomes, but also their title to epitomize the core nature of revolutions. Where historical conditions have met in a particular combination, para-digm cases of revolution have arisen.

Hence, the categorization that follows portrays a sequence in which the successive moments of resistance and upheaval moved from being putative revolutions to become central, 'historic' events, worthy of embodying the full potential for radical change in human societies. The case made out thereafter, over the course of Part I, is that movements of history and global development have now undermined the possibility for revolutions to repeat that central, 'historic' role.

Reformation revolts against centralizing monarchies: their character and associations

What I call 'Reformation revolts' occur between the beginning of the fifteenth and the end of the seventeenth century and are, of course, associated with the spread of Reformation ideas and the resistance to established authority which these underpinned. The long Bohemian/Hussite uprising, the Dutch revolt against Spanish/Habsburg power and the English Revolution, or Civil War, are the prime instances of the type. Less obviously, the French Wars of Religion and certain movements within Germany and Switzerland during the Religious and the Thirty Years Wars can be assimilated into the category, since they too are marked by resistance to centralizing authority in the name of Reform. Concurrent with these, but not sharing Reformation ideas, are the Frondes in France, and the Basque and Catalan uprisings against Spanish absolutism. Yet these belong with the Reformation revolts both chronologically and in terms of their target: the encroaching power of nascent absolutist monarchies. I have chosen, that is to say, to give priority over other challenges and changes that are concurrent with it, to a particular kind of nascent 'revolution' in this period. The grounds for that choice are that, even though there are a number of contemporaneous challenges to authority, it is the true Reformation revolts that most obviously bring together central features of revolution: crisis of power, challenge and change.

For a number of reasons, this chapter will have to give more detailed attention to these revolts than to the other, later categories of revolution. For one thing, some of them are relatively little known-about in their own right. Yet, as the overall point of the book is to discuss what impact and meaning revolutions can have in the world of the twentieth century and beyond, it is difficult later on to give these early 'revolutions' the attention they deserve. Finally, they constitute a group of 'proto-revolutions', which enable us to see what will make core cases of revolution by tracing the gradual appearance of the important features.

The very word 'revolt' marks the way that this group is on the margins of the category 'revolution'. One reason is their tendency towards secession. Their Protestantism is often directed at the establishment of separate, free areas for the dissident believers, on the margins of larger regimes, notably the Habsburg Holy Roman Empire. Hence, from the point of view of contemporaries and historians they are 'revolts' against the existing government rather than attacks upon its heart. This does not, of course, prevent the state in question from deciding that the insurgents' challenge is not to be borne. The Reformation revolt aims not so much to seize and alter a pre-existing territorial power as to pull away from it, leaving the core as it is. This point is brought into relief by the concurrent instances (the Frondes etc.) of *more explicit* opposition to the centralizing monarchy. The revolutionary prospect of producing change in the political sphere is mitigated by the possibility of *dispensing with* the given political authority, rather than restructuring it – as if revolutionary intentions and state power have not yet met in the same ring. These are revolutions *avant la lettre* so far as their intention to produce change is concerned: they are not focused primarily upon the transformation of society via the capture and redirection of the *existing* structure of power.

An associated reason that makes this group distinct among revolutions is the transcendent focus of the 'revolutionaries'. They frequently declare for freedom *from* existing authority and address their aspirations to the next world. This distinguishes them from the revolutions of a century later, which – as the historical sociology of revolutions (especially the work of Tilly) teaches – increasingly proposed a transformation of the *present*, secular world through the exercise of the *present*, given state power structure. Because of their secession and their marginality, these 'revolts' are also vulnerable to takeover by forces from outside – as indeed happened as the big powers moved into the power vacuum of the Thirty Years War. With the exception of the English Revolution, they are relatively ineffective in altering the trajectory of development of the pre-existing state. Yet, ironically, the non-Reforming revolts that do explicitly confront growing absolutism also fail to redirect it – not least because they lack the ideological coherence that Reform gave to the more separatist-inclined Reform movements. In the sixteenth and seventeenth centuries, state-transforming ideology had not yet locked horns with the state itself.

Apart from their association with Reform and expanding monarchy, historically speaking these revolutionary episodes have to be set alongside three other tendencies: the rise of autonomous commercial towns governed corporately, according to a variety of local rules and 'freedoms', by their own wealthy elites and trading associations (what is referred to in the jargon as *Ständestaat*);[1] the (complementary) development of early commercial and financial capitalism; and the persistence of peasant revolts against power external to region or village.

The spatio-temporal character of the different phases of capitalist development has been the special subject of Fernand Braudel (1984) and the theorists who have followed in his footsteps. Their best-developed historical study of capitalism to date (Arrighi 1994) has explored the evolution and growth of commercial capital as it shifted focal point over the fourteenth to the twentieth century. His approach allows me to integrate

commercial capitalist development into a spatio-temporal categorization
of revolutions. He observes, for example, how capital became wealthiest,
and had most impact, where it graduated from merely commercial activity to the greater profitability of financial investment linked to political
powers (Arrighi 1994, ch. 2). Thus, from the thirteenth century, Milanese,
Venetian and, especially, Lombard bankers were bank-rolling monarchs
– including, latterly, their own. In Florence, this produced a circle of
conspicuous princely expenditure which underwrote the Lombards' ever-
more advantageous loans abroad and ever-more dispendious state activity
at home. The Genoese version of this arrangement went further (pp. 109–
26): finance escaped its territorial base to reap the profits of Habsburg
loans and military conquests in Spain, South America and Northern
Europe. Revolt first meets capitalism, however, when Dutch towns, having gained a monopoly over profits from trade in and out of the Baltic,
deploy their surpluses in profitable loans to *all* sides, their adversaries
included, in the post-Reformation conflicts of the latter part of the sixteenth century.[2] This 'cycle of accumulation' existed because Dutch
capitalism was able to maintain a highly beneficial arm's-length relationship to state powers: Spain, squandering loans to send troops in from
outside, the Prince of Orange, financing his own campaigns to take
command of the Netherlands, and England, resisting Spain in other parts
of the world.

That nicely judged distance from established political structures can
only have reinforced the tendency towards secession from political authority within the Dutch Revolt itself. But it epitomizes, as well, how we
should understand the relationship between capitalism and 'revolution' at
this stage. Capital is a mode of social organization and a basis of power
which across Europe has contended with the political and military power of
states; where it is strongest, it limited the territorially grounded power of
states (Tilly 1993). Though it may have weakened the authority of princes,
or underwritten their power with its surpluses, I do not believe that it steers
the overall direction of the revolts.

In itself, the peasant revolt is an event well known in history: from as far
apart as China under the emperors,[3] to Feudal Europe, the French 'Great
Fear' of 1789 (Lefebvre 1973), to its special peasant role in twentieth-
century colonial revolutions. Yet, as Mousnier shows (1970, pp. 305–48),
to judge from their organization, leadership and ambitions, in the troubles
of the sixteenth-century, peasant revolts tend to be passive, conservative or
secessionist. The Peasant Insurrection of 1524–5 appears as a *continuation*
of long-established practice, quickly repudiated by a Reformation movement which favoured the virtue of obedience among the poorest members
of society. However, the paradigm sixteenth/seventeenth-century case appears to be the peasant revolts which struck France whenever the rising
absolutist regime wavered in its pursuit of more central control and more
effective taxation. These episodes of resistance derive from the traditions

of communal self-protection which belonged to local networks closing ranks against impositions from outside. They were in fact a response to pressures inherent in the growth of the centralizing, war-making French monarchy (namely its steadily growing taxations) and they actually forced concessions from the state at times when it was itself weak (Bercé 1990). Yet, even though they may have contributed to revolutionary situations, they were not conducted as revolutions: the various upsurges ended whenever local 'freedoms' were acknowledged or negotiated, and the peasant '*Croquants*' themselves cleaved to the myth that the king would grant (or had indeed already decreed) their just demands.

> Such riots were characteristic of a social order in which the subject was attached to his locality by a network of group and community ties, and the king was still revered for his love of justice rather than loathed for his greed for money. When that old social order disappeared, the riots went with it. They had expressed, in spectacular fashion, the values of a traditional and customary culture. (Bercé 1990, pp. 242–3)

It is right, then, to see peasant revolt as a separate social practice, with a distinct chronology of its own, which has been given various closing dates.[4]

The three tendencies I have discussed which coincide with 'Reformation revolts' (namely towns, capitalism and peasant revolt) alter the character of the revolts to a greater or lesser extent in particular instances. They imply, as well, that in their historical incidence Reformation revolts are not *merely* Reformation revolts. Yet, since, taken together, Reformation, civic humanism/*Ständestaat*, capitalism and peasant revolt observe different chronologies and different spatial configurations, they cannot be taken to be the same. Hence, my decision to take the Reformation revolt as the specific type of revolution for this early period, but to observe the distinct mix present in any particular outbreak.

Bohemia, the Netherlands, England: the changing impact of Reformation revolts

For a number of reasons, I should like to examine instances of the Reformation revolt more fully, before moving on. For one thing, Reformation revolts have been relatively little considered in the classic analyses of the nature of revolution, which tend in consequence to misrepresent the events and narrow their own focus. Secondly, as I will show, they exhibit more clearly than the later 'paradigm' instances a feature that is in fact central to an understanding of the historical significance of revolution itself: marginality in relation to a number of other structuring socio-political forces. The meaning and varying extent of revolutions' marginality are, indeed, one of the abiding themes of this book. Thirdly, their historical differences and impact indicate the conditions which allow some (usually later) revolutions to achieve greater historical impact – and thus become 'paradigm' cases. Reform-revolt cultures have a way of surviving as counterpoints to the political order in the core states of Europe, sites where resistant values embodied in later revolutions proper can be fostered. That has been a role performed by Dutch, Swiss, Scottish and US Protestant societies.

The 'Hussite' revolt of 1419–36 figures here as the first religiously constituted mass movement against established authority (Heymann 1955 and 1965, Krejci 1983). Earlier English, Wycliffite elite challenges to orthodoxy concerning the legitimacy of a corrupt ecclesiastical authority were taken up at the other end of Catholic Christendom by the Czech John Hus. Whilst he himself was burned at the stake in 1415, a largely urban popular movement took shape around the 'utraquist' ideas he had formulated concerning the sacrament.[5] When, in 1419, their demands for freedom of worship were denied, they openly challenged monarchical authority by throwing Prague's so-called Romanist councillors, who had been appointed against the town's wishes, out of a window at the town hall (the 'First Defenestration of Prague').

This popular challenge chimed, however, with the resistance that Czech royal boroughs and feudal nobility had already been mounting against the Bohemian monarch's attempts to impose his authority and raise money from them. These middling elite groups, too, had been attracted to Hussitism. When, in the same year, the crown of Bohemia was inherited by the Holy Roman Emperor, Sigismund, the ambitions of higher authority took on a larger prospect, but also a wider and more disparate range of attention. The combination of Czech nobility, town elites and urban reformers successfully resisted two 'crusades' sent against them by Imperial, Catholic authority. Bohemia and Moravia were brought back to the fold only in the course of the 1430s, with the negotiation of the Compacts of Basle (1433–6), which accepted, but limited, the right to preach outside the Church and reversed some of the seizure of Church property which had taken place during the revolt. This settlement occurred largely because the 'moderate' establishment within the Hussite movement sued for peace with the Romanists, rather than continue their association with 'extremist' popular movements. Rather than monarchical power reimposing itself from above, then, it was *intra*-rebel tensions between the territories controlled by the different religious tendencies that shaped developments for a further decade, following the death of Emperor Sigismund in 1437. Then in 1458 a Bohemian nobleman, George of Podebrady, got himself elected as king. Though doctrinal dispute continued, not least from the Papacy away in Italy, challenges to authority on the ground ceased. In reality, then, the implosion of resistance with the acceptance of the Compacts of Basle had marked the end of the revolt.

The Hussite Revolt brought together a combination of social groupings, all embraced by the Czech language, which was unlikely to occur so early anywhere else in Europe: a late-medieval nobility jealous of its freedoms; successful urban development; and the drifting, potentially dissident, population born of expanding and dispossessed peasantry. Between such groupings, common cause could be made: against royal power, for religious freedoms, in pursuit of the pickings from confiscating Church property, and in defence of the dignity of the lower orders. What is more, these forces had only to resist a weak monarchical authority operating at the edge of its range. This combination did indeed initiate a sudden, profound, deliberately provoked crisis about legitimate power. But it was quite untypical of the period. The experience was not seen elsewhere for over a century precisely because the combination of effective forces to mount this kind of challenge was so hard to find.

Moreover, the challenge itself was muted from the start. The monarchical authority so challenged always had the choice of letting matters rest. Also muting the challenge was the revolt's powerful inclination to secede from the sphere of political power, rather than confront it and transform the society more widely. This is evident in two features of the Hussite Revolt. The most successful rebels militarily speaking – those who took off to found the new city of Tabor in 1420, or the Adamites who seceded in turn from the Taborites – were more or less utopian secessionist movements. And the rebels avoided military action away from their own area, until the threat from outside forces seemed to make it unavoidable. We can say, on the other hand, that the Hussite Revolt possessed the defining features in resistance and in intention to produce crisis and change. Directions for change were there in plenty: starting with Reform of the religious life, but including egalitarianism, separatism and the redistribution of Church property.

Finally, however, this first 'revolution' misfired with its historical context. The prime premise for that claim is that the Revolt did not – perhaps could not – consistently combine forces to confront an established state authority. Hence the challenge fizzled out in local by-ways only to be repossessed in due course by central, and (from 1526) even Habsburg authority. That incapacity was confirmed by the parallel events of the early years of the seventeenth century. A temporarily weakened Habsburg monarchy was apparently forced (in the 'letter of majesty' of 1609) to renew the religious freedoms of hallowed memory. Within a decade, however, the bulk of the Bohemian nobility threw in their lot with anti-Protestant conservatism by electing Archduke Ferdinand as king. Protestant resistance to the subsequent imposition of Catholic orthodoxy was isolated, internally divided and short-lived. The 1618 Protestant Diet of Prague expelled the Catholic governor (in the 'Second Defenestration of Prague'). A period of renewed independence – and Calvinist reaction under a new elected king, Frederick of Bohemia – was swiftly brought to an end by the Emperor and his various allies from across Europe, at the Battle of White Mountain

(1620). The second Bohemian Rebellion is rightly taken more as the tinder to start the Thirty Years War than as a revolution or revolt in its own right. Rebellion had, once again, proved susceptible to internal schism; and, this time, monarchical power barely faltered.

The story of the Netherlands is different, in that there revolt did produce secession and a long-standing, autonomous state. Yet other features are comparable, even though events take place a century later. The Netherlands too had been subjected to a loose late-medieval government, which the Dukes of Burgundy were seemingly trying to tighten up at the moment when Duke Charles the Bold suffered military reverse at the Battle of Nancy (1477), conceded the 'Grand Privilege' and died, leaving his territory to be divided between French and Habsburg sovereigns. The unification, by the accession of Charles V, of Habsburg lands in Spain and Germany initiated a great extension of Habsburg sovereignty, but that too was constrained by recognition of the rights and freedoms of Netherlands Estates, nobility and towns. Thus, the Transaction of Augsburg of 1548 represented the continuation of the relative autonomy of the elites within this wealthy, developed sector of Europe. In this legal and customary framework, civic humanism developed further than elsewhere in Northern Europe (van Gelderen 1992, pp. 19–30). Once the Netherlands fell under the authority of Philip II, however, the financially stretched Habsburg-Spanish administration began a determined attempt to modify these freedoms by imposing orthodoxy and taxes.

The first points of contention, the introduction of the Inquisition and the imposition of renewed religious hierarchy, were not only matters of religion, but also of local power and independence. Though they provoked popular, religiously inspired resistance (in the form of widespread image-breaking in the 'Iconoclastic Fury' of 1566), it is hard to maintain that the policy, or much of the resistance to it, was primarily a confessional matter. On the one hand, extreme Protestant heresy had already been quite effectively suppressed under the previous emperor (G. Parker 1985, p. 37). On the other hand, what had been offensive about the reorganizing papal bull of 1559 (*Super Universas*) was that it imposed from above an albeit necessary reorganization of ecclesiastical powers across the territory of the Netherlands. To the fears of the surviving Anabaptists and Calvinists was added the dislike among nobility and town elites for inquisitorial practices that were 'a threat to their autonomy and privileges concerning jurisdiction . . . [and] were widely considered to be in conflict with traditional notions of justice' (van Gelderen 1992, p. 36).

Even though this is another 'Reformation revolt', then, to interpret its character and impact we have again to look to the other, overlapping forces for change: the resistance of middle-level nobility, the strength of corporately governed commercial towns; the development of early commercial and financial capitalism; the strategies and needs of the Habsburgs' rising absolutist state. The Netherlands, as Charles Tilly remarks, 'epitomized the conjunction of capitalism and the Renaissance' (Tilly 1993, p. 55, Schama 1987). Even though it may be natural to attribute the 'First Revolt' of 1565–8 to the provocative policy-preferences of Philip and his oppressive governor, the Duke of Alva, we have to see them as merely a rather striking instance of what the Habsburg monarchy, and others, were doing in other parts of Europe over this period: extirpating religious groupings whose loyalty could not be trusted; extending the central administration; mopping up haphazardly granted local freedoms in a 'regularization' of the legal system; trying to tax whatever sources of wealth could be found. The Netherlands situation merely showed these tendencies of absolute monarchy writ large. The 'central' administration was thousands of miles away, with its eye on the Americas and the Eastern Mediterranean and the core of its values in the southern European Counter-reformation – hence the tendency to import officials and military commanders from Spain. The temptation to tax this, the wealthiest margin of the Spanish-Habsburg empire, was quite irresistible, and cumulative.

Thus, once resistance had been set off in 1565, Habsburg-Spanish rule would find itself caught in a spiral of military endeavour and fiscal need, each provoking another wave of resistance. Alva's successes in 1568 encouraged him to proscribe the leaders of the First Revolt and to claim the spoils needed in the royal treasury by pushing through the States new taxes, which, when the States temporized, he imposed unilaterally. This stimulated support for the rebels, who harried the authorities from abroad and (in 1572) mounted a full-scale invasion. Defeating that invasion, while fighting off the Turks in the Mediterranean, brought on the 1575 decree of bankruptcy. In 1568 the king was already telling Alva: 'It is more than necessary to arrange for there to be a fixed, certain and permanent revenue from those provinces for their own maintenance and defence, because clearly the money for it cannot – and will not – continue to come from here' (quoted G. Parker 1985, p. 114). By 1574 (before bankruptcy became official), he perhaps saw that the military-fiscal spiral was fatal to the cause of the monarchy: 'if we have no money, our position at the conference table will prove even more difficult. . . . I think that the Netherlands will be lost for lack of money, as I have always feared. . . . We are in great need and our enemies know it well' (quoted G. Parker 1985, p. 166). Financial collapse permanently undermined Spanish military effectiveness and reputation. In the mid-1570s, long-unpaid troops turned to other, ill-disciplined ways of trying to collect or replace their unpaid wages, to the point that mutinous armies became a notorious pestilence in their own right.[6] The cause of order and stability then became that of the rebels. The States and the Prince of Orange's party seized the initiative, met without royal permission, and negotiated the Pacification of Ghent of 1576: a pact of mutual assistance and guarantee of free movement, unimpeded commerce and freedom from religious persecution.

While, as in Bohemia, the difficulties inherent in the long reach of the monarchy's power can be seen as decisive in the challenge to Habsburg-Spanish power in the Netherlands, the drives towards change from the rebel side, though unmistakably present, are again plainly diverse and muted. The impulse behind Netherlands-wide political co-operation remained the maintenance of long-standing, local powers held in the towns – a fact which Spanish policy successfully exploited to wheedle away the southern (later Belgian) part of the Netherlands. Inherited political representation in the provincial and national States was conducted so as to protect local and sectional interests which joined forces only when Philip's military and tax policies gave them a shared grievance (Koenigsberger 1971a, pp. 114–15). When Gouda, for example, joined Orange's rebellion, its main priority was to obtain protection: town leaders hoped to mollify Orange himself, and to *diminish* religious pressure from over-enthusiastic reformers (Hibben 1983, pp. 67–100; see also Koenigsberger 1971b). The explicit challenge to authority was not against monarchy as such, but against the recent 'misuse' of it. In due course, that produced the claim to repudiate a particular king. In the act of abjuring Philip's rule, therefore, the States claimed to be the guardians of the *pre-existing* rights of the communities, empowered to repudiate a prince who tries 'to oppress and molest [his subjects] and to deprive them of their ancient liberty, privileges and customs and to command and use them as slaves' (van Gelderen 1992, pp. 110–65, quotation p. 150). This was Renaissance civic republicanism allied to the local power networks bequeathed from the Burgundian period. It did not entail a wish to reject monarchy. Once Philip was rejected, indeed, the dominant politics of the rebels (that of the Prince of Orange) was devoted not to the construction of an autonomous, national unit, much less a republic, but to finding an alternative monarch, well connected in the royalty of Europe, who would accept the throne under terms that preserved the freedoms of the towns and the States. This produced the futile, uncomprehending flirtations with the Duke of Anjou and the Earl of Leicester.

As for the Reformation elements, these too do not readily lead to a challenge and restructuring of political authority. The dominant Protestant attitude was that obedience to secular authority should be matched by tolerance of a divergent private faith on the part of authority (van Gelderen 1992, pp. 102–9). Among the militant Protestants, we find again a temptation to secede rather than construct an alternative government. Thus, the radicalism of the Committee of XVIII in Ghent, by persecuting Catholics in the town and taking their proselytism to other parts of the southern Netherlands, succeeded in driving a wedge between Catholic and Protestant provinces. Similarly, Calvinists in England were to find themselves in a tense relationship with monarchy, even though their instinct was to preserve it. Calvinism's preference for its own, presbyterian government succeeded best where Calvinists seceded and set up independent republics (Tuck 1993, pp. 202ff.).

In short, this Protestant revolt, like the Hussites', was an element within a wider situation chipping away at authority. The main determinants, at this time as in Bohemia a century earlier, were the capacity of the Imperial monarchy to integrate territory into its common structures and the strength of resistance from established, partly autonomous political groupings. We should not ignore the fact that one of the strongest impulses for change came from the side of authority itself: Philip's wish to bring the administration of the Netherlands into line with that being developed in the rest of his extensive empire. Neither Hussites nor Netherlanders willingly challenged, or eventually modified, the state power ranged against them; both preferred privacy or secession. Yet one revolt, the Dutch, succeeded; while the other failed. The striking difference in this case is the wealth and commercial prosperity of the area. On the one hand, this made it more important to the financial health of the Habsburg monarchy – which could not so easily let the problem alone. On the other hand, it equipped the resisters better to organize the defence of their own territorial integrity from their own financial resources (rather than yielding their financial advantages to the dispendious empire), and, if the need arose, to break away from the monarchy altogether.

England is the exceptional one among these Reformation revolts. The English revolution did bring about a transformation of the society and the state which ruled it. It has therefore always been easier to treat it as a revolution proper – even if it was not (any more than that of France later) a transformation away from monarchy or even from a version of absolutism (Clark 1986). It is as a result more widely known-about – and less in need of detailed presentation here. Not that the epithet 'revolution' is not debated (Clark 1986). Aylmer (1987, pp. 204–5) pursues the problem of nomenclature in the contrast between the limited *impact* associated with a rebellion and the deeper effects associated with a 'revolution'. This confirms the tendency emerging from the present pursuit of classifications: to downplay dissident beliefs, and use impact upon an identifiable regime and the society it governs to establish a conceptual boundary for revolution proper. In the longer term, the English Revolution did usher in the radical transformation of the British state in the late-seventeenth and eighteenth centuries. On the other hand, the theses of Conrad Russell (1990) and John Morrill (1976) successfully undermined the presumption of a general revolutionary impulse in society at large. This is just the ambivalence we find in other Reformation revolts: challenges to government that will readily settle for private religious rights, or complete withdrawal. As Barry Coward (1986, p. 30) puts it: 'The English Revolution in 1648–9 was led by men who were conservatives in social and political attitudes but who were religious radicals.' If we examine the constellation of forces in the field to challenge authority we find in England a very similar picture to the others. Looking at the conditions for radical change produces the same result, but with two crucial differences: the spatial disposition of the centres of authority and challenge; and the functional effectiveness of the authority created in the crisis for the needs of the new, commercial socio-economic processes.

The English Revolution falls into the category of Reformation revolts partly because it occurs in a period – though towards the end – when that is the most evident form taken by 'revolution'. The *internal* evidence of specifically Reform elements in the Revolution is much more debatable. The crucial role of Scottish Presbyterianism in bringing the king's government to war and bankruptcy in 1639 is indisputable. But those same Protestant interests made common cause with the king a decade later, whilst it was Irish Catholicism that mounted another, costly revolt in 1641. Likewise, the commentary of Sommerville (1986) demonstrates that, in the early seventeenth century, counter-arguments to absolute royal authority were promoted by English Catholics as well as Protestants. The thesis of a subversive and incipiently democratic Puritanism, associated primarily with the prolific earlier works of Christopher Hill (1958, 1964, 1965) can be taken to demonstrate the *presence* of a new, religion-grounded, ethic that was sceptical of authority. If formulated sufficiently loosely, such attitudes can be shown to be held in common in Puritanism and across the range of anti-royalist activity: as Hill wrote of Cromwell, 'In retrospect perhaps the most important fact about Cromwell was his irreverence, his subversion of degree' (1986, p. 61). Manning (1991) pursues that idea in his studies of popular involvement in the Revolution. But all this leads *away* from Reform as a privileged factor in the Revolution's character as a revolution. Manning concludes that: (i) the subversive lessons of Puritanism impinged upon only some of the middle ranks of society who turned against the king (pp. 39 and 241); and (ii) that, the revolution once unleashed, it was the lower orders that pressured elite leaderships in London and in the provinces to resist any fightback by the king's government. We can see in this the transformation of the Protestant revolt into a class conflict about which groups could maintain (and should dominate) the social order – though, in the provinces at least, this could equally well be seen as localism resisting central authority as such. In sum, discriminations of belief may in the end be immaterial: it was thanks to the Catholicism of Spain and France that the association between Catholicism and the extension of monarchical power came to be a theme of the whole of seventeenth-century European history.[7]

If we turn from Reform, and look around in seventeenth-century England for forces to challenge or alter authority, we find, then, various others. One was the practice of common-law judges, who, like the Dutch States, claimed to defend principles and rights acknowledged by precedent and usage. They were party to a general division of authority between custom, parliamentary statute and royal privilege, which no government was able to overcome (Sommerville 1986, pp. 89–108). That underwrote, for example, the elite's ultimately successful resistance to the king's attempts to impose 'illegal' taxation. More broadly, an impulse towards the values of legality and legal reform can be plainly seen in the work of Parliament under the protectorate (Gaunt 1986). The Leveller movement has often been seen as seminal (Macpherson 1962, pp. 107–59; Manning 1991). But that is more for what it anticipated in later centuries than for the impact it actually had at the time: its spell of influence in the late 1640s was brief, and depended crucially on capturing the political voices of a disgruntled army.

On the other hand, given its central role in forcing a break with monarchy, the army itself must clearly rank as a major motor of change from the mid-1640s until 1660 and beyond. The role of the army most plainly suggests points of comparison with the forces promoting change in other parts of Europe. For it indicates *general* conditions for change. On the one hand, the original prompt for the army's intervention in national politics was inadequate pay and indecisive management of the military apparatus which the rebel camp had brought into existence. The English army's intervention is much more thought-out than that of the mutinous Spanish in the Netherlands – even though, by 1660, the army itself proved inadequate to the task of government. Yet does it not stem from the same structural demand developing within the contemporary state, whoever was running it? Armies had to be managed and paid for. The Habsburg monarchy failed to do that. So did the French state during the times when lawless soldiers were provoking peasant revolts. Likewise, Charles I failed to provide for his military expenditure in the wars of 1626–9, 1639 and 1641. And so did the Long Parliament.

All over Europe there was a clash between financial resources and felt military needs. This was a condition for change that operated equally upon monarchies and upon any regime, such as the Long Parliament, that sought to replace them. But how did this make for a 'revolt' in one case, 'secession' in another and putative revolution in the third? The difference lies in the spatial dynamics of the cases. In England, the monarchical state was challenged at the centre of its power (England – and also, arguably, Scotland) as well as its periphery (Ireland). Unlike the Spanish-Habsburg empire, England was a state with territorially confined power. It was challenged from within, and had nowhere to look for alternative financial or power resources. To return to the expression used in connection with Bohemia, England is the first putative case of 'revolution' which did not 'misfire': the forces for change cornered the state in power and there were no alternatives to radical change.

We can link this conception to the spatio-temporal mode of analysis found in Braudel and Arrighi by looking at the way the English state *was* transformed over the longer term. Focusing upon the role played by early financial capitalists, who were to be crucial in the future global position of Britain and the form taken by the British state, Brenner (1993) has applied the Marxist view of the English Revolution to evolution *within* capitalism and in the power centres of the English state. The interests of what he calls 'new merchants', those investing in the Americas, fell outside the established framework of the contemporary colonial trading corporations. He describes how, unregulated under royal privilege, they formed alliances with established, rural aristocratic interests and directed pressures, from the edge of visible politics, on points of leverage within Parliament and the City. Because they did not enjoy *direct* benefits from the monarchy, they organized politically on the margins of the monarchical state, in alliance with a commercially enterprising minority of the landed aristocracy, embraced religious radicalism and worked their way into positions of influence in the Corporation of the City and in Parliament. Now, the new merchants had little need of the old-style, state-sponsored monopoly. What they required of government – and got by the time of the 1688 settlement – was a modernized legal framework for property, and an aggressive, centralized state which kept its hands off the free market at home, but developed diplomatic and military means to defend English trade around the globe.

This account identifies a major, and unique, force for change in England in the seventeenth century: the needs of a new organization of finance capital which, by combining financial strength with global naval power was to accede to the dominant position of Dutch capitalism over the coming century (Arrighi 1994). Arguing in the manner of Tilly (1990), we can say that the English state had the same financial needs as others in Europe at the time, but was dealing with a particular, new version of capitalism, which – more than elsewhere – needed a certain *kind* of state to develop and to use its coercive potential in a particular way. Whereas in the Netherlands the state was kept on a tight rein by capitalism, the English state was *encouraged* to centralize its tax-raising and to develop its war-making capacities. This it did impressively over the years after 1688. A generous public finance, which was nonetheless effectively constrained by Parliament, was put in place: it was integrated with financial capital through the rolling perpetual public debt, and used to fund the numerous wars in defence of British trade worldwide – starting with the French war from 1690 (Brewer 1989).

This discussion of three 'Reformation revolts' shows each in turn approaching closer to something we will want to call 'revolution'. Yet it is not the Protestant belief system that gives the English case its claim to be revolution. For, whilst its appearance promoted a new questioning of established authorities, that belief system itself would as likely accommodate separatism, private religious rights or a doctrinally discreet authority. Rather, the 'revolutionary' aspect is to be seen in the impact of insurgency upon structures of authority and of rule. And that impact is more a function of the evolving spatial organization of societies Europe-wide. Resistance impacted upon authority where it and new social forces for change had no alternative but to confront one another and restructure government in the process. Where Habsburg authority could simply withdraw, it did so.

Where local powers, Protestant and otherwise, found room to opt for an alternative monarch, they would settle for that, thus ensuring that their existing room to manoeuvre was preserved. Where new commercial forces for change could get by in the space left by preserving weak government, they were content. But where new forces for change could not be met by a repositioning of that sort, resistance met head-on with the very character of government, which was explicitly overhauled in the process.

Thus, in England, the monarchy could not withdraw or relocate to other parts of its kingdom: it had to live with the social forces of commerce and localism. This it did magnificently: on the one hand, 'an extraordinarily powerful centralized state, organized for the more or less explicit purpose of enhancing England's international power' (Brenner 1993, pp. 713–14), on the other hand, 'a compact, financially effective state, containing royal power' (Tilly 1990, p. 124). To survive, English government had to shadow expensive organizational and military developments happening in Europe; though it could be required to do so in a fashion (inexpensive, primarily naval) specific to the country's island location on the edge of the European continent, and suitable also to the new commercial capitalism arising in its territory. Reformation revolts are 'pre-revolutions', I conclude, in the sense that they present modes of challenging legitimate power and are seed-beds for ideas of a radically changed political and social order. But they tend to lack some vital requirements for 'a crisis about legitimate power over society tending to produce an upheaval and change'. For that, conditions must exist where forces inducing change confront a focal point that can be the site of overall change. That focal point must be organized government, sufficiently near at hand not simply to withdraw, and sufficiently well developed to be the channel through which general social and political change can be pursued – usually, that is to say, a state. In the absence of a single governmental order which a putative revolution may meet, crisis and change are diffused.

This, I submit, is the basis of the connection made, within the historical sociology of revolution, between the development of the state and the appearance of 'revolution'. No institution can better the state, with its ambition to preside over a whole society, as a focal point for *society-wide* crisis and change. Viewing revolutions in history, then, the meeting of resistance and the organized management of society emerges as a crucial marker to distinguish paradigm instances. But it is, of course, a possibility that only appears 'in history'. We are entitled to cluster instances of revolutions proper around the spatio-historical circumstances that permit the pursuit of 'general social and political change' – which, in the history of the world stemming from Europe and its expansion, means, of course, the rise of the state. That finding entails, on the other hand, that even though various revolts may be called 'revolutions', by students or by participants, they will not belong at the heart of the category of 'revolution'. In such cases, internal features of resistance and pursuit of change may be present, but the target or the scope of change is too occluded for the designation to fit. That is the case, as we will see below, even for quite a number of putative 'revolutions' in Europe in the nineteenth century.

Constitutional-republican revolutions and the crises of absolutism

One autonomous but related factor which I have not so far considered in its own right in connection with Reformation revolts is absolutism itself. The degree to which it impinged varied in the different cases: nascent, but distant, in Bohemia; present, but as much in the aspirations of the monarch as in his real powers, in England. But, equally (as Kimmel 1988 makes clear), absolutism was not viscerally hostile to Reform (did not north German and Scandinavian princes turn it very nicely to their own advantage? – Steinberg (1966)). And, again, resistance to absolutism was equally a factor in *non*-Reformation revolts – such as in the Basque country in the 1630s or in Catalonia and Portugal in the 1640s. The particularist preservation of late-medieval privileges and freedoms seems the common ground in both Reformation revolts and other upheavals against absolutism. In short, Reform was not necessary to prompt resistance to absolutism, though the presence of Reform changed, and strengthened, the ideological material of that resistance.

Moreover, Reform alone never *overcame* an absolutist regime. That distinction rests with the later group which I shall outline here: 'constitutional-republican' revolutions. That is the main reason for considering absolutism in relation to this, later category of revolution – and consigning Reformation revolts to the group of (at the time) relatively ineffectual counter-impulses as absolutism rose to power. On the other hand, studies of early resistance to, and crises, in absolutism do indicate the long-term weakness which more than anything was to leave absolutism vulnerable to these later, constitutional-republican revolutions: the tendency towards fiscal crisis.

Fiscal crisis, combined with population pressure, has been advanced as a key element in *all* revolutionary breakdown (Goldstone 1986 and 1991). Certainly, it can be considered as an inbuilt tendency within absolutist regimes, to the extent that they sought to muster power – first and foremost military power for use at home and abroad – on the basis of the more or less unreconstructed, provincial power structure of the nobility, who were well placed to retain and expend resources for themselves. Absolutist regimes often assembled their power whilst straddling the simultaneous erosion of rural power structure and status relations by the commercialization of rural landownership (P. Anderson 1974). Given absolutism's persistent fiscal Achilles' heel, it is plausible (after the event) to anticipate that revolution was merely waiting in the wings to overturn it.

Yet it needed more than resistance from Reform ideologies (where indeed they *were* hostile to the authority of the monarchical state) to provoke revolutions that would unseat absolute monarchy. A degree of broader social upheaval, making more widely based resistance to absolutism possible, was also necessary; and, were that to arise, common Reform ideology could help to bring those pressures together. As Kimmel's *Absolutism and its Discontents* puts it: 'Revolutions . . . require at least several alternative political ideologies that might serve different groups as visions of the future. Religious dissenters frequently, but not always, provide such an alternative vision' (1988, p. 194). In short, the 'discontents' that, in Kimmel's study, absolutism was subject to, were real enough; but they did not by any means link Reformation revolts to absolutism or its historical fate. The stronger link lies with the later group of 'constitutional-republican' revolutions.

Given their greater prominence in studies and theorizations of revolution, it is not necessary to give such extensive treatment to what I am calling constitutional-republican revolutions as was given to Reformation revolts. Their central feature is their focus on overarching programmes for rational restructuring of the political order on the basis of values of justice and public well-being. Constitutions are, therefore, their most obvious (and, in the case of the United States, their most enduring) element. That does not mean that constitutional projects appeared before other features of revolutionary situations, some of which were already familiar in the proto-revolutionary Reformation revolts. Resistance to new/revived taxation; challenges to the legitimacy of authority; rural unrest; even dissenting religion: all these are present in constitutional-republican revolutions. Yet, projects to inscribe founding, rational principles for the existence of the state are commonly an early feature in the upsurge of constitutional-republican revolutions, and some version of them is commonly an outcome. Hence the name 'constitutional-republican': the term 'constitutional' refers to that conception which supposes that government has, or should have, clear, coherent principles susceptible to written form and broad social agreement; the term 'republican' refers to the associated belief that the foundations of such a set of principles must be in some sense the good of the public – the *res publica*.

Setting aside the borderline case of England, the first explicitly constitutional-republican revolution was, of course, the American Revolution (or War of Independence) from the early 1770s, followed by the French Revolution, and then by a flurry of sympathetic European revolutionary uprisings: the Netherlands and Dutch-speaking Belgium from 1787 and 1790 respectively, Germany and the territory of the Austrian Emperor in the early 1790s, Ireland from 1798, Spain in 1820. These are the group classically identified – by Palmer (1959), and Jacques Godechot (1965) – as 'democratic' and 'Atlantic' (or 'Western') revolutions. This is the category of revolution that during the nineteenth century *threatened*, even if it did not actually overturn, monarchies from Belgium, to monarchist France, to Germany, to Italy dominated by the Papacy, to Russia, to Austria/ Austro-Hungary, to Spain. In the minds of some (Arendt 1965), their common ground in ostensibly universalizable, liberal principles which are still with us today has given them a claim to be the *only* true revolutions. Though they do represent a coherent group, which share a number of features and are chronologically adjacent, that is going too far.

The chief internal feature of this group is their impulse to formalize, in secular terms and often at a very early stage of the revolutionary confrontation, the role and powers of the state. The US Declaration of Independence is plainly a classic of the genre; the French republican constitutions would also be (had they not been so often overturned); the less well-known Belgian constitution was widely taken as a model. The discourse of this constitutionalizing is, of course, the law (primarily Natural Law) and jurisprudence – lawyers being prominent among the elites involved in these revolutions. In addition, the framework of state power they tend to produce is individualist, in the sense that (in keeping with much of later Natural Law thinking) it assumes that society has to be founded on the basis of individuals possessing transcendent qualities (such as self-interest or the urge to self-preservation) which are ethically irrefragable. These individualistic tendencies are intimately connected, therefore, with a challenge to, or crisis within, an older status structure.[8] In that sense, too, constitutional-republican revolutions are, of course, 'liberal': they tend to underwrite a society extending to individuals a clear field of negative liberty.

Are they, therefore, also 'bourgeois' revolutions? Following the cleavage of Marxism and anti-Marxism, this has been the central, not to say obsessive, issue regarding English Revolution historiography (Pocock 1980, Richardson 1989, Stone 1972). Yes, in the sense that their individualist post-revolutionary regimes have embraced the liberalization of private-market activities where the bourgeoisie have enjoyed the benefits of freely developing their resources. No, in the sense that members of the bourgeoisie have not usually been politically dominant in 'bourgeois' revolutions – in the case of France, that honour goes to the lawyers, as pointed out long ago by Burke and, more systematically, Alfred Cobban (1974). No again, in the sense that a capitalist bourgeoisie has not always needed, preferred, or in the short term gained from this kind of liberal revolution. Thus we find bourgeois capitalist classes patronizing, and profiting happily from, secessionist outcomes (the Netherlands, Switzerland) or from authoritarian mercantilist monarchies (Bonapartist dictatorship, nineteenth-century Prussia, Franquist Spain).

No matter has been more centrally discussed in the historiography of Marxism and its opponents: but without a definitive outcome. Many an organic link has been identified between constitutional-republican revolutions and the priorities of bourgeois life, the interests of capital or the structural form of the capitalist mode of production: but none of that has shown that the interests, the involvement or the support of the bourgeois classes belongs to the *inherent* nature of the liberal-constitutional revolution (Comninel 1987, Lewis 1993). Some Marxists have even gone so far as to identify an entirely different regime, such as the Napoleonic or the Fascist, as the one most natural to the bourgeoisie (e.g. Poulantzas 1973, 1978). Though common and close, the links between the bourgeoisie and any particular liberal-constitutional revolution depend, it appears, on the sort of dynamic that Galtung (1974) expounded in game-theoretical terms: where they may win as a class, the bourgeoisie can side with revolution if conditions persuade them that their interests are better served by instituting universal, liberal rules, rather than by cleaving to earlier patrimonial channels to power or sticking with the pre-existing (albeit unsatisfactory) authoritarian basis for law and order.

It follows that constitutional-republican revolutions were not inherently *anti*-monarchical. A monarchy adapted to the general 'public' interest was a possible outcome for the French Revolution, and did emerge from the Belgian. On the other hand, these are the revolutions that *did* unseat absolutist monarchies in the late eighteenth and nineteenth centuries. Over and above their character as movements, therefore, their striking place in my historically modulated categorization is their success against the pre-existing, centralizing European monarchies. These are revolutions which *do* hit the target: the pre-existing state itself, even if they do not always fatally wound it. But having set out the central features of constitutional-republican revolutions, we must, of course, deal with the grey areas around. In keeping with the key role I give spatio-temporal circumstances, their conceptual grouping in relation to the European 'type' can in fact be accounted for by their timing and location in relation to the growth of state structures.

Most strikingly, there is the case of the American Revolution, the most 'constitutional' revolution of them all, but one which appears not to live up to my last stipulation. It did indeed successfully challenge, and undermine, arguably the most powerful European monarchical state of the day. But its challenge was made far from the seat of British power, and relied upon the possibility of secession, rather than the direct transformation of the existing state (Heale 1986).[9] The American was a 'constitutional-republican' revolution taking place in particular spatio-temporal circumstances. Instead of generating social and political change *through* the given state, it produced a replica of national territorial government, improving on the European original in the safe space of the North American eastern seaboard. Hence, it occupies a hybrid role at the time, even though in subsequent history its post-revolutionary state became the flag-bearer for the very type of liberal-constitutional state that emerged in this period.

A different spatio-temporal account can be given for two other groups of nineteenth-century 'constitutional-republican' revolutions: those in Latin America, and those in Central Europe. From 1808 to 1825, rebellions espousing the same liberal-constitutional principles as those in Europe took the field against Spanish rule in the Americas. The intention of the revolutionaries was to spread a republic from Argentina and Venezuela right across the South American territory that Spain had brought together under its rule. Indeed, this aspiration places these revolutions within the bounds of another category: the national liberation revolution – which I deal with below because I see it as flourishing only a century later. In the event, separate republican territorial entities emerged: Argentina, Venezuela, Bolivia and Peru. As in North America, spatio-temporal circumstances in South America produced revolutionary secessions. But here they instituted much weaker republican territorial states. Again at a safe distance from European state power (and a weakened power at that), 'revolution' had aped the terms of the constitutional-republican revolutions of Europe, but in socio-political orders far less well integrated both territorially and ethnically. Finally, somewhat later in the period we should take account of the Mexican revolution. As I will explain further below, it too appears like a cross between a late liberal revolution and an early national liberation struggle. These Latin American revolutions emerge, then, as shadows of the constitutional-republican type, and forerunners of the national liberation type before their time has come.

The Central European revolutions of the middle decades of the nineteenth century exhibit a parallel marginality, under converse forces. They again advanced constitutional-republican aspirations for change; but these were pitted against *powerful* governmental orders located *alongside* the territories rising in rebellion. The 1830 Polish revolution, for instance, was directed against their own 'Congress Kingdom', a technically distinct state but ruled by the Russian Tsar, which had been created in 1815 by the Congress of Vienna as the triumphant monarchies settled the affairs of Europe at the end of the Napoleonic Wars. It was, in reality, then, a creature of Russian absolutism, with the support/collusion of the other foreign monarchies. And challenging it merely brought in the full force of Russian military power, the loss of even token independence and the migration westwards of Polish republicanism – which is a separate story to be taken up in chapter 6. Much the same pattern recurred in 1848 and in 1863. The revolutionary wave of 1848 again echoed constitutional-republican demands and form – indeed, it can once again be seen to spread from a renewed republican uprising in Paris. Yet, the pattern was repeated: weak forces for change emerge to meet stronger, adjacent state powers which might make a tactical withdrawal but would only return later with redoubled force. The constitutional Hungarian government that emerged in March 1848, for example, while the Austrian authorities were busy recapturing their capital from their own rebels, was already running into trouble over financing its army, when a year later a revived Austria brought independence to an end militarily. The 1860s constitutional settlement, consisting of constitutional equality between Hungary and Austria, quite satisfied the Hungarian elites.

As if to echo these implications of the distribution of state power in nineteenth-century Central Europe, the Vienna constitutional revolution, which did of course take place at the seat of an existing state's power, could be speedily suppressed with a force of 70,000 Austrian troops. For some, indeed, the implications of the structure of power in Central Europe seem to have been evident at the time: Palacky, founder of the Czech revival, admitted that if Austria had not existed, it would have been necessary to invent it for the 'crucial task of protecting the smaller nations of the Danubian area' (quoted Wandycz 1992, p. 157). The spatio-temporal situation of nineteenth-century revolutions in Central Europe consigns them, in short, to a marginal position in two categories: they were too weak and subject too well to powers from outside their territory either to get far along the road of a constitutional-republican order or to establish national independence from the states around.

I maintain the view, then, that one thing does distinguish the constitutional-republican category from those before and after: they did confront core, leading states in their own territory; they are *not* marginal. That fact gives them a central place not only in any historical categorization of revolutions, but also among the *meanings* of 'revolution'. The French Revolution, and whatever others of that ilk might occur from then on, haunted the thinking of revolutionaries and 'reactionaries'[10] in nineteenth-century France, Germany, Italy, Spain and Britain (Domergue and Lamoine 1991, Mason and Doyle 1989). Moreover, that debate was formative to the entire discourse about revolution, which will be the emerging topic of the next three chapters. What we will have to evaluate, over the course of the book as a whole, is how the centrality of nineteenth-century constitutional-republican revolutions has shaped our understanding of both revolutions and history – and to what extent it should continue to do so. On the other hand, if we cast doubt on the notion that liberal-constitutional revolutions are inherently bourgeois, we cannot, by the same token, define them as 'class' revolutions. This is ironic, since it was precisely nineteenth-century historical experience that gave rise to the idea – and not only among Marxists – that *all* revolutions belonged to certain classes. This question of revolution and class will reappear in the next chapter.

As a final precaution, we should note that the strong historical association between absolutism and revolutions does not imply, as we have seen in Central Europe, that the latter was *always* the death knell of the former. Constitutional-republican revolution was neither necessary nor sufficient to bring absolutism to an end. Scandinavian absolutism in Sweden and Denmark, in their distinct international situations, passed directly from a (markedly populist version of) absolute monarchy to constitutional versions (Mann 1996b, Østergård 1990). Notoriously, Prussian absolutism managed to side-step constitutional-republican revolution in 1848 and adapted extraordinarily well to the contemporary pressures of urbanization and capitalism. It formed an effective military-industrial complex around a

modernized military nobility, a much admired legally systematized administration, and corporatized monopolistic industrial capital. Germany estab-
lishes a 'constitutional-republican' state only from 1917–33, as a direct
consequence of external defeat. And that still showed the effects of earlier
successful absolutism. It was a limited constitutional revolution only long
after its Western European neighbours, and in circumstances which allowed it to be swiftly challenged by the residues of the aristocratic-military
bloc, the forces of the 1920 Kapp Putsch. This was supported by the
renegade *Freikorps*, which went on to form the basis of Nazi populist
militarism. As against this nostalgia for absolute power, the revolutionary
challenge from the Left, in the Sparticist rebellion of 1919, was widespread
but unco-ordinated by a working-class leadership which, the Sparticists
apart, had preferred to reach an accommodation with the military-industrial
complex. The unusual strength, adaptability and long-term residue of absolutism in Germany are, once again, attributable to that country's marginal position alongside state development in Western Europe. Developing
late, in rivalry with them, it adopted a military nationalism that allowed it
both to impact on its rivals and to command mass support. Other revolutionary challenges in Germany were short-lived and ineffective. In the end,
it was deliberate restructuring by victorious foreign states after 1945, rather
than any internal revolutionary events, which put an end to the traces of
Prussian/German absolutism.

Communist ('social-democratic') revolutions

Earlier in this discussion, it was not clear whether opposition to absolutism
should appear among the defining features of Reformation revolts or be
linked to later revolutions. In the same way, it is not easy to place democracy among the core features of constitutional-republican revolutions.
Hence, the concept appears here: on the cusp between the earlier liberal
revolutions and the later 'communist-democratic' ones. The prime difficulty is in fact to associate democracy with revolution at all. After all, real
contemporary democratization, in the familiar (albeit flawed) sense of
liberal-democratic parliamentary regimes, has usually *not* come about in
the wake of any sort of revolution. As for the expression 'democracy', until
a century ago it was used largely by *opponents*, pejoratively, to refer to a
desperate state of anarchy and disorder.

   If we are to associate democracy with revolution, with which category
should it go? The claim for constitutional-republican revolutions to enjoy
that honour is based more upon the *ideas* they generated than upon results.
That is to say, that the concept of 'democracy' was prominent among the
aspirations and slogans that were voiced in the various nineteenth-century
constitutional-republican revolutions. On the other hand, from the start,
there was little or no coherence as regards what species of democracy

might come of revolution. In the seminal instance of 1790s France, there were in play at least three versions of what we might call democracy – none bearing the title 'democracy' – which we might call reformed monarchism, radical constitutionalism and the 'revolutionary' government.

Reformed monarchist government – giving the hereditary monarch a defined role as executive and commander-in-chief, subject to the oversight of the Assembly representing the nation – was an option up to the time of the 1791 constitution, which enshrined it. And beyond then, indeed, in so far as it was again in prospect with the Bourbon restoration of 1815 and the 'liberal', Orléanist revolution of 1830. Once the king was sidelined in the 1790s, however, we can say that 'radical constitutionalism' dominated: a national constitution with a sovereign National Assembly narrowly elected by the wealthy minority of 'active' citizens. This was 'liberal'-democracy in its most pejorative, i.e. narrowest, form. The 1793–5 period gave rise to an alternative version of the post-revolutionary state, which did open up power to the urban lower orders to an unparalleled degree and evince a high degree of popular mobilization. The lower classes took a previously unparalleled part in national politics, showing a democratic potential inherent in the Revolution itself. But this was not, in truth, so much democratic *government* as a transient hotch-potch of emergency measures which seemed necessary to extract support and obtain mass commitment for the war effort. The fact that it was called 'revolutionary' government at the time, however, has licensed something of a myth about a 'truly revolutionary' and *therefore* democratic, interventionist, form of government.

Thus, the period 1793–5 presents *possible* directions for the French, or other, revolutions: the representative franchise, popular power, social welfare, stronger community/nationhood. But these were possibilities which nineteenth-century conservative and liberal reformers did their best to contain or head off. We are left to conclude that democracy is opened up as a historical possibility by constitutional-republican revolutions; but it is not inherent in them. That is not to say, on the other hand, that the *possibility* could not, and did not, prompt democratization *outside* the setting of revolutions – partly to *buy off* risks of further revolution elsewhere.

'Social-democratic' and 'communist' are titles given by revolutionaries themselves to a number of revolutions that occurred in the first half of the twentieth century. They can be more thoroughly associated with democracy from an earlier stage to the extent that they were grounded in well-organized mass movements. Furthermore, from the start they explicitly embraced a widened, 'social' version of democracy, with stated intentions and projects for action (public guarantees of welfare, expropriation of the wealthy, restructuring economic systems for the good of all) which were very plainly pitched at the benefit of a large, poor majority of the population.

On the other hand, revolutions in this category were rare; and they were rarely successful. Germany and Hungary in 1919–20 were rapidly scotched by foreign intervention and lack of effective popular support. Yugoslavia in the late 1940s might fall within the group, and likewise Ethiopia in the 1970s (Tiruneh 1993). Given its narrow, elite base and conservative nationalist objectives, the concurrent and adjacent instance of the Ataturk revolution in Turkey (to which I will return in chapter 4) cannot be counted in their number. Cuba became known as a 'communist' revolution, but began as something quite different (DeFronzo 1991, pp. 171–6). Only Russia and China, albeit massive events in their own right, qualify plainly as successful instances of the type. Both were self-styled 'communist' revolutions, where Leninist party apparatus was essential for success and subsequent government. What they actually delivered by way of democracy can be indefinitely disputed.

Two further features, which affect their historical place and meaning, need to be brought out about these successful instances of this category of revolution. They bring to an end regimes which are at best ailing absolutisms; and both occur on the margins of the existing state system. These features are connected with each other.

The mix of state structures and social forces for change in the communist revolutions seems to be either over- or under-stated versions of those found in the earlier cases of constitutional-republican revolution. Commercial development and/or the high bourgeois classes associated with it are minimal and poorly rooted: politically isolated[11] and heavily dependent upon Western Europe in Russia; barely existent among the native Chinese population. The working class was correspondingly isolated[12] – a situation which, of course, could only invite disciplined, centralized Leninist leadership. In both countries an enormous, far-flung and illiterate peasantry was easily the largest proportion of the population. These were a far greater force for change than in the earlier constitutional-republican instances. Yet, the direction of change which the peasantry most naturally embraced ran counter to that of the other forces for change, such as they were: the peasantry's strongest political urge was for their own, local autonomy (Mousnier 1970). The very weakness of the internal forces for change in these communist revolutions invites us to expect more instead from the wider global conditions for change.

In terms of the broader state system of the time, both Russia and China appeared marginal, only just keeping up with the leading states – and they were so regarded by the others. The mystique surrounding the person and authority of tsar and emperor in no way made up for a lack of effective administrative, financial and military power that belied their claim to absolutism. In short, these were revolutions against soft targets: the greatest difficulties were not in obtaining power from such weakened regimes, but in holding on to power, and governing the territory that they had once claimed to rule.

Given their spatial marginality and the paradoxical combination producing their revolutionary change, it is appropriate to ask why these revolutions appear so historically meaningful. The answer may lie in the sheer numbers that Russian and Chinese revolutions embraced. But still, why should revolutionary collapse, and disorder in two poor, marginal areas of the globe appear so overwhelmingly significant for seventy-odd years of the twentieth century? To answer 'the Cold War', though valid as far as it goes, is to shift the puzzle elsewhere. It only reminds us of the perception common to both sides about these revolutions: advocates and opponents agreed that these *were* history-making.

A fuller answer to this question lies at the heart of this book. Perception mattered more than real amounts of power mustered by the revolutions in question. Sometimes, I will suggest, *perceptions* of revolutions are a greater political force than their reality. For most of the twentieth century, upheavals on the margins of the world stage, which have produced at least as much disruption, political weakness and suffering where they have occurred as they have created forces for change in the world at large, have been seen as powerful models of the opportunity for, or threat of, a general transformation. They have been assimilated to a version of the 'classic' revolutions of the previous historical period: supposedly formative moments of the one-way change at the core of modern experience; instances of what is to come and of ways to get there. Perhaps the history-making power of these communist/social-democratic revolutions (and others) has always been grounded upon a systematic misconstrual of their spatio-temporal role. Yet, conversely, what power must be possessed in the twentieth century by that which symbolizes progressive, irreversible change for these revolutions to inspire and/or threaten as they have?

National liberation revolutions

Between 1945 and the mid-1970s a large number of colonial territories obtained 'national' independence through organized resistance to the metropolitan power, and sometimes to its allies also. The 'national liberation' struggle brought together resistance to a Western colonial power, aimed to establish the independence of the given colonial territory as a democratic nation, and commonly led to independence as a recognized sovereign nation-state. Prime examples would be Vietnam, Indonesia, Malaysia, Cyprus, Algeria, Kenya, Guinea-Bissau, Angola, Mozambique, Bangladesh.

For some time the national liberation revolution seems to have been systematically confused by the discourse of inter-state relations. In the Cold War context, where communist revolutions were held to be the possible future for societies worldwide, national liberation revolutions in the colonized world were readily absorbed into the global struggle between liberal-democracy and communist revolution. So, this category is easy to mix with the previous one, and hence other cases might easily be added to the list above. Yugoslavia's communist revolution occurred as German invaders were ousted. Though the country had never been formally administered by a European colonial power, China's revolution (like that of Vietnam) took place as the colonial Japanese invasion receded. Likewise, Mexico's revolution from 1910 to 1931 mixed constitutional-republican ambitions with the wish to exclude the semi-colonial power of the USA. The Jewish insurgents' success in ejecting Britain from Palestine certainly enjoyed the reputation and enthusiasm of a Jewish 'national liberation' to create the state of Israel. South Africa's long mass resistance to the apartheid regime succeeded in overturning the existing state in the 1990s, *and* produced a functioning multi-party democracy; on the other hand, its properly *colonial* power, Great Britain, had effectively been pushed aside early in the century by the long-term outcome of the Boer War (i.e. independent Boer rule).

Though this is an extraordinarily difficult group to separate out, the central features and common circumstances are distinctive enough to justify using it as a category in its own right. The established state is always a faraway metropolitan power, whose administration of the territory observed little, if any, of the democratic elements installed in the metropolis. This is what gives so much scope to rural and peasant revolutionary forces – a feature that is more striking still where, as in partly colonized or non-colonized territories, colonization/modernization has impacted less on rural life (Wolf 1969).[13] In the post-war period, where the category of national liberation revolution most belongs, all the colonial powers' administrations were in incipient crisis from lack of economic resources, legitimacy and power at world level. In national liberation revolutions, there is always an uneasy alliance between 'national' elites (i.e. a native minority trained and/or influenced by the 'advanced' values of a colonizing Western power) and traditional, rural power-holders whose position has often been left intact, or indeed *used*, by the colonial administration. This revolutionary alliance often broke down after independence, as secessionist movements and/or central government by one or other regional ethnic group surfaced.

As in the case of communist revolutions, we find a soft target in the state that is to be overturned by these revolutions. Post-war European colonial nations were in no condition to enforce their imperial power across the globe, and in the face of US hostility – even if they did not wake up to that fact until well into the 1950s (or, in the case of Portugal, the 1970s). In national liberation revolutions, elements in the countryside count more as forces for change than ever before. Commonly, far more effective military opposition can be mounted against the colonial government from the loosely controlled rural areas than in the underdeveloped urban centres.[14] Urbanization has progressed little (though *pre*-colonial, *non*-Western commercial development may well have survived, albeit in a depleted condition – as it did in India or North Africa). 'Modern' industrial capitalism is often narrowly based upon extractive industries (oil, mining) whose ownership lies in the colonizing state, though its local management may be partly in native hands. The impact of any native commercial middle class as a force for change is, therefore, very limited. Given the presence also of Westernized 'national' elites, we find again, therefore, a deep tension over the *direction* of change. Finally, with this category – as with communist revolutions, only more so – we are likely to feel that the predominant conditions for change lie in the larger, global situation rather than in the forces for change within the territory itself.

Contemporary revolutions

Beyond stipulating that they have happened in the recent past, my cat-egory of 'contemporary' revolutions is the least easy to define. Indeed, it is the very diffuseness of the spatio-temporal trajectory of revolutions to-wards the end of the twentieth century that provides a key problem on which this book reflects. Since 1979, revolutions have appeared in Iran, Afghanistan, South Africa (which I have already referred to as a national liberation revolution), Central America and across a swathe of Central and Eastern Europe. How are we to assign any historical definition to so diverse a group, facing in so many different directions? That is why I will say little here by way of definition, but discuss them much more fully in chapters 4 and 7. Nonetheless, we can, I believe, divide contemporary revolutions into two sub-groups, which can be characterized, very loosely, as the anti- and the pro-Westernizing. That permits some broad general-izations, particularly about their situation in relation to global conditions of change.

Iran and Afghanistan belong in the first, *anti*-Westernizing group – though with significant differences between them. Both cases began with an attempt at a *top–down*, modernizing revolution: the Shah of Iran's 'White Revolution', and the reforms of Mohammad Taraki and Babrak Karmal in Afghanistan. In both cases, the main force of the revolutionaries declare their deep-rooted *opposition* to a certain, dominant version of modernization, epitomized by the West. Forces for change do not at all cohere: they are split between modernizing elites in the early phase and anti-'modernizing', more traditional elites. In the case of Iran, those anti-modernizing groups are strong in the town bazaar and in certain, religious cities (Foran and Goodwin 1993). In Afghanistan, they are grouped around rural clans and warlords. Yet, revolutionary hostility to modernization has not prevented Iran at least from belonging, twenty years later, to the modern world (the outcome in Afghanistan is still too confused to judge). Both these revolutions happen in the very borderlands of the Cold War, areas into which, both before and since, West and East funnel war materi-als by the ton. So these are, once again, revolutions where the external situation probably accounts for more of the overall conditions for change than do the forces within the societies in question. We shall find that to be the case also in the *pro*-Westernizing revolutions.

The pro-Westernizing revolutions around 1989 are more numerous, and struck home more in the West, where they seemed to represent revolution's return to square one. Though the details vary, the events exhibit certain common features (Brown 1991, East 1992, Prins 1990). All prominently include mass demonstrations against the incumbent communist party, undermining its legitimacy, and claiming 'Western' human rights in a broad sense. Though there are differences of degree in this, there is little bloodshed: typically minor instances of coercion trigger a combination of public demonstrations of anger and a loss of nerve on the part of those in power. The ruling communist parties accept a major reformation, notably subjecting themselves to open elections which they lose – though many have recovered a share in power since (D. S. Mason 1992). This absence of retaliatory measures on the part of the regime suggests an intriguing common feature in the forces for change: they include the *internal* collapse in the morale of the ruling elites (Horvath and Arpad 1992). Following the upheaval, the new power-holders pursue a mix of Westernizing measures and nationalist political rhetoric. The former takes the form of privatization, free-market reorganization, opening barriers to the world market and seeking to join Western inter-state bodies. The latter strategy – barely compatible with the first – entails a firmer assertion of national identity and independence, most obviously directed against Russia.

A more-than-ever striking feature of these revolutions is the extent of exogenous conditions for change. Collapse follows a long period of relative economic decline throughout the Eastern Bloc, and occurs in sequence following, and partly as a result of, the withdrawal of the overarching structure of Soviet power. Russia's hopeless, embarrassing involvement in Afghanistan is the trigger, which prompts the USSR to withdraw from military commitments to support regimes abroad. All but one of the states overturned is heavily in debt to the Western financial system. Eastern European states seem at best to have staved off popular dissatisfaction by borrowing to ease the material situation of their populations – a disastrous strategy for long-term economic stability. Following their revolutions, all have felt the magnetism of integrating themselves into supra-national bodies in Western Europe, and reorganized along the lines of blueprints from abroad – such as the International Monetary Fund.

By comparison with the four categories I defined earlier, this 'contemporary' group is confusingly diverse. These revolutions occur in widely separated locations and with widely different directions. That, indeed, is a prime motivation for the reflections of this book: revolutions have left the geographical setting which gave them coherence and, partly for that reason, moved beyond the singularity of their previous aspirations. The extraordinary hybridity of the most recent case of all, South Africa, embodies to a fault the perplexing combination of elements: a pro-Westernizing revolution like those of Eastern Europe, in a country which had been isolated from the international system and where ruling class morale collapsed; a national liberation struggle against a regime grounded exclusively *within* the territory; a constitutional-republican revolution effected through elections as well as through insurgency; a non-communist revolution which could not be imagined without the impact of external forces from across the world – public opposition in the West (which adopted South African blacks' struggle as their own), the price demanded for rejoining the world market[15] and the hostility of non-Western states affecting the strategic situation in the southern end of Africa.

Conclusion: the problem of revolutions in history

In each of the historical periods where I have placed a category of revolution, the character of 'revolution' has been different. The basic features which I included in my initial definition – deliberately provoked crisis of legitimate power, upheaval and socio-political change – have been present. But the forces in play and the direction of change have varied enormously. Likewise, the appreciation of putatively revolutionary episodes by contemporaries and historians has been different. The international organization that was readily espied behind communist and national liberation revolutions disappeared from view when revolutions were discovered that advocated Westernization or rejected communist materialism.

Given this degree of evolution, both the interpretation of 'revolutions' and the manner of their explanation have to be considered as evolving according to some historical direction. Indeed, because interpretations given them by contemporaries evolve, the *effects* of revolution evolve also. Thus, explanation and the constructions placed upon revolutions by historical actors have to be examined in parallel for any overall historical pattern of evolution. Accordingly, the next chapter considers how theorists have accounted for revolution. The third chapter then proffers an account of how the revolutions have themselves been caught up in a long historical trend. This lends a direction to the changing appreciation of their character and impact.

2

Why Revolutions Have Occurred

Introduction: explanations and logical possibilities

The implication of chapter 1 was that 'revolutions' was a fluid category of event: a set in which certain instances held a paradigmatic place for reasons to do with their time and location, rather than their character in the straight-forward sense. The way that revolutions had to be defined and appreciated as historical events shifts over time. Hence, the approximate correlation – very approximate at times – between the categories of revolution I put forward and periods of history. Rather than categories, this chapter surveys the numerous explanatory accounts of revolutions that have been developed by students of history and society.

An explanation is more than a categorization, of course; but it cannot be wholly extricated from definitions and categories. A change in the definition of objects of study will alter the focus any explanation will take. So why should not accounts of revolution themselves shift in response to movements in history? The assumption behind this book is that at the present historical moment we find ourselves precisely in a position to reassess revolutions and historical change more generally. The aim therefore is to embrace not only the changing paradigm *cases* of revolution, but also the *concepts* and *explanatory accounts* and how they suit different historical moments.

If we have it in mind that explanations of revolution may evolve over time, we do not simply have to be left floating on a tide of ideas that follow chronologically – one damned explanation after another, as the weary old definition of history has it. A survey of past explanations of revolutions presents us with a selection from which we may go on to put together a view that suits our times. Properly arranged, it can also map out the range of what is possible; that is to say, it can identify by logic the extent of the field within which explanation may be formulated. Within that field, there is, in point of fact, a loosely identifiable evolution among explanations over the course of the last two centuries: away from views that saw in revolutions the prospect of human groups helping along a benign overarching social progress; and towards views that saw them as a process beyond human making and direction. But that is not the main driving force behind the exercise pursued in this chapter. Rather, I want to set out the *logical* possibilities within which a view of revolution and of historical change may be reformulated for any historical moment, and to consider what might influence choices made within those logical possibilities.

I contend that there are three dimensions along which accounts of revolution may range. This chapter is arranged around these dimensions – set out in the order that makes them easiest to grasp, rather than the order in which they surfaced in theorists' notions about revolution. First, there has to be some kind of breakdown in the pre-existing order of society. It is proper to presuppose that there are mechanisms *sustaining* a social order, just as much as there may be others that may *destroy* or *transform* it. So where sudden, radical change occurs, it is to be expected that some such sustaining forces have broken down. In principle, breakdown might have occurred at either social or political levels. But, given that revolution entails the *deliberate* intention to produce change, political breakdown will usually appear the more central.

The second logically possible dimension of any account must be some overall direction of change. At one time the exploration of this dimension of change used to be found in a 'universal' history or in a 'philosophy of history' – exploring an ontological case for there being a particular overall direction in history. My introducing 'some overall direction of change' as a 'logical possibility' in accounting for revolutions does much less, of course, than the traditional philosophies of history, which are now largely discredited precisely because of the grandeur of the factual claims they propounded on the basis of limited, a priori premises. Yet, an overarching direction is evidently something that it is logically proper to *look for*, even while remaining ready to acknowledge its absence if need be. Some findings might include the further claim that the overall direction was towards a better condition in the future; that is, the concept of 'progress'. That is going further still from the modest claim I am making at this stage, which merely concerns what it is logically appropriate to seek in explaining revolutionary change. It would not be *incompatible* with my claim to discover that there was some benign overall direction of change; but it is not the same idea.

Thirdly, an account of revolution may expect to find that behind the event lies the capacity of specific agents to produce effects: 'agency'. In saying this, I make no prior claim that there actually *are* agents or that they are *effective* agents of the direction that change takes. Still less do I intend to take up a fixed particular position within the perpetual agency-structure debate. I am merely claiming that, where events occur, it is logical to seek an agent of those events. *Mutatis mutandis*, where there occurs a 'deliberately provoked crisis, tending to produce an upheaval and change', it is proper to seek some agent, or agents, of the crisis and/or of the change.

The bulk of this chapter will survey different accounts of revolution that have been advanced, organizing them around those basic, logical categories of the dimensions within which, in my view, any account may move. It will also consider the circumstances which might lead those who consider a revolution to prefer to emphasize one category over another.

Breakdowns

The general idea behind breakdown accounts of revolution is of a prior, or 'normal', situation that comes to an end – with the revolution – when the forces sustaining the existing order have failed under the pressure of some initial circumstances. Many pressures could be imagined: bad harvests, invasion from abroad, inflation, administrative failure, intra-family rivalry around the monarchy, loss of wider consensus, etc. Clearly, a considerable range of forces could be discovered in the search for factors which induce a revolutionary breakdown. In one recent, influential study, for example, comparing the English Revolution with rebellions against Ming and Ottoman autocracies (Goldstone 1991), population growth has been given the central, initiating role in precipitating a string of instabilities, such as a fiscal crisis, as the state attempted to expand to deal with the population problem.

A particularly well-articulated instance of breakdown accounts can be found in the work of Jean Baechler, for whom protest itself always takes second place to the 'fundamental correlations' behind all of what he calls 'revolutionary phenomena'.[1] 'The problem must always be stated in terms of the maintenance or destruction of equilibrium or in terms of the interrelation of forces for its modification' (1975, pp. 134–5). At the fundamental level, revolutions always arise from some disequilibrium among the range of variable forces operating within society: political variables such as war, corruption etc.; economic ones such as mutations in the circuits of production; social variables such as methods of socialization, values and guiding ethics (pp. 135–76). The whole thrust of Baechler's work suggests a preoccupation with monitoring for signs of revolutionary breakdown, the better to head it off (e.g. 1975, pp. xii–xiv). Such explanations naturally emerged also in a debate in the decades after 1789 among those who, broadly speaking, regretted the fact that the Revolution had happened and so tried to account for it in terms of errors made by the previous regime or by others who might have acted differently (Hayward 1991, N. Parker 1990, pp. 161ff). In the absence of further development, the initial presupposition of a breakdown account will tend to be that the given revolution *need* not have happened: the existing order was good enough in itself to survive, but for the appearance, or mishandling, of the factors responsible for the breakdown.

However, worthwhile attempts to trace breakdowns in the pre-existing order will naturally run through a number of factors in play, and see whether they are themselves interconnected in a complex fashion. For this reason, de Tocqueville's account of the French Revolution remains the formative case of how to explain a revolution in terms of breakdown. De Tocqueville advances a startling thesis (de Tocqueville 1856) which was seminal for historical sociology: the Revolution had been brought about by the behaviour of the political order that it destroyed. For centuries, the French state had been taking away power and responsibility from the middle and upper levels of the social hierarchy. By undermining the power of the ranks beneath it, the state had appeared to offer greater freedom to all: freedom from the oppressiveness of other power-holders. But in reality this strategy was removing the capacity of *all* levels of society to wield power, for good or ill.

When, in the late eighteenth century, the state launched itself on a course of reform, de Tocqueville can then claim, its own previous actions had already destroyed society's capacity for mutual co-operation in support. Thus, instead of being able to draw strength from a wide range of social groupings still wielding influence over the whole, the reforms the state initiated merely inflamed internecine resentments between the different levels of a society which was now quite incapable of consensus and self-government. Rather than the dawning of any new age, the upshot of the attempt at reform was a murderous revolutionary interlude. In due course, Napoleon reasserted an authority not dissimilar to that which had preceded the revolution. French society was simply not fit for anything else. The true dynamic of the French history lies, then, not in the Revolution itself, but in the long process of state centralization, which it merely hastened. This conclusion epitomizes the 'breakdown' element of de Tocqueville's account: it is natural enough for a breakdown to be followed, sooner or later, by the resumption of 'normal working'.

Two important conceptions, pointing in certain plausible directions for the sources of a breakdown, can be found for the first time in the thinking of de Tocqueville. First, the Revolution was not merely a breakdown of state power produced by some *external* circumstance beyond the capacity of the existing order. Breakdown occurred in relation to the very object of government, society itself, which both resisted the state and itself failed to produce certain hoped-for effects. The relationship of state and society is given primacy, along with an expectation of some balance between forces within society itself. This is the concept of 'civil society': a realm potentially autonomous from the power of the state which rules it, possessing its own internal dynamics and possibilities. Breakdown may occur because civil society is out of balance with the state, or because of the failure of important political processes within civil society itself. Secondly, de Tocqueville is the founder of what we might call the 'statist' analysis of revolution;[2] that is, an interpretation which gives the state itself a crucial, or even a determining, role in the beginning of a revolution and/or in its outcome. The state may unwittingly let slip the most important implements of its rule, it may undermine the basis of its own power, it may generate (or even arm) opposition to itself.

The related concepts of functionality and of balance lie at the base of accounts constructed in terms of breakdown: 'functionality' in the sense that the focus of attention is on the role, or function, which a certain number of variable factors within the situation would *normally* fill in the whole; and 'balance' in the sense that the effects of multiple factors have normally to match one another. If a particular factor fails, or exceeds its place in the whole, one should expect a breakdown. That overall conception was influentially pursued, for example, by Brinton (1965) through the extended analogy of revolution with the sickness of an organism. The 'conflicts which are normal . . . to any Western society boil over into violence, and there is a revolution' (Brinton 1965, pp. 24–5). But Brinton, neatly turning the presumption of stability on its head, took it that a revolutionary process was *necessary* from time to time. Revolution is born out of endemic tendencies in society as a whole, which flare up periodically, as fevers in a human body, and have to be staunched in the revolutionary process.

From the starting point that there are a number of functional components to a situation where a revolution occurs, theories will naturally turn to a number of levels or areas of a society's existence (of the sort embraced by the comprehensive range that Baechler indicated) and look for any overwhelming forces, or any that get out of balance. These are what bring on revolutionary breakdown. Thus there is, for example, a strong literature of the social psychology of revolution. It can be traced to Lebon (1980), who – implicitly invoking early psychoanalytic notions of an upsurge of primal collective impulses – was the first to classify revolutionary behaviour, or a 'revolutionary mentality', as a psychologically abnormal, or neurotic, phenomenon. The approach tends to be associated with a presumption against group behaviour altogether. Since Lebon, however, the approach has been considerably refined (Feierabend et al. 1972). Gurr (1970) can be said to epitomize the systematic outcome of the approach. In his studies of 'political' violence, the business of society is perpetually to contain impulses towards violence in the pursuit of political purposes. The likelihood of political violence depends upon certain variables. It is spurred on by the extent of relative deprivation which potential dissidents feel; by the apparent absence of permitted alternative political strategies; by the cogency of dissident organizations; and by their normative justifications for violent resistance. It is made less likely by the reverse of those factors: the strength of normative or institutional supports for the status quo; and a proper degree of countervailing coercive force. Cohn (1962), using the concept of collective 'millenarianism', has developed a historical sociology out of the psychological explanation of breakdown. Talmon (1986), on the other hand, represents the continuation of a polemical strand within it.[3]

The concept of balance *between* forces, or between forces at different *levels* of the social order, is part of the natural apparatus of breakdown accounts. It belongs, of course, among the oldest of sociological concepts, to be found back in Montesquieu or Rousseau. If we consider also his 1835 comments on the young United States of America, the idea is integral to the corpus of de Tocqueville's work, from whom it was picked up by reforming liberals such as John Stuart Mill. With the French experience of breakdown fresh in his mind, de Tocqueville observed the way in which the political life of American civil society was fostered by participation and local responsibility. It was the lack of political sophistication to mirror the direction taken by the state that had brought about revolution in Europe, where 'legislators conceived the imprudent project of destroying . . . rather than instructing and correcting' the people (de Tocqueville 1968, book 1, introduction). A modern version of this is to be found in Huntington (1968), which identifies a number of parallel processes of change, which have to be kept in step if they are not to provoke a revolutionary breakdown. In particular, economic and social change can produce 'decay' in the authority of traditional holders and forms of political power (loss of legitimacy, intra-elite violence, corruption, sheer ineffectiveness). What Huntington calls the political 'gap' has to be closed by new, rationalized political institutions, clearly differentiated (in the modern manner) from other levels of social life, yet effectively integrated with them. If political change of that kind does not occur, alternative potential elites will arise in the resulting conditions of *anomie*, and challenge traditional power-holders for the positions of authority.

Breakdown may also be traced to global forces of some kind, whether or not in conjunction with other forces. Global historical change and the state system are evidently candidates in keeping with the historical overview that motivates this book. They stand at a boundary between breakdown explanations as I have defined them and accounts founded on an overall direction of historical change. It is therefore appropriate to explore that version of the breakdown in the context of the next section, and, in particular, after I have said something about the historico-sociological concept of modernization.

I observed earlier that the logic of breakdown theories leads easily to the expectation that things will in due course return to the *status quo ante*. If the idea that social and political institutions are functional is pursued in a sufficiently subtle and variegated fashion, it may even end by demonstrating that a true breakdown – and, hence, a true revolution – is impossible. Or, to put the point more clearly, something that *appears* to be a revolution is possible, but the newly created institutions simply end by mimicking the action of those they have replaced. The same *set of functions* has to be filled as before: only the names are changed to protect the illusion of a revolutionary victory. The revolutionary challenge is in due course outmanoeuvred by the larger necessities of the given society's structural components. This possibility was already contained in de Tocqueville's sanguine narrative, in which state centralization simply resumed after the 1790s, with a different autocratic head: Napoleon. But Weber's encyclopaedic analyses of societies past and present illustrate more fully how this conclusion may be reached.

Weber left his mark on social theory by correlating a number of different social processes. Notably, he added the ideas of status structure and political authority, in its different forms, to the economic and political functions within society at large. This rebalances the potential impact on the state of any forces of breakdown (e.g. class-economic evolution, popular politics) contained within society. Thus, within the authority function itself, he could postulate a supervening progression towards more and more rationalized, bureaucratized forms of authority, and conclude[4] that bureaucracy was almost bound to win out over revolution, or other forms of political challenge:

> Once it is fully established, bureaucracy is among those social structures which are the hardest to destroy. Bureaucracy is *the* means of carrying 'community action' over into rationally ordered 'societal action.' Therefore, as an instrument for 'societalizing' relations of power, bureaucracy has been and is a power instrument of the first order – for the one who controls the bureaucratic apparatus.' (Gerth and Mills 1991, p. 228)

In particular, bureaucracy was the inevitable corollary, and easily dominant partner, of mass democratic politics.

Weber turned this sceptical approach to revolutionary breakdown: 'Modern revolution is like modern warfare, which . . . *represents itself* as a mechanical process . . . but at the same time actually *is* a terrible unending test of *nerve* for the leaders and for the hundreds of thousands of the led' (1995, p. 231). Modern liberty had arisen in Western Europe (pp. 108–10). But it had arisen from 'a unique, never to be repeated set of circumstances' in which capitalism and economic individualism needed to be matched, and where values of scientific rationality, geographical concentration, and a peculiar mix of religious and popular values were also present. Russia was more likely by far to maintain a *continuity* of centralized, bureaucratic power.[5] In Weber's view, only the personal actions of the Tsar, in maintaining the war against Germany, had *brought about* a revolutionary breakdown in 1917 (p. 244): the outcome he expected was merely 'pseudo-democracy'.

We have now seen how breakdown accounts of revolution can be, and have been, put forward in various forms. What features in the events of a revolution might bring breakdown to the fore in understanding it? Though that may be a natural question to ask, it soon appears that it is not features of the *events* that guide the choice to emphasize breakdown. Clearly, where a pre-revolutionary society had been dogged by challenges and minor crises, or where it failed to operate as smoothly or 'successfully' as comparable societies, breakdown could be quite plausibly expected. And there have been times when given countries have been regarded as ripe for collapse – pre-1917 Russia, for example. The converse situation immediately prior to the revolutionary upheaval – that is to say, a strong trouble-free state and an uncontentious population – would suggest that breakdown was an unlikely version of events. That might equally be suggested, however, by a process of even, unchallenged *change*.

Hence, those – and there would have been many – who were impressed by the wealth, splendour and stability of the pre-revolutionary French state, or by its success against internal opposition in the troubles of a century earlier, could expect to be hard put to find causes for breakdown. And yet, as we have seen, breakdown theories, unpromising as they may appear as an interpretation, originate in the debate that followed the French Revolution. It was easy to render breakdown plausible by accounting for it with external forces, or unnecessary mistakes, or deeper, apparently *un*threatening processes with unexpected consequences. Any prima facie implausibility in the idea of breakdown was more than adequately made up for by ingenious, yet perfectly persuasive, interpretations of the facts. The possibilities within the broad logic of breakdown are too numerous for indisputable features in the events themselves to be decisive.

To understand the choice to adopt a given dimension of explanation, we could as well look for factors in the situation of those who *consider* it, the 'observer's' view, rather than what is in the *events* themselves. For breakdown accounts, we would often find a view either that the revolution could have been avoided or that it was not worth undertaking. Breakdown is an emphasis that comes easily, that is to say, to those who, after the events, dislike the revolution or its outcome and would prefer that it had not occurred. The revolution itself has, in their eyes, little positive about it, and is better thought of as the contrary of some other 'normality'. Those values were palpable in the case of breakdown accounts regarding the French Revolution. *Prior* to the events, on the other hand, breakdown can become the preoccupation of precisely those who wish to see a revolution occur – if need be, by bringing it about themselves.

In contemplating a revolution that has passed – or one that may happen in the future – the values felt must weigh at least as heavily as the plain implications of the facts of the case; for the facts are insufficient to determine the choice. 'Values' here cover, no doubt, that which seems preferable and worthwhile; but we should also include what the 'observer' *expects* to happen, or *wishes* to bring about. In the case of Weber, for example, the overwhelming apparent strength of bureaucratic mechanisms in late nineteenth-century (especially German) society could prompt such a version of breakdown theory *à l'outrance*, where 'real' revolutionary breakdown becomes impossible. Bureaucratization runs as a guiding thread through his thinking about the modern world: a mixed blessing perhaps, but an inevitability for sure. In Weber's eyes, for revolution to try to reverse that process was to court failure and the resurgence of bureaucracy in a worse form. A similar observation could be made about de Tocqueville's overall work: the concept of breakdown expresses his regret of the revolutionary period in France's history; yet, when he considers American democracy that same conception informs the contrary aspiration, so to guide the unavoidable coming of democracy that it may happen without upheaval.[6]

Change, progress and modernization

Underlying the search for this dimension in revolutions is the assumption that there *is* some discoverable overall direction to historical change. Revolutions can thus be regarded as steps along the way of that overall direction of historical development. As Kumar (1986, p. 20) puts it, referring to the dominance of this dimension in early nineteenth-century thinking about the French Revolution: 'The lesson drawn from the course of the French Revolution . . . was that revolutionary violence was at most an expedient, necessary perhaps in the conditions of particular societies, to hasten on the changes already being effected by more fundamental, long-term social and intellectual forces.' To that, as I pointed out earlier, may be also added the belief that the direction is *for the good*. The human beings in revolutionary events may, in principle, be thought either to be the passive playthings of the supposed course of development or to participate actively in it – though, in practice, this dimension seems to have most appeared among those who thought that humans *were* active in promoting change, which was itself progressive rather than otherwise.[7]

It was, of course, during the eighteenth-century Enlightenment that a belief developed in the progress of the human spirit towards greater rationality and better organization of both social and natural worlds (Sampson 1956). That belief was first attached to the interpretation of the French Revolution by Condorcet's *Sketch for an Historical Picture of the Progress of the Human Mind*,[8] and the idea of the manageable, beneficial 'progress' of history survived very well in the nineteenth century. It underpinned much subsequent writing of history, which often suggested that century's industry and economic liberalism were the high point of historical development – earning it the contemptuous title of 'bourgeois history' from Marx and other critics (N. Parker 1990, ch. 4).

A progressive view of history has often underwritten social science itself, whose founding fathers, Saint-Simon and Comte, both incorporated progress into a history of the world where the French Revolution took its place (Manuel 1962). This nineteenth-century heritage enshrined the progressive interpretation in a specifically *European* experience of the first half of the nineteenth century.[9] An implicit norm was drawn, primarily from fusing together the history of that period in just two European countries: the *political* revolution in France and the *economic* so-called 'Industrial Revolution' in Britain (Kumar 1976). Saint-Simon's utopian speculations were typical. He claimed that progress would be realized when political transformation (as found in the French Revolution) was combined with urbanized industrialization (as found in Britain).

In the twentieth century, Marxism has, of course, been far and away the most influential theoretical framework to place revolutions in a progressive historical movement. But in Marx's version of progress – unlike that of the Enlightenment – the dynamic towards improvement does not advance evenly. There is indeed the familiar, long-term overall progress in the rise of human society's productive capacity (Cohen 1978, Shaw 1978). But substantial advance happens only after long periods of orderly but progressive management by established exploiting classes. It does not take place without revolution involving the exploited classes. At revolutionary moments, progress is concentrated and accelerates towards a new, historically 'more advanced' form of society.

Just like the breakdown dimension, some evidence for the dimension of progress in a revolution can usually be found. It may then be construed in many different ways, all consistent with the events themselves, which depend at least as much upon the perspective of the observer as upon the facts of the case. The actual interpretations of the French Revolution that Marx offers vary, for example, across the decades that he considered it – and visibly did so according to the prospects that the French Revolution could act as a stage along the road that Marx himself aspired to encourage: the arrival of a class- and exploitation-free society in the hands of the proletariat. When, in the early 1840s, the bourgeois elite can be seen running the show in the Orléanist regime and the popular opposition seemed strong, Marx views the French Revolution as a moment when the bourgeois class claimed power. This is the period that saw the composition of *The Communist Manifesto* and *The German Ideology*. Later, as that version of bourgeois politics lost out to the top–down autocracy of Napoleon III, it appeared increasingly to Marx that the progress made by the Revolution had been on a more abstract level – such as the abolition of barriers to the free market – and that the bourgeoisie themselves had been unwitting parties to that shift, which left behind a continuing need for governmental centralization. (In fact, Marx comes together with de Tocqueville over this tendency.) This period produces Marx's classic political analyses, notably *The Eighteenth Brumaire of Louis Bonaparte*.

Thanks in large part to the work of Weber, the concept of modernity has, in the twentieth century, taken the place that progress held in the nineteenth century's conception of any overall direction in history. Because of its use in organized twentieth-century social science – particularly the post-1945 American variety – modernization has the appearance of a more neutral, analytical category than progress. On the other hand, modernity too is grounded in the historical experience of the European world. And the normally expected out-turn of modernity looks similar to many nineteenth-century European versions of 'progress': a society of multiple, highly differentiated roles with a prominent place for individuals; 'rationalized' socio-economic organization based on the pursuit of utility and exchange in an extended market; formalized political power in sovereign nation-states.

But the concept of modernity implants real differences into the discourse on revolution and history. Whereas the concept of progress of itself was used optimistically, for narratives of movement towards a better life, 'modernity' has always been a more ambivalent destination: the road to Durkheim's *anomie*, Tönnies' loss of community, or the alienation of the cash nexus (in Georg Simmel's *Philosophy of Money* (1907) out of Thomas Carlyle responding to British industrialization). Even Weber's positive, rationalistic account of modernity recognized a hollowness in its domineering, individualistic rationality, and the seed of a pluralistic arbitrariness in its values (Lash 1987). Modernization appears an easier historical course to define and identify (Gellner 1964). But, in an important sense, compared to progress it is also goal-less: a transition, rather than a sequence of improvements towards fulfilment. Even then, accession to a condition of modernity may be more hazardous than the progress expected in the older philosophies of history. For 'modernity' takes the form of a set package of changes required of a society in order for it to be realized as a society. And it is a package that, more often than not, appears from some outside model which presents itself complete as a 'modern' society. In short, modernity constitutes a marker of a peculiarly destructive kind: challenging the coherence of the existing, inherited order with a model of an alternative which the given society has to become in order to be validated as a 'proper' society at all.

All told, to find revolution at the boundary between the modern and the pre-modern worlds encourages logically distinctive combinations of breakdown and historical movement: a revolution that distorts the potential gains of an inevitable transition, for example (as Weber feared the Russian Revolution would do); or one that attempts to hold back an unwelcome movement; or one that impedes, or accelerates a transition that has fallen behind. In short, with the concept of modernity, revolution sits more ambiguously at a point in historical movement where things may go wrong, or come to a halt or be diverted. Movement towards modernity suggests a *break* in the old progress, a historical opening with many (often unwelcome) destinations. In relation to the explanation of revolutions, then, modernity has the role of 'progress break': a moment when overall historical movement is opened up to progress, reversal or diversion.

We can again trace this progress-break version of historical movement to the thinking of de Tocqueville. He took the view that the French monarchy had undertaken a process of change that would be its own undoing. De Tocqueville thus suggests that a revolution may trip up the course of deliberate improvement – even if the change in question is an apparently welcome one, such as enlightened reform. Much of the sociology of revolutions owes its inspiration (Richter 1969) to his dictum that:

it is not always when things are going from bad to worse that revolutions break out. On the contrary, it more often happens that when a people which has put up with an oppressive rule over a long period without protest suddenly finds the government relaxing its pressure, it takes up arms against it. (de Tocqueville 1856, p. 196)

The very dynamic of change, which modernity suggests, entails, that is to say, a risk of revolution that can hold back the process. Huntington 1968 (discussed above) can, for example, be thought of as an instruction book for governments on how to avoid this pitfall as they advance, as advance they must, towards modernity. The perception of revolution as a breakdown on the road of modernizing change is found equally in Chalmers Johnson, expressed in the language of post-war American structural-functionalism: revolutions are 'one form of social change in response to the presence of dysfunction in the social system' (Johnson 1964, p. 10).

The progress break of modernity can be seen in the categories of a more historical sociology, in the work which Barrington Moore undertook in the aftermath of the Second World War, at the moment when it appeared that a global challenge from fascism could often be dressed in the clothes of the progressive revolutionary tradition (D. Smith 1991). Moore identified social forces, for and against change, which have to be negotiated in the larger historical spaces of the history of different countries – England, France, Germany, Italy, China, Japan, India. According to Moore, breakdown and distortion of the step towards modernity happen where these forces are deployed in the wrong balance. Moore starts, *à la* de Tocqueville, from the observation that states do attempt to modernize. According to Moore, the state is most likely to achieve its aim where the transformation of rural agricultural society has undermined the traditionalist landed aristocracy and broken up the power of peasant society.[10] Under those circumstances, modernizing commercial classes dominate socially, and the state can succeed in the 'modern' political integration of the masses; that is, democratization. If the power of rising and falling classes is not so fortuitously balanced, however, the modernization of the state is held back. Revolutionary peasant insurgency may challenge the state in its entirety, leading it towards open authoritarianism; or the state may stay locked in the conservative hands of older, landed classes. Such a state may then also be at risk from fascism's autocratic route to 'democratizing' mass society: an 'attempt', as he puts it, 'to make reaction and conservatism popular' (Moore 1967, p. 447).

In Moore, the progress break of modernity puts revolutions in an ambiguous place *vis-à-vis* historical change: they may occur at the leading edge of a historic transition, but they will often be *on its margins*, in places trailing behind the transition already apparent elsewhere, where the social forces are poised against it. This ambiguity is turned decisively in the negative direction in the equally seminal historical sociology of Skocpol, in which revolution emerges as predominantly a breakdown that occurs on the trailing margin of the highly competitive, modern system of states. In a nutshell, Skocpol's argument is that competition between states drives forward the centralization, bureaucratization and development of states, as much for military as for economic reasons. Some states fall behind in the race (this is particularly visible after military defeat) and are driven to pursue centralization, while increasing the extraction of wealth from the societies they rule at a pace which outstrips the resources of their own, weak power structure. In particular, they undermine the delicate balance of power between rural nobility and a rural populace capable of breaking loose of all control. All this brings on a crisis and the breakdown of state power. In the face of that threat, previously marginal urban elites then step in to take over the crumbling state structure. But their resources are quite unable to unite all the dissident elements of society politically, and they in turn are driven to resort to building up the structure of the state on even more rigorous, centralized lines than before. Thus we find republican and/or democratic movements, in France, Russia and China, which end in intrusive, centralized administrations under the exclusive authority of Napoleon, Stalin or Mao.

Skocpol had placed revolution in a bigger, transnational process of the modern world – the growing state system. There, it takes on the role of a mishap occurring to players forced into an untenable position from which they can emerge only through a process of revolution that reconstructs oppressive state power, flying in the face of its own avowed purposes. Skocpol's work, with its emphasis on state-building and rebuilding in a larger global structure, has undoubtedly shaped much of what has come out of the sociology of revolutions since (Skocpol 1994). Its capacity to situate revolutions spatially as well as chronologically is, indeed, something I have tried to emulate in categorizing them in chapter 1. And later I shall want to take up, and reconsider, the concept of modernity spreading across the surface of the globe through competition between different areas. We should note that, as it stands, it has so used the concept of historical movement as to remove from it most of its earlier, albeit unthought-out, optimism. But the most widespread complaint made against Skocpol's work at the time and since has been that it mishandled the role of human ideas and ideology.[11] For, in effect, to view revolutions as a progress break in such a powerful, supervening structure as the international system was to undercut in advance all claims made for the exercise of the will in revolutionary events.

The will of human agents

It is obvious enough that it is always difficult to combine the idea of will and agency with that of overarching causalities or structure. Hence, to put it simply, the more the structure bulks large in the understanding of a revolution, the less there is space for the power of specific agents who may be said to shape revolutionary events. To that extent, there may well be more emphasis on the dimensions of breakdown or overarching direction of a revolution among those whose values or aspirations place less faith in intentional action on the part of potential revolutionary agents. But that is only the start of the story, since the logical possibilities leave open many routes whereby agency may nonetheless complement structures. Accordingly, among theorists and historians, then, we find hardly any who attribute a revolution solely to the will of certain agents: what would they have to say as theorists or historians if they left structures out of the picture? Yet, there are many possible formulations of structural forces in history, or in a breakdown, with room for different degrees of agency from various types of agents. So we do find many theorists and historians whose version of the revolution locates the will of agents *within spaces* in the structures of history or a society in crisis.

I have argued elsewhere that much of the culture created in the French Revolution was precisely an attempt to formulate the terms whereby a collective agent could be seen making history in the Revolution (N. Parker 1990). It is not too much to say that the entire nationalist tradition of thought is carved out of that need (Kedourie 1960, O'Brien 1989). A nationalist thinker and activist such as Mazzini adopts late-eighteenth-century efforts to formulate expressions of the shared, public, or 'general', will, which represents the society as a whole in active terms, and makes of it a rational, united 'nation' to take its destiny in its hands – as the French did in their Revolution. As with other socio-political events, there has always been a good deal of abstraction involved in identifying the wills at work in a revolution. The German philosophical debate in the aftermath of the French Revolution illustrates that well, with Hegel as the *ne plus ultra* of the tendency (Ritter 1982, Shklar 1976) and, significantly, a figure whose influence revived in the aftermath of 1917 also. In that debate, abstract agents, from the emergent rationality of the human species downwards, were defined and given more or less convincing substance.

In the context of the French, and later, revolutions, however, Marx's combination of progress and will is by far the most suggestive. The formulation turns upon the relationship between the wills of participants in revolution and the uneven progress of human productivity, referred to earlier. This is no place to re-run analysis of the *locus classicus* of Marx's theoretical position, the 'Contribution to a Critique of Political Economy', even though its economy of expression has rightly justified its canonic status. Suffice it to say that in Marx's view, revolution enters into the dynamic of progress because it enables the active intervention of the exploited classes into history. Conflict between classes may be inherent in the set-up, but that alone could not bring about a revolution. Rather, when the structures of established 'relations of production' begin to falter, notably to become less productive, they lose their rationale for the society as a whole. Extraordinary – revolutionary – action to impose a different set of relations is then possible: but it is also a necessity, so that the overall historical movement of progress can resume. In a revolution, a previously exploited class overturns the dominant, privileged classes, takes over the political order and organizes society's productive forces. Marx and later Marxist historians[12] have argued that is visible in the 1790s, as the bourgeoisie took political command, to organize the market, and then the urban poor tried also to do so, to initiate a more socialized economy. But in exercising their will to change things, these revolutionary agents are also getting *back into step* with overall progress.

Crucially for Marxism – and, indeed, for the history of the twentieth century – that formulation about the will of humans in revolution was, of course, restructured by Leninism, which, for most of the twentieth century, had the success of 1917 to its credit and the power of the Soviet system behind it. If social revolution required social classes to enter actively into a struggle for progress, reasoned Lenin (1902), that cannot happen through their spontaneous resistance to oppression, or their wish for short-term relief of their economic sufferings. 'Modern', specialist skills in organization and leadership are called for, which can only be provided in a party of 'professional revolutionaries': not a class in their own right, but the genuine, effective, organized 'vanguard' of the proletariat. Equipped to resist suppression at the hands of the authorities, they could engage in the struggle alongside the workers, whilst also pursuing the radical, long-term solution to *all* the workers' present sufferings: namely, the defeat of capitalism itself and the transformation of society's production into a democratically controlled socialism. Under various titles ('the dictatorship of the proletariat', 'the leading role of the party', and so on), this conception of professionals 'leading' the will of the masses was the legitimation of communist parties, in and out of power, right up to the 1990s.

The political underpinning is not in doubt in this version of the will of human agents in a revolution. It is a view of revolution in which the will of specifiable agents is very much to the fore *because* it fits the aspiration to create a new order and the intention to promote revolution in order to achieve that. Rather than the French, the battleground of historical interpretation over Lenin's version of things has, naturally, been the Russian Revolution. The account of the Revolution which Trotsky represented (notably from Trotsky 1957a) was formative. Coming from the same background in the active promotion of revolution, on grounds of the very same values and aspirations as Lenin, he did not at all discard the dimension of will and action. He *re*asserted that the will and agency of a class *had* been predominant in the event of the Russian Revolution. But, in his view, that active role had been stopped (temporarily, he hoped) when a bureaucratic caste had taken over the leadership of the temporarily exhausted Russian proletariat. Trotsky and his followers, both theoretical and political, continued to believe that classes (and especially the working class) have a greater potential will for revolutionary action than any bureaucratized communist parties could be capable of. Thus, he regarded the direction in which the Russian Revolution was led by Stalin after the mid-1920s as *counter*-revolutionary (Trotsky 1957b): the working class needed to be given its head, and its power has still to be directed consistently at worldwide revolution. Given his preoccupation with the conditions for the working class to exercise their will to revolution on a world scale, Trotsky gave intellectual impetus to all the later accounts of revolution, economic development and inter-state relations.

A substantial body of twentieth-century humanistic Marxist theory and history has sought to locate in revolution manifestations of the more or less united will of exploited classes. Lukàcs, a minor player in the Hungarian communist revolution of 1919, has been an intellectual leader and a major inspiration. In the years following that failed revolution, Lukàcs reflected on what might be the twentieth-century proletariat's particular relation to historical change (Lukàcs 1971). He argued that the absence of human agency – that is, 'alienation' – is a predominant condition of *all* actual history because the power of human will is suppressed by social forms. Most of the time, that is to say, most human groups are unable to exercise wilful agency over the social forms they must live. This intellectually and existentially unsatisfactory situation may, however, be reversed in so far as a large and strategically powerful enough social class has the potential to transform society without the need to reimpose the discipline of powerlessness upon humanity. The working class, because of its position and its capacity for non-exploitative productive relations, has that potential. Therefore a *socialist* revolutionary situation could give one group, the proletariat, the unique role of being both creation of the previous, alienated social conditions and the knowing agents in their future transformation. It is in that rather particular kind of revolution that human agency is envisioned by Lukàcs.

The profound difficulty behind all this debate, as can readily be seen, is how to construe groups and their will in revolutionary events – or any others. The inherent difficulties in giving a definitive answer are the same as those we found in chapter 1 over the 'bourgeois revolution', but in more abstract terms. Do we look at the participants, leaders or those who gain – and how long after? Do we refer to identifiable members of a given class (no straightforward matter to determine in itself) or to some abstraction linked – often with difficulty – to empirical groupings: such as common patterns of communications, class interests, class identity or identifying values, exploitative flows, or modes of production (Giddens 1973, Mann 1995, Roemer 1982, Wright 1978)? I will return to the theoretical question in chapter 5. What are immediately relevant here are the many studies of revolutions in the mid-twentieth century which have sought to identify the groups in revolutions and specify the nature of their existence and their will. Humanistic historians, who have examined the real history of revolution or social resistance, have been numerous. The influential perspective of E. P. Thompson was to find a will to mount effective resistance in the distinctive culture of the lower classes (Thompson 1963, 1971 and 1994). Whilst vigorously rejecting Thompson's refusal to take social structure seriously, Craig Calhoun (1982) approached comparable manifestations of a popular will to resist or rebel with the same intention of putting flesh on the human will in revolutionary situations. Shared popular culture became a lightning conductor along which normally unexpressed hostility to real enough oppression may be carried into powerful acts of resistance.

It has appeared from these examples that the will of particular agents might be understood or demonstrated if the structural conditions underpinning their belief systems and social action could be properly explicated. The analytical historical studies of Charles Tilly, starting with the Vendée rebellion (1964), have accordingly tried to identify the rationale of collective social action in its given context. Tilly has, as he put it, been 'doggedly anti-Durkheimian' (1978, p. 48), by rejecting the presumption which I referred to earlier in the context of breakdowns: of a 'normal', stable, functional balance in which revolution is merely an interruption. For Tilly, resistance, like all other forms of behaviour, has *purpose* behind it.[13] In particular, he is interested in those instances of violence where a 'challenging group publicly lays claim to some space, object, privilege, or other resource . . . and the agents of the government forcibly resist their claims' (p. 180). This is 'contention': openly demanding, with or without violence, some of the resources held by those with greater power. Contention has a purpose, the claim it expresses, and it can be studied in its own history (p. 232). Revolutions can then be seen as moments when the contention of various social groups is mobilized in the struggle between two or more blocs 'effectively exercising control over a significant part of the state apparatus' (p. 190).[14]

This combination of the structural with the human will has an unexpected corollary: the structure emerges as a necessary stage for the effective *existence* of the agents whose wills are deployed in revolutionary action against it. Tilly's lengthy studies of France and England (1986 and 1995, Tilly et al. 1975) do indeed explore the ways that resistance and revolution have gradually taken on new forms since the middle of the eighteenth century: forms which have been *made possible* by the national stage which states themselves have been busy creating. To parody an oft-repeated dictum of Tilly himself: 'The state makes the nation, and the nation can then mount a revolution against the state.' There appears, that is to say, to be an affinity between the forms of agency that may be discovered in a revolution and the structures of state power which are evolving across historical time and space. And this implication is developed by Tilly himself (1993), who, on the basis of extensive comparisons, has examined different zones of Europe (Dutch, Iberian, British, French and Russian), each with its distinct historical path through state formation and a distinct pattern of resistance and/or revolution. As European state power was forming, from around the middle of the sixteenth century, both actors and the targets of their contention evolved. Put schematically, the earlier segmented societies, where contention was communal and took place either between patrons and clients or over dynastic succession, have gradually been superseded by consolidated societies with national states that are subject to challenge from coalitions of classes.

The formation of the state and of capital which thus reshaped the means, and refocused the targets, for 'contention' is, of course, the same development which, in the previous chapter, historically so privileged the relationship between revolutions and states. To adapt the account originating in Weber and pursued primarily by Giddens (1985), we may say that the modern state's very success in monopolizing/excluding violence within its territory created a social arena in which challenges to established patterns of power and privilege could be seen, on both sides, as challenges *to the state*, and, in that sense, as revolutions against the general, established order.

Tilly's perspective on the position of the human agents in revolution does not, then, yield a *generally valid* conclusion about what will on the part of which agents may do what in revolution. Rather, it points to how a student of revolutionary events might look for the will of agents: human agents would find a specific place in revolutions according to place and historical moment. Though Tilly may indeed have found in state-development a scheme to place revolutionary agents up to the present historical moment, amid contemporary talk of the end of the nation-state there may not be a place in future for agents in the terms Tilly identified for the previous few centuries. Whilst adopting Tilly's spatio-historical findings in the next two chapters, therefore, I shall want to consider afresh what framework for the will of human agents is conceivable at the end of the twentieth century.

Conclusion: historical trends and changing perspectives

My theme in this chapter has been that accounts of revolution can be expected to take up a position in the three explanatory dimensions: breakdown in the pre-existing order; an overall direction of change; and the agency of specific agents within the event. We have also seen that, to some analysts, at different times and places it has seemed difficult or impossible to find room for one or more of these dimensions. Others have insisted on emphasizing one dimension over the others. It is not obvious why the different emphases should emerge as they do.

As regards the three explanatory dimensions themselves, the fortunes of progress and of agency, in particular, have waxed and waned across the last two centuries. Take the progressive direction of history. It grew out of the Enlightenment, but was most powerfully formulated around, and in the long aftermath of, the French Revolution. Then, during the nineteenth century it was divided among contending claimants to the true path of

progress. In the twentieth century, it was most effectively claimed by admirers of revolutions in the collapsing overextended empires where, away
from the European birthplace of Enlightenment optimism, progressivist
'progress' was soon no longer recognizable.

The notion of agency has had an even more embattled career. Consistently acknowledged – though disputed between political tendencies – in the
century following 1789, it has hardly survived at all as an explanatory
dimension among theoretical commentators in the context of the twentieth-
century extra-European revolutions. To be sure, the concept has been com-
mandeered by hollow claims for the 'leading role of the Party' under
communist states. But many in the broader public, and of course the would-
be practitioners of revolution, have followed a different attitude from theorists: constructing a view or a political position in terms of their own, or
others', capacity to be agents who bring about change through revolution.
The dominant discourse of historical sociology on revolutions has been
largely negative about agency.[15] In the light of commentary upon Russian
and Chinese revolutions, there has been a powerful impulse to deny the
possibility of human agency altogether.

Weber and Skocpol epitomize this rejection of agency, and share an
irritation with what they see as the political blindness of voluntarist revolutionary activists. One wrote from early-century Germany where welfare
bureaucratization had co-opted the possibility of social change. The other
wrote in the light of the heady, failed aspirations of Americans during the
anti-Vietnam campaigns of the late 1960s.

> The question of whether any material development, let alone today's high
> capitalist development, could preserve these unique historical conditions
> [which account for the appearance of 'modern liberty'], let alone create new
> ones, needs only to be put for the answer to be obvious. And there is not the
> faintest likelihood that economic 'socialization' could encourage the growth
> of inwardly 'free' personalities or 'altruistic' ideals. Do we find the slightest
> traces of anything of the kind amongst those who . . . are borne along by
> 'material development' to inevitable victory? 'Correct' Social Democracy
> drills the masses in the intellectual parade-ground step and . . . refers them to
> a paradise in this world, making of it a kind of inoculation against change for
> those with an interest in preserving the status quo. (Weber 1995, pp. 109–10)

> as neo-Marxists have come to consider class consciousness and party organ-
> ization to be the key problematic issues about revolutions, they have become
> less and less interested in exploring questions about the objective, structural
> conditions for revolutions. (Skocpol 1979, p. 16)

> The lack of fit between Marx's theory of revolutions and the actual historical
> patterns of social revolutions suggests more insistently than many contem-
> porary Marxian socialists want to admit the need for rethinking some of the
> basics of Marx's approach. . . . Even if, *especially* if the working classes of the

advanced societies should become politically self-conscious revolutionaries . . . they would still have to contend with the repressive capacities of
existing states and with the possible threat of new forms of state domination
emerging unforeseen and unintended from actual revolutionary transformations. (Skocpol 1979, p. 292)

As I have discussed the logically possible dimensions of explanation for
revolutions, it has always been clear that the facts of the case alone will not
account for the emphasis on one dimension over others, or for their combination. The great excess of facts in history and social science precludes a
choice based solely on the examination of revolutionary events themselves.
In any consideration of revolutions, therefore, values must also count in the
choice of emphasis made – as they did for Weber and Skocpol in their
scepticism about the stated intentions of contemporary proponents of revolutionary change. For those whose common sense disposes them to think
that humans can and will do some of what they aspire to, however, aspirations and intentions must matter in human events such as revolutions. A
presumption of effective human agency is not, that is to say, solely a
prejudice in the minds of active proponents of resistance (who believe they
themselves can achieve their revolutionary intentions): common sense too
insists on recognizing agency as a category in the field of human action. So
the removal of human agency from the categories that explain revolution
begs for explanation itself.

To understand why emphases within these explanatory dimensions should
be adopted as they are, we need, in short, to consider both the facts of the
case(s) and the perspective of the observer. We could seek to match the two
sides of the issue together. On the one hand, we could ask: what do revolutions have to look like to inspire in those who consider them a particular
pattern of emphases for explanation? Conversely, we could ask: from what
position are the 'observers' likely to consider that revolutions manifest
each of the different dimensions we have identified?

There may be a pattern in this. In the twentieth century, revolutions have
occurred in the third and fourth categories I set out in chapter 1 ('com-
munist/social-democratic' and 'national liberation'); that is, they have occurred away from the West. Concurrently, theorizations have increasingly
lost contact with the dimensions of progress and the agency in revolution.
In the next chapter, I want to ask whether the pattern of incidence of
revolutions themselves may not be behind this. Though I have yet to account for it, revolutions appear to have obeyed a tendency to occur further
and further from what seemed to be their Western European heartland. On
the one hand, has this altered the balance between the dimensions which
may be found in them? On the other hand, has it placed observers, including
social science and modern social theory, in a situation which prioritizes the
explanatory emphases which they opted for?

3

The Trend in Revolutions

Introduction

In this chapter I want to develop a hypothesis about the relationship between where revolutions occur over the course of historical time, and the impact they have. The notion of impact here includes the degree to which they may bring about genuine, or intentional, change; their effects upon other states; *and* the impressions they give. The argument has a number of stages.

First, I extrapolate from theories about the spatio-temporal distribution of forms of state and power. This process is embraced under the term 'modernization'; even though that term itself does not have a definitive, hard-and-fast content. The spatio-temporal distribution of forms of state and power, of course, implies a lot about where revolutions, which by their nature challenge, or alter, forms of power, may occur and also what direction they may take. Putting these two together, I can then argue that, as the position and character of revolutions change over time, the strength of the different dimensions of explanation (as debated in the previous chapter) will tend to change also. This accounts *inter alia* for the declining force of the progress and agency dimensions in our understanding of revolutions.

But, if over the course of time revolutions tend to give a different impression to 'observers' of revolution, that in turn will change their 'impacts'; that is, the impressions both of outside commentators and of those involved in processes of change. The net result of this evolving spatio-temporal situation is that the direction of change, including deliberate, willed change undertaken by human agents, evolves over time also. Not only does it become harder to identify direction and agency at all; direction and agency themselves become more diverse as revolutions occur in different locations. They appear, I shall argue, to move in the direction of *different* 'modernities'.

This accounts for the changing appearance of revolutions over the twentieth century. But it also sets a problem about where, and in what form, revolutions could be expected in the twenty-first-century future. That will be taken up in chapter 4, and then, using a different approach, based more on the *meaning* of revolutions in the discourses of history and change, will be considered further in the second half of the book.

'Modernization' on the stage of history: the implications of theories

Whilst modernization, as I shall argue later, should properly be regarded as a shifting, synthetic category, it is the best term to embrace, in a fairly open-ended way, the possibilities we have to choose from in trying to understand the long-term process by which the present world came about over the course of 'modern' history. In that wide sense, then, I take all the theories concerning the global extension and evolution of social forms to be theories about modernization. They can be divided into, on the one hand, those that consider the *spread* and boundary *interactions* of systems, and, on the other, those that consider evolutions *within* or *between layers* of given systems.

The leading exponents of the former are the theorists and historians of the 'world economies', the 'world system', and so on: Fernand Braudel, Immanuel Wallerstein, Giovanni Arrighi. That whole body of thinking stems, of course, from a European, and then a Western reflection on the different forms of 'civilization': Vico, Montesquieu, Hegel, Marx, Spencer, Toynbee, etc. But this group of recent studies starts from two manifest priorities of the modern world: the economy and states – both natural targets of revolutions. They have also generated determinedly dynamic modes of interpretation, in which the systems perpetually spread and change.

Braudel's enormous historical study was been devoted to the way that different 'worlds' have formed within, and then overstepped, the European space. The crucial conception in his dynamic of historical change is that of the capitalist city in its 'world-economy' (Braudel 1984, ch. 1). By their internal diversity and unprecedented inventiveness, certain cities have occupied, one after the other, a commanding role over their own expansionist economic sphere, obtaining wealth and directing developments in a way that their rivals could not achieve. Over the course of modern history, Venice, Antwerp, Genoa, Amsterdam, London and New York have been such focal points, as each in turn developed economic ambitions with an incurable need, and capacity, to overreach the existing boundaries of their existing economic relations. In the sense that they always reach further out *into* the world, these centres of gravity are 'world-economies', even if their structuring influence has not in fact covered the full extent of the globe. The final effect of their 'world-economies' has been the appearance of a single, world economy centred first on Europe and then on the United States. On the basis of this historical work, we may envisage a complex transformation, spreading across the globe and coterminous with 'modernity'. The process has been *historical*, with contingent by-ways, strategies, struggles and plain accidents.

What is the relationship between this kind of overreaching economic sphere and the target of revolutionary challenges, namely political and social orders? It is significant that two out of Braudel's five world-economy cities – Amsterdam and London – have been central winners to emerge from a revolutionary process. But we must not leap to conclusions. More generally, it is clear that there is both symbiosis and tension between the dynamic extension of a 'world-economy' and the political life of the state. Braudel's own account of Amsterdam (1984, ch. 3) illustrates both. The city funded Dutch growth, secured the position of the rebel state (through, for example, a near-monopoly of maritime transport for all the other European economies), and imposed some terms on how the emerging Dutch state could operate. Yet, a century or so later, it seems to have been the narrow greed of Amsterdam's moneyed elites that undermined the Netherlands' own global power base: the V.O.C., or Chartered East India Company (1984, pp. 221–35). What we have, then, is a dynamic of development which extends across the space of Europe and the wider world, opening up – and sometimes also closing – political options. The same could be said for the City of London as Brenner (1993) described it (see chapter 1): helping the formation of a new state, but from the sidelines, and only on terms.

In spite of differences with Braudel (on, for example, the historical significance of earlier, non-European empires) the picture given by Wallerstein's 'World System Theory' is fundamentally similar: an expansionist, capitalist dynamic, emanating from Europe, shapes patterns of economic activity *and* the powers of political institutions across the surface of the globe (Wallerstein 1979, 1983, 1984). Wallerstein's 'systemic' logic is, on the other hand, a distinct addition to the Braudelian picture. It postulates much more explicitly that the system as a whole is a mechanism for the extraction of surplus wealth generated in economic processes and its transfer across the world, from exploited 'periphery' to favoured 'core'. This entails an inescapable complementarity of roles within the growing world system of political-economic power. Different zones may sit at the top of the hierarchy of accumulation, or they may be confined to a more or less disadvantageous position – wholly exploited, or exploiting only at the price of being exploited in their turn. Thus, different parts of the world vie for roles; but with limited options, due largely to the givens of their geopolitical position. Wallerstein's account, however, can only provide a step in our discussion. Notoriously unamenable to human agency, it operates essentially at a level *above* the pressures and challenges that occur *within* as small a territorial unit as a nation-state, which is the stage on which revolutions mostly happen.[1]

The more recent theorization of Arrighi offers something of a bridge to that level with its interrelated concepts of 'territorist' power; of 'systemic cycles of accumulation'; and, finally, of the 'world hegemony' of one state after another sustaining an 'ordered anarchy' in the world system of states (1994, esp. pp. 27–36). Taken together, these concepts allow us to maintain the idea of different *forms of power*, in political and socio-economic spheres, in tension with one another and different *political entities* (i.e. normally, states) interacting in a basically stable competition. The dynamic between states (and, for that matter, other forms of the political) and the burgeoning world economy is contained in the contrast between 'capitalist' and 'territorist' 'logics of power'. In the one logic, that of capitalism, the final purpose is the control of wealth, regardless of where it may be in spatial terms – though power over territory may be important to success. In the other logic, control over space is precisely what counts, though it may be necessary to have access to wealth as a means to that end. It follows that capitalism may sustain, make use of or obstruct the given territorial-political control, according to the particular circumstances; and vice versa.

Over the course of Europe's modern history, a sequence of situations has developed in which state and capitalism have achieved a symbiosis. At such moments, thanks to the political structure of the state, surpluses could be recirculated in a way that increased the profitability of capital. Likewise, the profits would assist the maintenance or expansion of the territorist state. The Florentine state, for example, taxed and spent the surplus of its commercial entrepreneurs; but they, in their turn, lived off the military strength and esteem which that gave to their country. Since early on in modern European history, however, the cycles of accumulation have operated *within the very working* of the system of states, because (as Braudel's image suggests) capitalist accumulation reaches out beyond the territory of the given state to repatriate profit. The Genoese, for example, briefly acted as financial agents beyond the confines of the empire for the territorist ambitions of the Habsburgs (Arrighi 1994, pp. 109–26). Their profits were made possible by the workings of the international system of the day. It is Amsterdam's and, later, London's role as the clearing centre for the whole of Europe's trade – and then for that of the whole world – which epitomizes, however, the special, hegemonic position that a territorial power could acquire while sustaining a cycle of accumulation on its territory. In those instances, even without any formal central governance for the system of states, *all* the other players in the system (be they wealth-acquirers or territory-acquirers) had to fall in with the dominance of the territorist-capitalist centre: that is, first the Netherlands and then Great Britain. To try to challenge the hegemony of that centre and its global channels of wealth and power was to risk a general collapse from which all could expect to suffer.

By this stage in my discussion, we have the necessary concepts to envisage a 'modern' extension of interrelated political entities and centres of market power. The many players in the set-up *do* have choices, but they are constrained. There is only so much scope to occupy, or to invent, certain roles, together with matching political and economic forms. To ignore those constraints would court the risk of exclusion from the overall set-up, or damage to that set-up, with consequent dangers to all. To challenge Amsterdam in its heyday would mean leaving the then modern financial/trading system.[2] The competitive–co-operative logic of this long, complex game could shape the options at any particular political and economic time and place, even while the system as a whole retains the broad, expansive and accumulative features which characterize modern Western history. There is, therefore, plenty of room in this globalizing overview to fit the evolution *within* or *between layers* of given political systems. The route to an account of the spatio-temporal distribution of revolutions now lies through theorizations of those layers.

For the lower, less global analysis that revolutions call for, we need to supplement the economic and state/territorial conceptions of power that appear in the various global pictures I have considered so far. It is certainly advisable to incorporate from the start additional categories of power, such as those Michael Mann has employed in his long study of the development of European political forms. The categories of ideological and political power are especially apposite (Mann 1986).[3] In conjunction with what Mann refers to as 'economic' and 'military' power, these two categories permit us to track the pressures (whether or not they threaten actual revolution) put upon established forms of power, particularly those at the possible point of revolutionary events: where state and society meet. For Mann's categories disaggregate state–society power relations: into military-coercive, ideological-discursive, and political-calculative.[4] In theory – and, indeed, 'in reality' when we look at many an instance of revolution – existing political powers could be separately challenged and/or changed in respect of one or more of these forms of power.

That said, it is the studies by Skocpol and by Tilly which set the specific agenda for any account of the modern spatio-temporal distribution of states overwhelmed by revolutionary challenges. The former gives priority to the breakdown, partly self-induced, of states which are subject to excessive pressures by the competitive international system. The pressures of competition are both military and economic – each state being aware of, and trying to overcome, its military and economic weakness relative to the others. But, like any breakdown, these are clearly the *combined* effect of the pressures themselves *and* the ability of the states they impinge upon to withstand them. In Skocpol's analysis, the vulnerable states are surviving 'agrarian bureaucracies'. States of this type lack well-developed administrative and coercive power within their territory, being instead dependent upon a potentially recalcitrant nobility to maintain the rural social order, and extract and pass on taxable wealth – so far as they are willing. Such states, that is to say, already lack certain modern mechanisms of power and are internally weaker for it.

To link that style of analysis with the theories of the *spread* of modernity, we need simply to ask: what may lie behind the location of states such as Skocpol considers? Prima facie, military pressure upon a state is more likely to come from a more successful neighbour, which will more easily infringe its literal boundaries or the boundaries of its influence. In the lead-up to its revolution, France is close to a successful military rival in Britain; similarly, Russia is close to Germany; and China is close to Japan. But the spatial incidence of competitive pressure does not operate solely in terms of simple proximity. The external, competitive pressures are present in the system as a whole, and so will impinge upon different states according to a more complex spatial logic. Russia had been under competitive pressure from France and Britain too. And China had already fallen apart as a consequence of pressures from faraway Britain, France, Germany and even the Netherlands.

We can, I suggest, best understand the incidence of competitive pressure *à la* Skocpol through a concept of the world spread of the modern European capitalist world, as described by Braudel et al. For in those models, dominant, advanced states, and their capitalisms, reach out into the world as a whole. Thus, Britain competes with France not solely because they are neighbours, but also because the capitalism of each country needs to get a hold on the Americas. Britain and France compete with Russia economically and militarily in the Mediterranean/Black Sea, before Russia finds itself competing militarily also with its Japanese and then its German neighbours. As Orlando Figes puts it, 'The First World War was a gigantic test of the modern state, and as the only state that had failed to modernize before the war, it was a test which tsarist Russia was almost bound to fail' (1996, p. 810). China competes militarily and economically with various powers from Europe which impose pseudo-colonial conditions of trade upon it, and then has to compete militarily with Japan – which has been competing in turn with those same European powers and the USA.

In short, external pressures occur according to the complex spread, in tandem, of modern global economic *and* state power. We can capture this with the metaphor of a 'ripple of modernity'. The advanced centre spreads its influence in different, but mingling waves; each wave may then bounce back and interfere with others. Thus US/European pressure on Japan 'bounces' off into Japanese pressure on China. I will return to the possibilities of this analogy later.

We can say something similar about the spatial incidence of the *internal* factors in Skocpol's model: that is to say, about the survival of agrarian bureaucratic society and those power structures which prove inflexible under the attempts of the embattled state to increase its competitive capacity in the state system. But to do so, we have to use a wider categorization of forms of power – such as we find in Mann. If peasantry and rural nobility survive too long for the good of the state, that effect must belong largely to economic, political and ideological forms of power. The military power of the state will not alone be able to counter these unpalatable socio-economic facts within the state's territory. For example, as Moore teaches, the peasantry are primarily undermined by the spreading economic market, which simply did not extend into the hinterlands of rural France, Russia or China, so leaving a potentially autonomous peasantry in place. Or again, the political position and ideological strength of *ancien régime* rural nobility survived in spite of the proselytization of a modernizing Enlightenment, centred on London, Edinburgh–Glasgow, Paris and other urban centres.

Much the same can be said regarding the surviving political and ideological forms of power in pre-revolutionary Russia and China. There are global ideological and political pressures, emanating from the West; but they had not reached far into the power-base of those countries' predominantly rural societies. We should in no way belittle the autonomous complexity of such local political and ideological by-ways. Read (1986) offers an instance with great reverberations for modernist ideologies across the globe: the literary stir created by the 1910 *Vekhi* (landmarks) collection which, while advocating a return to the inner religious life, formulated a *revolutionary* religious belief. In the subsequent debate, it was Lenin's anti-intellectualism (in *Materialism and Empirio-Criticism* – 'one of the crudest and least philosophically sophisticated of the contributions' – p. 174) which triumphed; whilst the passion for the inner life joined the mainstream of modernism further west. The ideological story of China's Taipeng rebellion is more bizarre. From about 1846 till the final recapture of Nanking in 1864, the 'God Worshippers', an *anti*-materialist social order of hybrid Christian-Confucian belief led by failed Confucian scholar Hong Xiuquan, ruled a part peasant, part ethnic-minority force of thousands, capable of continuous war against the Manchu emperors. Hong himself had got his Christianity from partial renditions of the Bible into Chinese, prepared in the 1820–30s by independent-minded Western missionaries in Canton (Spence 1996, pp.14ff). But, crucially, he failed to maintain good relations with the Westerners based in Shanghai, especially the British, who found the God Worshippers' customs unorthodox and Hong Xiuquan's claim (as Jesus Christ's younger brother) to world dominion both heretical and diplomatically inadmissible. Here, then, was a strangely changed ideological offshoot of European 'modernity', turned to mysticism at its head, yet inspired by the belief that the Chinese must recover themselves by ousting the embattled Manchu order and adapting selected Western ideas and/or technology.[5]

The implication of my reasoning is that we may account for the spatial distribution of revolutionary crisis and change in the Skocpol model by extending our idea of the global spread of 'modern' pressures, to include political or ideological ones as well as those that are military or economic. In the spirit of world-system theory, military, economic, political or ideological pressures can all be said to spread across the globe over the course of modern history, though each has to be kept analytically distinct in order to track differences between their spread in any particular zone.

As I mentioned in chapter 2, Tilly's studies of resistance, revolution and state formation also use a spatial model (set out in full in Tilly 1990). It adapts the familiar divide between eastern and western Europe into something more of a cluster. Capital, the crucial ascendant form of non-political power, grows in a long strip of commercial development running from south-central to north-western Europe. Each state developing in Europe must find a way to accommodate to it. In the heart of that strip, where capital in commercial cities achieves too much independence from the state (e.g. in the Netherlands), the power of the state cannot establish itself, or extract sufficient resources to sustain its coercive-political form of power. Conversely, where, away from the strip of European development, commerce remains weak (as in Hungary, Russia or Spain), coercion by the state and aristocratic landholders effectively suppresses capital, achieving extensive control, but over backward, impoverished peasant economies. The most *successful* state-formation, on the other hand, takes place *alongside* this strip of commercial development, neither within nor too distant from it: notably, in France and England. But it is there also that the earliest revolutionary confrontation is likely to occur. State coercion and capital are in balance: their relationship may well have to be settled in an overt contest. But a mutually beneficial accommodation can be reached after such a conflict. The outcome is what Tilly calls 'capitalized coercion', where, at the price of ceding some freedom to urban capitalist society, states secure access to large domestic financial and military resources.

The lesson of this spatio-temporal account of state formation via revolution is to reinforce the earlier point that if economic power and state power (in its military, political and ideological forms) are held apart analytically, we may identify their separate, yet interrelated spatial extension within Europe. Tilly's account of European revolutions relates the differing incidence of revolutionary changes of power to the different zones of state-formation and compromise between coercion and capital. Thus, France achieved 'capitalized coercion' in a 'modern' socio-political balance: initially by the state consolidating a centralized, national order of rule, and then by the resolution of the resultant imbalance of political forces in the revolutionary collapse and re-formation at the end of the eighteenth century. Britain's path to statehood also placed it 'astride both coercion and capital' (Tilly 1990, p. 132), after its seventeenth-century revolutionary upheaval formed 'a compact, financially effective state, containing royal power, placing a parliamentary coalition of landlords and merchants in substantial control of national affairs, leaving landlords and parsons the regulation of local business . . . advancing the conditions for agrarian and then industrial capitalism' (p. 124).

Where the balance of commerce and coercion was different, one or other of them won out easily and there was no strong post-revolutionary state. Holland's 'capital-intensive' path produced highly decentralized, civic-corporate power, which, until well into the nineteenth century, confined conflict within minor dynastic contests of the older, 'communal' form. Spain's 'coercion-intensive' mix weakened its cities and its global military power, leaving internal political contests in the hands of aristocratic or military elites right up to the second half of the twentieth century. In these circumstances, state coercion and capitalism's demands had not met face to face, and thus been resolved.

That brief examination of the conceptual possibilities in theories of the historical global spread of the 'modern' world, paired with intra-country comparative analyses, puts us in a position to hypothesize the spatio-temporal distribution of revolutionary change. On the one hand, there is the secular expansion of the world system, which should properly be disaggregated into modifications in different forms of power. That is to say, though they are interrelated and do maintain a rough alignment, 'modern' military, economic, political and ideological power all exhibit distinct dynamic tendencies in spreading across the globe. On the other hand, the incidence of specific revolutions in their particular location can be grounded in the pressures and drives in states and their societies.

Breakdown, progress, modernization

To link the spread of, and interactions between, global systems to revolutionary upheavals and evolutions within given countries' systems, we need to develop a concept of how the internal level interacts with the global. I propose to interpret the power structures that are 'internal' to a given country or area as 'conduits' of various of the pressures generated in the higher-level, global system. This entails that such pressures impinge internally upon the different societies and that a reaction is forthcoming from within. In this way, the concept of a 'conduit' for external, global pressures goes some way to account for the incidence of the breakdown that makes for revolution. On its own, however, it does not, indeed it is not intended to, fully account for breakdown: for pressure alone does not predetermine the manner or the outcome of these responses. Thus, once I have expounded the notion of a 'conduit' of pressures that prompt breakdown, I shall go on to consider how, if at all, these impacts from the global pattern are reflected internally within a given country and, in particular, how that may affect the dimensions of change and agency which can figure in any revolution.

The simplest impact, and the closest to the Skocpol model, occurs where the developing state, as a dominant military force in the area it rules, experiences pressure from adjacent areas – or, of course, from areas further afield if they have reason to operate militarily at a distance. Plainly, we could identify such military pressures equally in other historical situations, with much less developed centralized states – such as that which European feudal military power placed upon the Ottoman Empire at the time of the Crusades. But in our modern history, it is *states* that prove best at wielding military power and hence most experience the pressures of military rivalry. Given that the state depends also, and increasingly (as expensive modern organization and military technology develop), upon wealth – extracted in tax and/or borrowed – new developments of *economic* power can also funnel pressure in upon the state. In the simplest case, the state will be bankrupted by its military needs and unable to extract enough wealth from the society it rules, or to impose its wishes on that society's holders of economic power. Alternatively, the state may be weakened by rising in-debtedness abroad at the hands of the global system of extraction and exchanges – as was seventeenth-century Spain (and likewise a host of late twentieth-century states).

However, the state's ideological and political power may also be chal-lenged by pressures from the expanding global system. The need to com-mand ideological power is implicit in the very notion that political authority has to sustain legitimacy. While it may (so long as there is little movement of ideas across territory) do that on its own 'internal' terms, such internal isolation is less and less feasible in the modern world. The positions of English, French and Russian monarchies were undermined by ideas coming from, respectively, Holland, the USA and Western Europe. So the state must make a more or less successful show of matching these ideas – as the French monarchy attempted by its agricultural market re-forms, or the tsar did (less convincingly, perhaps) with the 'liberalization' of the Duma. Otherwise the state's ideological position will be impugned. Finally, the political strength of the state has to be seen as a matter of not only addressing a number of interests within its territory, but also juggling inter-country impacts upon those interests. For 'internal' groups can be weaned off their own state by wider processes of change which alter their interests. Thus, in 1688 the restored English aristocratic/commercial elite saw that its interests were better served by the Dutch-Protestant connection brought by William of Orange than by the French-Catholic one that had supported the later Stuart kings. Or, again, successful independence-minded British subjects in North America saw their advantage in more open access to the Atlantic trade than Britain was prepared to allow them in the 1760s.

In each of these instances, the state can be properly described as the 'conduit' through which pressures – military, economic, ideological and political – are registered from the world spread of modernizing forces. For it is in the state that the pressures manifest themselves and cluster. In *some* cases, the state into which these pressures flow will be altered only after it has collapsed in revolutionary confrontation. But, of course, the preferred solution of any system or institution is a mix of resistance and adaptation. Though the pressures will most likely be universal, then, the states' responses will vary: from more or less successfully suppressing the effects of pressure; to bending before it becomes evident; to reforming in time to head it off; to repression; to overt confrontation. The last three strategies may or may not end in a revolutionary challenge. Or, indeed, there is the intriguingly hybrid response, 'revolution from above', which Ellen Trimberger studied (1972, 1978) in Japan, Turkey, Peru etc.: where a section of the existing elites steals the clothes of modernizing revolution learnt from abroad to fight other, 'anti-modernizing' forces at home. But it is the revolutionary out-turn which makes the meeting of internal power and modern global pressures most obvious for us to see. If it is the place of states in the modern world to be the conduits of world-level modernizing pressures, that is to say, it is the nature of revolutions to be the least likely, but the plainest, most dramatic *response* to those pressures. It is that which has given scope for an understanding of revolutions in terms of a breakdown *accompanied by* progress, in which the parties try to catch up with, or otherwise respond to, 'modernity'. A revolution, I conclude, is one kind of event that may occur as political systems, most probably states, react to the pressures they register from the expanding, modern global system. That is not, of course, the *whole* character of any particular revolution; but it goes a long way to explain why the incidence of revolutions is distributed as it is.

Political systems can be exposed to pressures either from above or from below. But, clearly, the combination of *both* is particularly likely to occasion a breakdown of the system's overall authority. And this can occur whenever spreading modern military, economic, ideological and/or political forms of power force the political system into greater than usual efforts. For the times when a system has the greatest need to exercise its powers are precisely those when those powers are most likely to be tested to destruction. This observation fits well the incidence of what I called, in chapter 1, the 'constitutional-republican' and the 'communist/social-democratic' revolutions. Skocpol's achievement demonstrates that perfectly for France in the first category, and Russia in the second. But the picture of self-destructive efforts to match external pressures also fits the wider range in Tilly's account. The English state, for example, confronts militarily pressures from Spain, France and Holland; tries to keep up with the political and ideological advances of its absolutist rivals; negotiates with difficulty the ideological pressure from continental Protestant religion; and has to reach a new accommodation with its London-based capitalism. In one area after another, these pressures weaken it so much that it survives only after transformation in a full-scale, revolutionary confrontation.

This notion of a conduit applies equally well to cases where revolution does *not* occur. So the Habsburg-Spanish state acts just as much as a 'conduit' of pressures; but there are fewer, because the international spread of Protestantism had not reached to its ideological centre, and commercial capital was little developed there. As a result, unlike England, the Habsburg-Spanish system continued to exercise the essentials of its coercive, military power and of its ideological authority.[6] Finally, the notion of a conduit also encompasses the way that quite a number of potential, or incipient, revolutions, especially in my categories of 'reformation revolts' and 'national liberation revolutions', seem to 'misfire' by comparison with the central, paradigm instances of France and Russia. In these instances, trans-country pressures are felt and responses from above and below bring on revolutionary confrontation; but the revolt often does not meet, overturn and reform the state itself.

Change and will in the face of modernity

The claim that revolutions occur where states are conduits of the pressures from the expanding, modern global system does not, of course, mean that the impact of such external pressures is the end of the story. First, as we have seen, these pressures do not by any means *always* produce a full-scale revolutionary confrontation between a state and the social forces it claims to rule. Reform, diversion and/or repression may prove to be perfectly adequate responses. Secondly, where revolutionary confrontation does occur, the players in the situation may act, and interact, in a variety of ways. There is a great deal more to understanding a specific revolution than any necessary and predictable outcome determined in the global system. To acknowledge and incorporate the global dimension in an account of the incidence of revolutions does not, then, oblige us to believe that the force of the global system closes off all the possibilities in the revolutionary situation. We do not have to go on to adopt that tendency within the global manner of thought found in theorists such as Wallerstein or Skocpol. To take only the latter, it is true, as she shows, that both France and Russia end up, after their revolutions, with a stronger, more centralized state, as required to sustain an international position. But the differences between the two outcomes remain legion. Those differences could be the result of a number of specific features particular to each case. Some will concern the global position of the state in question: for example, France's capacity to challenge comparable European powers during the nineteenth century compared with Russia's limited possibilities in a twentieth-century global order already fully embraced by British and US power. Secondly, differentiating features may arise from internal elements: such as the relative strength of French enlightened and legal elites by comparison with those in Russia.

Thirdly, the full story of a revolution will have to combine together the change and agency dimensions. There are plainly numerous specific historically significant human actions, with their associated outcomes, in any actual revolution: Louis XVI's imprudent, inept action in attempting to 'escape' Paris in June 1791 irretrievably damaged the prospects of the monarchy's inclusion in the new 'republican' order;[7] Stalin's use of his position as Party secretary to create a network of patronage that crucially undermined his rivals by the time of Lenin's death, thus enhancing the long-term prospects of an autarchic, one-country strategy for the revolution as a whole. At a level of explanation closer to the structural, we can repeat that the scope for change of one country at one time is likely to be different from that of others. Once post-revolutionary France had been re-incorporated into the European state system, the French state could very well envisage participating fully in the colonial economic expansion of contemporary European nation-states. This option was not available to post-revolutionary Russia, largely landlocked and in a world economy dominated by competition between large industrial producers. So the direction that Russia apparently could, or should, follow in the first decades of the twentieth century resembled, instead, that of turn-of-the-century Germany or the USA. To make the point in another way, for an early-twentieth-century state in the throes of breakdown and change, Germany and the USA were powerful models of the 'modern' future.

So the change dimension of a revolution is not merely the product of the global system, with agency excluded. Both change and agency have to be seen in the larger spatio-temporal context, which may favour or exclude certain possible directions and conscious choices. When a revolutionary challenge is made within a society, it opens up the prospect of many possible futures. Given that the pressure from more advanced parts of the world has contributed to the initial crisis, the participants in a revolutionary challenge will usually express a wish to 'catch up'. But with what? Some participants in the French Revolution looked across the English Channel at the shape of the future; others looked across the Atlantic; others, again, returned to a more or less misconstrued version of the world of antiquity (Baker 1990). Participants feel the need to declare where they are going and what future condition they expect to arrive at. But how do they determine that? In sum, whilst it is easy to speak of revolutions, in short-hand, as a moment of 'transition to the modern condition', to those *in* the revolutionary situation, who register the pressure from more 'modern' forms, it has never been obvious which model of modernity to follow or what reorganization is needed achieve it.

We can take the point about agency further. There are features of modernity in itself which *force* upon participants the pursuit of unprecedented outcomes. I pointed out in chapter 2 how modernity must intrude as a 'goal-less' import in the societies upon which it exerts pressure. The 'de-traditionalizing' effect of modernity tears up the basis for past forms, and casts social actors into looser, open webs of inter-communication and inter-dependence stretching out beyond any visible group (Giddens 1990).

By leaving social practices 'disembedded' in this way, the modern world *imposes* imagination, invention and choice upon social actors who must accordingly give new form and reason to what they do. From a more gloomy perspective, one may see the same restless pressure to invent emerging as the 'disenchantment' of modernity delegitimizes the order of the universe as given: 'Awareness of the world's contingency and the idea of order as the goal and the outcome of the *practice of ordering* were born together, as twins; perhaps even Siamese twins'(Bauman 1992, p. xii). Yet if modernity forces some creative invention, it also offers terms in which to formulate such innovations: starting with 'rational prognosis' (as identified by Koselleck 1985, pp. 12ff), by which the future can be designed according to the givens of the present world and human purposes and benefits. In short, when global pressures of modernity push change upon those societies where there is scope for revolution, this structural effect is concurrently evoking the need for agency to choose and modify modernity as given.

We can add a structuring aspect to that articulation of agency in response to the spread of European/Western modernity. Broadly speaking, the nearer a revolution occurs to the centre of expanding European/world modernity, the greater is the scope for human agency to make a manifest, deliberate choice of, and impact on the direction of, 'progressive' change. That possibility has to be set out through a number of steps.

Clearly, the idea that revolutions occur in response to the world spread of a system suggests that we can differentiate revolutions that are nearer 'the centre' of the system from those that are further from it. This is possible even if one keeps in mind that the spread of the system is a complex 'ripple' rather than a simple, singular expansion. Other things being equal, to be nearer to the centre is to have a greater potential impact on the core, and to be present when the direction of the system *as a whole* is less firmly established, more open to modification. The comparison of the USA, France and Russia brings this out. The North American colonies were too far from Britain and its major colonial interests (in the East) for their secession to destroy the most successful commercial state of the time; but it did, after a lapse of time, chip away at the ideological underpinnings of 'old regime' power in Europe more generally. On the other hand, the collapse of France – the most manifestly powerful absolutist state and right at the centre of attention in Europe – fatally undermined the credibility of any unreformed absolutism in the nineteenth century and forced to the fore a new dominant European model of the solidaristic nation-state uniting military, political and economic strength. By contrast, the long-anticipated demise, a century later, of Russian absolutism did not bring forward an effective alternative to the dominant model in modernity's new North American heartland. That continued to develop unnaffected. In brief, the more 'central' revolutions may more easily appear to be at the head of any dominant direction which historical change is taking, and to offer a greater impact and a wider scope for choice and innovation to the participants in the particular revolution. In this sense, it is easier to see the French Revolution as an event in which human agents consciously take a lead in historical change.

Prima facie, we can then draw the following rough conclusion: more 'central' revolutions will tend to participate in the current direction of overall modernizing change and to show more scope for human agency. A number of conditions make a revolution more 'central' to the system, for the purposes of this hypothesis. Other things being equal, a revolution that occurs nearer the simple, geographical centre of the system would indeed be more central; but to reason thus is usually to take the geometry of centres and zones too literally. To be involved earlier in modernization will also make for 'proximity' to the centre in the present sense. More subtly, a revolution that has a greater strategic potential to impact on the centre, and/or the others involved in the system, is more central. This is more likely where the revolution occurs in a country with a more crucial, less easily replaceable role in the working of the system. Furthermore, a revolution that reacts to and manifestly takes part in modernizing change across the board – in military, economic, ideological and political practices – is also more 'central'. Finally, having the greater potential to impact on the system offers a greater prospect of participating in the overall direction of change associated with the spreading system. This is so in either of two senses: first, to be nearer the centre increases the chance of emulating the centre as a model (as England did with the Netherlands); secondly, to have a greater potential impact offers the prospect of shifting the direction of change emanating from the centre.

Where it is more feasible for a society to join in, and modify, the direction of overall change, it follows that internal forces promoting revolution may come together around a programme that can find a place in the dominant global direction of change. That in turn increases the prospects of alignment between pressure from *outside* for change, the overt preferences adopted by *internal* forces for change, and the direction a society may *actually be able to take* after a revolutionary breakdown. Hence, to be near the centre increases the possibility of a revolution exhibiting, at one and the same time, a response to modernizing pressures; an alignment to overall global modernization; *and* conscious agency in pursuit of such change. 'Central' revolutions, as I claimed above, are more able to exhibit deliberate leadership of the overall direction of modernization.

Two further points are required before developing the above argument with later revolutions in mind. I have endeavoured to underline that the spread of the system is a complex 'ripple' rather than a simple, singular expansion. That is to say, the spread of the system can be disaggregated into – at least – military, economic, ideological and political levels. This is initially a theoretical precaution. But in many instances it can be seen that the different levels *are* operating with a degree of mutual autonomy.

Britain was a centre of political power in the early twentieth century, even after it had lost much of its economic power. Similarly, Paris has for centuries been a world ideological influence, even during those times when French political and military power has been very much in doubt. It follows that modernizing waves at different levels may very well cross one another's paths; that is to say, they may emanate from different 'centres'.

Finally, all this indicates why it is necessary to treat 'modernization' and 'modernity' as synthetic categories (and, accordingly, put them in quotation marks at times). At any given moment, certain military, economic, ideological or political forms appear to have the capacity to dominate others or demonstrate greater strength than they. This itself is a function of the complex of developments at the level of the 'modern' world. By exhibiting such comparative strength these forms appear to belong to the future: that is how they can acquire the epithet 'modern'. But the relatively autonomous spread of different forms, possibly from different centres, makes it impossible to stipulate authoritatively and for all time one set of successful, and hence 'modern', forms. The features of the 'modern', therefore, cannot themselves be regarded as fixed and certain; they are a result of the outcome of unpredictable trans-country rivalries.

Revolutions and modernities

With the passage of time, this point about how modernity cannot be fixed is likely to weigh more heavily upon the direction taken by revolutions. So I want now to examine more closely the evolution of change and agency in revolutions as the dynamic I described earlier takes them further from the centre of modernity. In this context, the French Revolution must be regarded as truly quite exceptional, even though not entirely unique. For that one particular revolution took place at what appeared to be the centre of the 'advanced' world. It is therefore a quite misleading exemplar of the nature of revolutions and their impact on history.

It is now possible to look back and qualify the claims to be leading human progress that were made on the basis of the French Revolution. But, given the proximity of the revolutionary shock to the centre of the then modern system, participants and onlookers at the time were in no position to see any weakness in such claims. For twenty-five years, French military power could threaten the combined forces of the older monarchies. French republicans managed to win over progressive political and commercial elites in Belgium, Germany and Italy. The Napoleonic continental trading system functioned for a decade and a half. Ideologies from the Revolution challenged established European power structures for decades after that. On all levels of power, then, France was a visible success: the strategies pursued explicitly in the name of this revolution yielded results. In this way, the French Revolution exhibited with unique force the explicit, conscious power of human agency over the direction of modernizing historical change.

If we compare *any* other revolutions, we find that their claims to take a conscious lead in history are weaker by virtue of their relative 'distance' from the centres of the expanding world system. The Dutch revolt took an impressive economic and ideological lead. But it occurred before any capitalist centre had found a strong political base. Its political and military impact was thus soon muted by the survival of larger military power in the older states of Europe (notably Spain and France) and the rapid ascent of English financial power, successfully integrated with a more centralized and better-funded state. The time-bomb of the American Revolution made relatively little impact upon economic or political forms in the European centre of world power until, one and half centuries later, it was backed by a world centre of economic-financial power. In its day, the Russian Revolution, on the other hand, was far more persuasive, and could appear to rival the French. It made a substantial ideological impact across the Western world. But the hoped-for economic preponderance never materialized from within the isolation that was imposed on it by the global system as a whole. Fifty years after the event, the Chinese revolution has produced a weighty military power which sits on the side-lines of world military conflicts; its ideological influence has always lagged behind that of Russia. It *may* be about to produce a persuasive economic model, though that is unlikely to overtake the USA, Europe or Japan.

I argued above that the more 'central' a revolution was to the heart of the expanding world system the greater degree of historical direction and human agency it could be expected to exhibit *vis-à-vis* the system as a whole. It is now necessary to qualify that claim, in the light of what has just been said regarding the ambivalence of 'modernity' at any given time. This amounts to taking seriously the 'ripple' metaphor used earlier: modernity spreading on different levels at different rates from different possible centres. Ripples, one should add, bounce off objects and interfere with one another. This metaphor gives an altogether more complex picture of modernity's spread. It implies that modernity at different levels may impinge upon any part of the world from different locations. A common route for post-French Revolutionary constitutional thinking was not the French republican model, but admiration for the *Belgian* constitution. In the 1950s and 1960s, in spite of Sweden's military neutrality, its 'Nordic', corporatist model of economic and social cohesion gained ideological ground across Europe as a whole. In short, the pressures arise from the challenge of seemingly different modernit*ies*.

If pressures do emanate from different modernities, then the structure of pressures promoting breakdown, of the available possible directions of change, and of the room for human action within any revolutionary response will be all modified. I should like to illustrate this further ramification of the ideas of this chapter with the example of revolutionary movements in Latin America. The choice is prompted by the peculiarly close-knit post-colonial relationship of that part of the world to the Europe-based world system (Cardoso and Faletto 1979).[8] For most of the last two centuries, the continent 'has been a major importer of ideas, ideology, social theory and doctrine' (Castañeda 1993, p. 179). So persistent has been the failure of the notion of national resistance movements in South America, that some now even see it as the graveyard of the very idea that national politics is the proper focus for resistance (Garretón 1995). Latin America had initially been held by colonizing European states (Spain and Portugal) of a type that early on fell well behind their European neigh-bours. It was then lost, earlier than other colonial regions, and felt the greatest impact of modernity 'relayed', as it were, via the USA's *anti*-European development. Latin America presents three notable twentieth-century revolutionary struggles: in Mexico, Cuba and Peru.

A common feature in the revolutionary politics of Latin American coun-tries is the pattern of limited modernization left in the wake of the conti-nent's early, absolutist Iberian masters: constitutional models of initially French (but later US) inspiration, approved primarily by weak educated elites, atop a state with stronger military than civilian constituents; large peasant/Indian populations dominated in the countryside by the wealth and direct power of large estates (*haciendas*) which were originally worked by forced labour; limited commercial/urban development. Within this setting, small, very wealthy civilian or military elites have usually been able to hold the state to protect their own narrow interests.

Thus it was the misuse of the formal provisions of the constitution by Porfirio Diaz (the president for thirty-six years) that sparked the initial point of conflict to start the Mexican revolution. When Francisco Madero challenged Diaz's continuation in power in 1910, he successfully mustered support from the peasantry and the middle and working classes, which had been created by late-nineteenth-century US-stimulated development. But, in a violent, conspiratorial political environment, with only limited, suspi-cious loyalty from his mass supporters in town and country, Madero was soon assassinated and replaced by a military strong man, Victoriano Huerta. During the First World War, Mexican 'national' politics then became the plaything of manipulation by the Western powers, especially Britain, Germany and the USA. But only the latter (the largest, and closest, of the three) could effectively impose its ideological and political power (backed by occasional military intervention), which it did in the constitu-tion of 1917. Many crucial moments in the progress of the Mexican revolution were played out in US politics (e.g. when President Wilson opposed Huerta) or in the US public arena (as when Villa, the peasant leader, was lionized by the US press). But the intrusive force of US political modernity had its limits. Carranza, the US-favoured president who followed Huerta, was assassinated in his turn only three years later. Political cohesion was only re-established through the implementation of the constitution as undertaken by a part-Indian leader, Lázaro Cárdenas, who secured major concessions to peasant interests in the land (notably by the entrenchment of their *ejido* communes into the constitution), formalized workplace protection for workers, and the nationalization of central economic assets. Some of the autonomous capacity of peasant forces still survives, as when, in 1994 after the signing of the North America Free Trade Agreement, a new *Zapatista* movement (bearing the name of the South's great peasant leader in the revolution) successfully pre-empted the implicit challenge to the peasants' rights in the land by taking control in the Chiapas region. [9]

Mexico illustrates the mix of political forms that can emerge from a revolution on the confused outer limit of differing versions of Western modernity. The shallow establishment of *any* central state by the European colonial powers met with a flow of political and ideological pressure from a later, capitalist-democratic power centre to the north. On the face of it, the Mexican state, in whoever's hands it may be, is severely constrained by the dominant, modern international system. This forces the state power itself into passive acceptance. So there is little sign of the politics of the Mexican state successfully making free, deliberate choices. And yet, the combination of an underdeveloped state and a position at the outer limit of differing versions of Western modernity created the space for a hybrid combination: patrimonial politics, a US-style liberal constitution, strong entrenched corporatist political movements, and insuppressible secessionist tendencies in the remoter parts of the territory (Laurell 1992). In Mexico's revolution, we find a confused picture of attempts to 'catch up' and of the effects of deliberate human agency. But the impact of its greatest modernizing pressures, US politics and capitalism, is muted, even though Mexico has never really been able to set off in any of the dominant modernizing directions of its day.

Cuba's situation resembles Mexico's, except in the island's territorial extent, the level of economic development, and (crucially) the *timing* of its revolutions in the global scene. Its *hacienda* agriculture had been more thoroughly developed, commercialized and integrated into the European and US markets before (later than in the case of Mexico) Spain's formal authority was shouldered aside by US intervention to 'support' the Cuban Revolutionary Party formed by the romantic-liberal revolutionary, José Marti, in a rebellion against colonial rule. US *military* as well as political intervention made its first appearance immediately when, in 1899, American forces excluded the rebels from government and created their own short-lived military administration. In the resultant settlement, Cuba was left with a constitution approved by the US, which (by the inclusion of the US Senate's 'Platt Amendment') went so far as to formally permit the US to intervene for 'the maintenance of a government adequate for the protection of life, property and individual liberties'. Cuba had passed from the hands of one modernity (Spanish colonial administration, primarily sustaining the security of the large estates) directly into the hands of another: US-capital ownership of production, a US-approved constitution and US-dominated politics. Throughout the first half of the twentieth century, the US ambassador ran the Cuban president a close second for title of most important figure in internal Cuban politics. In short, as Luis Aguilar puts it (quoted in Bethell 1993, p. 40):

> Lacking any tradition of self-government or political discipline, with a low level of public education, and impoverished by the war [of 1902], the Cubans found themselves trapped between growing American control of land and sugar, and Spanish domination of commerce, virtually guaranteed by the peace treaty between the USA and Spain. Politics thus became the principal avenue to economic improvement and one access to national resources. Consequently, political parties quickly became . . . co-operatives organized for bureaucratic consumption. . . . Old colonial vices, political corruption, local *caudillismo* and disregard for the law reappeared quickly.

As in Mexico, the impact of modernization from the north had its limits. The constitution alone did not make the state, which continued to operate according to habits of the narrow elites formed from the military or from local, *comprador* wealth. During periods of relative weakness in the economic or political dominance of US power, internal forces in Cuba could take off in a different direction out of keeping with US approaches. Thus it was that, in 1933, as the US recession undermined both the island's prosperity and the strength of the USA as a model, the American ambassador was forced to accept the *Septembrista Putsch*, and a 'radical' new leader from the lower levels of the military, Sergeant Fulgencio Batista. By 1940, with the USA heavily involved in war, Batista was even able to revoke the 1902 constitution. On the other hand, what the USA could not do at the time through its direct political and economic impact, was to happen in any case in the context of post-Second World War US-centred economic growth: a reversion to corrupt, clientelist politics, latterly even presided over by Batista himself after his return to power in 1952.

On the other hand, greater and greater integration in the US economy also made for pressures in the direction of breakdown, as the urban population was squeezed by the inflationary effects of US-dependent growth without any effective reform or social protection from a corrupt, inadequately developed state. But, as in Mexico, development in, and control over, the countryside remained a weak point for any Havana government. Thus, in 1959, the removal of a dictatorial, albeit formally elected, Latin American president was once again to be undertaken by forces operating in the rural areas, with wide acquiescence across Cuban society but active support primarily from the peasantry. Under favourable internal economic and political conditions, the tiny force of exiles led by Fidel Castro (a previously failed revolutionary from a wealthy planter family trained as a lawyer and formed in left-wing urban politics) could achieve mass recruitment in the rural areas and face down a demoralized national army. This is a mix of forces for change quite particular to the Latin American margin of modernization: European-style urban liberal or socialistic political radicalism, uncontrolled transnational capitalist economic growth, the failure of an ill-developed state infused by the corruption of big money, and country areas never properly incorporated under the central power of the state. It gave room to Cuba to limit the *political* impact of its modern northern neighbour, and Cuban revolutionary leaders the pretensions to change the course of their history. 'History will absolve me,' declared Castro defiantly at his trial after a *failed* uprising in 1953.

If the Cuban revolutionary experience begins to depart from the Mexican after 1959, that can be attributed to the greater scope for a consciously different historical direction offered by the appearance on the world scene of a *third* putative version of modernity (after that from Spain/Europe and from the USA), the Soviet model. Until the late 1980s, Castro's post-revolutionary Cuban state developed to exploit the space this offered in the ripples of modernity. So long as strategic and military rivalry reigned between the Soviet Union and the USA, the former was, for example, willing to take up the output left by the withdrawal/exclusion from the USA of Cuba's sole significant export, sugar. Likewise, the Soviet Union offered the Castro regime an ideological and political model which, far from its Russian heartland, could be adapted to Cuban experience. The expropriation of large property and surpluses made in sugar exports paid for Latin America's first manifestly effective programme of mass education and health care. Mass organizations developed during the 1960s, which achieved the previously impossible political incorporation of the majority of the Cuban population, were modelled on Soviet experience and headed by a 'Marxist-Leninist' Party which dominated the newly formed state bureaucracy and was given a Soviet-type 'leading role' in the 1976 constitution.

The Cuban revolution sustained a certain *independence* in relation to *both* Soviet-style modernity *and* its alternatives.[10] In spite of constraints put upon it by Soviet foreign-policy priorities (Castañeda 1993, p. 81), diplomatic relations among the 'non-aligned movement', military assistance to left-wing governments in Africa, and civilian assistance to regimes[11] more or less impressed by the Cuban social experiment effectively secured a safe, even prominent place for this tiny, dissident state on the edge of the biggest twentieth-century source of pressure from modernity. More ambiguously, however, by a widespread covert support for guerrilla movements, the Cuban model of how to incite the rural population to overthrow the state managed to present itself as an effective 'South American' route to democratize and socialize the state. This element of the Cuban 'model' held its own ideologically and politically for two decades.

But it never successfully replicated the Cuban experience. To Castro, and others, the collapse of the Soviet Bloc plainly brought to an end Cuban-style room to manoeuvre into a new historical course.[12] Yet, Cuba had been exceptional even before that point was reached. Its case shows *the limits* of the creative opportunities, as well as the *possibilities* for human agency through revolution on the margins of contending modernities. Military power (in US-assisted counter-insurgency wars); the besetting distance between urban and rural populations or movements; and global (again, US-led) economic change across Latin America, which was to expand, and incorporate the urban population (at the cost of locking their fate into the international financial system and its demands for state budg-etary discipline): all these have blocked the replication of the freedom which Cuba's revolutionaries briefly possessed.

Indeed, so crucial was indebtedness to the collapse of the Soviet Bloc in the first place, that one might argue that by 1989 a secular change in the relative strength of *all* alternatives to modern financial power was showing itself in various locations across the world. Peruvian revolutionary history illustrates this point. The Latin American tradition of isolated, military coups with various political directions has flourished there. Thus the 1968 top–down, socialist revolution was reversed in 1975 by a conservative one. But from the 1980s, the impact of international indebtedness on govern-ment has been progressively more apparent. The mid-1980s government of Alan Garcia lost its popular support when it imposed austerity as part of a debt rescheduling package. Alberto Fujimori, the surprise winner of the next election in 1990, simply pushed further with the same political direc-tion. To deal with the consequent unpopularity, in 1992 he resorted to an executive coup, suspending the Congress and arresting many of its mem-bers. This left his own Cambio 90 party unchallenged in the subsequent election. But Fujimori could stay in power through the support of military and business elites for his strategy with Peru's international financial position. Military-democratic power, held in place with Western support, appears the only option for the Peruvian state. Yet, during the same period, South America's most successful mass guerrilla movement, the Sendero Luminoso,[13] established itself in both cities and the countryside, chal-lenged the central state, but was defeated. On the one hand, then, global financial pressures decree central discipline; on the other hand, globaliza-tion of the food market forces peasants from the land into the cities, where their support organizations readily become politicized centres of unsuc-cessful resistance (T. D. Mason 1990). As Castañeda has argued, South American politics, still lacking the basis of modern nationhood, has yet to form effective agents of change and find a distinctive political path which will challenge the destiny that to date the global system has imposed upon it from outside (Castañeda 1993, pp. 237ff).

Conclusion

From some recent models of the global patterns in the expansion of European/Western 'modernity', this chapter has derived conclusions about how difficult, and unusual, it must be for revolutions to exhibit with force the dimensions of historical leadership or deliberate human agency. France, while it provided the paradigm two centuries ago, was structurally very much the exception. Other revolutions have confronted the handicaps of 'distance' from the crucial centres of the system's spread. Though some (Russia, China, Cuba) have maintained a more or less convincing appearance of leadership and freedom to create new socio-political forms, the conditions against any departure from the direction forced upon the bulk of the world by global modernization have acted increasingly against them.

This sombre picture is complicated by the ambiguity, and consequent free play, within the processes of modernization itself. This has given scope for deliberate original developments in some circumstances. It has also created a complex picture of the various possible directions that revolutionary confrontation may represent at the end of the twentieth century. I will consider this in chapter 4.

4

Revolutions and Modernity in the Twentieth Century

Introduction

Up to this point, I have tried to interpret revolutions as one response – a rather unusual one, albeit the most historically visible – to pressures for change generated by the spreading of 'modernity', initially from Europe. It followed from this that a revolution which was more 'central' (in a rather particular sense) to the expanding system was more likely to succeed in shifting the direction of modernity, or overtly modifying modernity's constituents. As a consequence, early, central revolutions were more likely to realize the possibilities of finding a place in an overall historical direction of change by the exercise of human will. No revolution stood a better chance of doing this than did the French, which was 'early' and 'central' in every sense of those terms. Others might – as the Russian Revolution did – give a convincing appearance of imposing a new direction on modernity; but they were playing on a more difficult historical pitch. In mid-twentieth century, much of the Third World was plausibly seen as the potential arena for revolutionary challenges with worldwide impacts.[1] Yet, over time, that part of the globe too was always likely to be more restricted as a space for freedom to manoeuvre against spreading modernity. So these impressions were likely to be more short-lived. Exactly so has the Russian Revolution now come to many to seem like doomed opposition to the long-term global forces of modernization. The logic of my argument accounts for the tendency seen in the twentieth-century theorizations of chapter 2: to find less and less room in revolutions for the elements of historic direction and human agency. It is as if analyses of revolution have woken up gradually, over two centuries, to how unusual the French experience was always likely to be.

What complicates, and modifies, this picture of the historical movement of revolutions is the *diversity* within modernity itself. It has had a number of centres, one after the other, and sources of pressure for modernization on one level of social organization have been different from sources on other levels. With the passage of time, the centres of modernity have themselves spread out across the globe, notably shifting to the United States. Thus, in the twentieth century, 'modernity' impinges upon South America in different forms, from different directions, than a century earlier. That alone modifies the determinism initially suggested by the account I have developed: by giving space for social forms to respond to pressures without simply emulating the given model, or even to mix models and to innovate. In chapter 3 I took the case of Cuba because it was both striking and exceptional in this regard.

However, the rippling pressures of different versions of modernity entail a possibility that I now wish to explore further: are there any systematic patterns in twentieth-century revolutions which, by placing them *between* distinct versions of modernity, offer specifiable possibilities for the directions taken by revolutionary change? I will look at three groups of revolutions which exhibit this possibility: national liberation revolutions aimed against European colonial government; contemporary revolutions in the Middle East which appear to shift their societies *away from* the Western model of modernity; and contemporary revolutions in East-Central Europe which appear to shift their societies *towards* that model. Finally, I argue that under certain limited conditions, revolution can exploit the edges of competing versions of modernity to qualify or, occasionally, amend its given forms.

Mid-twentieth-century national liberation revolutions

In chapter 1, I identified the central features of these 'national liberation revolutions'. Resistance to a faraway metropolitan state came from an alliance of new 'national' elites and traditional, rural populations and power-holders, in colonies where only a few of the European developments of statehood had been installed. The principal historical moment of revolutions of this type was the period after the Second World War, when the metropolitan states were weakened in Asia and North Africa by the fact of their military defeats during 1939–45, and preoccupied at home with the after-effects of war. Though over two decades a large number of territories were surrendered without anything approaching a revolution, decolonization through revolutionary resistance set the pace – as the explicit confrontation in revolution tends to do – so as to encourage other decolonizations. Apart from instances of that, relatively straightforward type of national liberation revolution, we have to bear in mind that they can also occur against *secondary* governments, i.e. those that have taken over a colonial role where the earlier metropolitan state has withdrawn.

It is easy to overlook the fact that the mid-twentieth-century conditions for national liberation revolutions themselves arise from pressures on the metropolitan states occasioned by *internal* divisions generated within the spread of modernity. As Gérard Chaliand put it (1990 pp. 22 and 24):

> The power of the West and the political-military preeminence of Europe remained intact until World War II. But World War II shook the foundation of imperial Europe overseas just as World War I had shaken European empires in Europe. . . . [B]etween the mid-1950s and the mid-1970s . . . the West has almost always been politically defeated in the end while trying to keep the status quo. This had been due, above all, to a very important change: the domination of the West was no longer either legitimate or unavoidable.

The Second World War itself had been an internal struggle over 'modernity'. It pitched a group of relative latecomers to modernity (Germany, Italy, Japan) against a group of longer-established modern European states, which had developed the pattern of closed colonial trade and investment that was considered by late-nineteenth-century European states to be necessary to ensure industrial growth. This group of older European states found themselves in alliance with a newer version of a modern society, that of the USA, which was not ostensibly dependent on a colonial empire. Regardless of the bottom–up pressures within the colonies themselves, the division and crisis of European modernity were already pressuring the metropolitan states towards new industrial, trading and strategic arrangements. Such pressures came from the vivid experience, and economic after-effects, of instability within Europe during the first half of the century, and from the need to accept a post-war pattern of modernity in which the USA was dominant and industrialized Japan and Germany had to be accommodated. In short, national liberation revolutions can already be regarded as events made possible by the division and 'ripple' of Western modernity.

To that was, of course, added the long-term growth of forces for change within the colonized territories themselves. European education, encouraged with a view to forming cadres for the colonial administration, was a source of many national liberation leaders. Integration of the colonized economies created other forces for change, in populations offered the prospect of economic development and then squeezed by monopoly constraints on commodity prices. Meanwhile, compromise with traditional power structures, for the sake of maintaining rule, left intact sources of confrontation with the colonial power and provoked dissatisfaction among those still ruled by those traditional structures.

The survival and/or transformation of traditional power structures in the post-independence political set-up should remind us, as well, that there are *two* stories of modernizing challenges within the national-liberation revolution, not one. On the one hand, the 'revolution' is aimed at European, colonial governments, which are subjected to later modernizing forces from the post-war, US-dominated global environment. Like the early 'Reformation revolts' of chapter 1, this revolutionary story ends with *withdrawal* of the states in question, rather than their direct overthrow – though some ex-imperial states do nonetheless undergo more or less radical reconstruction at home (e.g. the French Fifth Republic from 1956, the Portuguese revolution of 1974). On the other hand, in a longer time-frame, national-liberation revolutions, by attempting to reform *pre*-colonial power structures, manifest the pressure to modernize *them*. Post-colonial India absorbed into its new, national federal structure, in some cases by force, the previous princedoms which the British Raj had been content to accommodate. Post-colonial Cambodia has witnessed the continuation of pre-colonial royal politics, in a modernized form supported by electoral legitimation.

Algeria is probably the classic case of a post-war national-liberation revolution. Pressure for effective, autonomous political structures came from within local elites who had been trained up for French citizenship and a subordinate role in the provincial government of the territory. The first two ex-liberation leaders to become presidents of independent Algeria, Mohammed Ahmed Ben Bella and Houari Boumédienne, had both been educated in Paris and served in French North-African regiments. Their Front Nationale de Libération united a French-trained leadership with a guerrilla army recruited from the rural areas whose native population had been displaced by France's extensive colonization. This latter, along with France's continuing hopes of economic gain from oil (a classic colonial extractive strategy), raised the stakes for the metropolitan state; which goes some way to explain why this particular decolonization happened only after a full-scale and bloody revolutionary war.

Thus, late-nineteenth-century European modernization had generated forces for change: the dispossessed in the territory; and elites with ambitions to emulate the colonizers' example of sovereign statehood. The new Algerian post-revolutionary nation-state adopted a direction of change intended to create a version of the modern state somewhere between the French post-war planning model and the Soviet socialist version. Like Latin America, however, the partial creation of a local state, honed by brutal war, created a military power which weathered better than the elements of civilian and/or democratic politics explicitly set up by the revolution. Thus, strategic political disagreement was initially resolved by Boumédienne's *military* coup of 1965, only two years after independence. Over the next two decades, Algeria settled into a centralized, oil-based economy run for their own benefit by an enclosed oligarchy formed out of the military hierarchy and, gradually, clan links which had survived the entire colonization process. Aspirations for a distinctive pan-Arab socialism notwithstanding, that indeed has emerged as currently the principal form of power left over from the earlier North African Arabic world which the European imperial state had displaced.

The Vietnamese national-liberation revolution presents the same scenario of forces: elites educated in Western Europe with aspirations to modernize in alliance with peasants never successfully incorporated by the French colonial regime. But there are three significant differences, all of which can properly be situated in the spatio-temporal ripples of modernity. First, the colonizing power had already been unseated once by a nearby rival modernizing state, Japan, whose occupation was the forming ground for the later anti-colonial forces. Though left in administrative control, French officialdom was thoroughly demoralized by the time the Japanese decided to take power directly in March 1945, only to create a power vacuum from which Ho Chi Minh's revolutionaries would profit. Secondly, French and Japanese occupations had here been imposed on a country with a historically well-grounded political and economic integrity, so that nationalist revival proved a strong political cement and the peasantry was to be a more coherent force for change and a decisive element in military victory (Popkin 1979, Scott 1976). Thirdly, this revolution happened in proximity to the global boundary between the Eastern and Western blocs, which were about to become two competing versions of modernity. In consequence, as the war ended, the primacy of the Soviet threat in US strategy, combined with President Roosevelt's sympathy for its 'people of small stature' imposed upon by the French, were decisive in creating space for the initial revolutionary seizure of power (Tønesson 1991). On the other hand, in this instance, unlike Algeria, the torch of imported modernization, and effectively occupation, was later taken up by the USA itself, in its role as the new post-war leader of a modernity opposed to worldwide communism.

The first result of this combination of circumstances was a protracted guerrilla conflict that began in 1943 against Japan and ended, in 1975, having been extended (from 1955) to confront US and US-backed native forces. The impoverished state which emerged from so long an internal war possessed little else than strong nationalist cohesion and a large, experienced army, which it continued to use after the end of the war to secure its position in South-East Asia. Secondly, in the course of the later twentieth century, the political actors in Vietnam's revolution can be seen to adopt a number of *different* directions of modernization. On to the French-socialist aspirations acquired in Paris by exiles such as Ho Chi Minh (as leader of the independent Democratic Republic of Vietnam, that is, 'North Vietnam') were grafted Western versions of free-market capitalism in the south and a (competing) more or less successful, Soviet model of large-scale industrialization integrated in the East European Comecon system. The collapse of the Soviet alternative in the late 1980s threw Vietnam back on a later Western model: competing in the free market for foreign capitalist investment and integrating its labour force into the global free market, under the approving eye of the IMF.

Anti-colonial national liberation revolutions do, indeed, suggest a systematic pattern, explicable by their position *vis-à-vis* versions of modernity and the possible directions for change which that offers. They emerge from a mix of the model of sovereignty imported from the European metropolis and the economic and social pressures put on the population by the demands of the colonizing society. On the other hand, the challenge to, and division within, Western modernization is itself a vital precondition of the revolutions' success, since it had previously undermined the economic, military and ideological strength of European imperialism.

However, depending on the spatio-temporal situation of the given revolutionary confrontation, division and competition over modernity extend the scope for variance *within* the national liberation revolution. Vietnam's revolution bears this out, by its resemblance to that of Cuba. Vietnam's too is directed latterly not against the original colonial power, but at the later, US world hegemon, which takes over to act as a conduit of imported modernization. Likewise, Vietnam's revolutionary forces for change exploit the creative possibilities within – but also bear the adverse effects of – the country's position in the Cold War contest between two mid-twentieth-century versions of modernity. Finally, in so far as its revolutionary transformation takes place outside the strict limits of anti-European decolonization, the Vietnamese case shades off to resemble another type of revolutionary confrontation altogether: one that can challenge late-twentieth-century, US-style modernity. Thus, during the 1970s, the Vietnamese revolution was thought, both East and West, to have the makings of a state crisis for the USA itself. But, as I shall argue in the next section, it is other areas of the globe, areas which have been less effectively colonized by Europe in the first place, which exhibit most strongly this late-twentieth-century possibility for mounting a challenge to Western modernization *per se*.

Anti-Westernizing revolutions

Whereas national-liberation revolutions were directed first and foremost against an identifiably foreign power, following the general dismantling of the colonial empires there have been revolutions which challenged, and transformed, established *internal* power structures within territories that had not been colonized in the first place. Revolutions in these societies of course met their own state structures face to face. But they were nonetheless directed against states which were acting as conduits of modernization pressures in the sense that I defined earlier.

Iran's history of political change to deal with the challenge from Western modernization goes back to the middle of the nineteenth century, when Amir Kabir, the first reforming chief minister, was briefly in power. This was the first of a number of short periods of liberal elite leaderships attempting to emulate Western liberal values and structures (Abrahamian

1982, Ghods 1989). Over the following 130 years, each such period of reform was suppressed by enhanced coercion from above. The state felt the pressures from Western modernization and alternated between emulation, co-operation and resistance.

For their part, the European powers imposed on Iran modernization favourable to themselves. The British tobacco concession, as agreed in mid-nineteenth century by the central Iranian state, is emblematic of this. It gave Iranian tobacco a route to the world market, but on terms that were beneficial to the British holders of the monopoly and often left the pre-existing, bazaar traders in a much weakened commercial position. These groups, who came together in an ancient institution that was at once economic, social and political, put up strong, intermittent opposition: as, for example, in the early 1890s, when violent disturbances created the conditions for another period of elite-led Western-style reform, culminating in the 'constitutional revolution' that in 1905 created a representative assembly, the Majlis. But that did not alter the unfavourable *international* conditions in which the Iranian state had to operate, or prevent more modern states from imposing their will over Iranian territory – as when, in 1907, the British and the Russian governments, agreed to split Iran into two spheres of influence. During the 1910s, this Western-Europe-style politics gradually came apart. Its end came with the creation, in the USSR, of a different, hostile version of European modernization. Emulating modernization from abroad now included a new socially radical alternative, opposed both by conservative forces inside Iran and by the international politics of the West. Iran's internal politics would be caught up in the space between Western and Soviet versions of modernization for the next six decades.

In the 1920s, and again the 1940s and 1950s, Iranian society produced resistance from below which was more or less explicitly associated with the Soviet alternative to European modernization. Each such outbreak was put down by an Iranian strong man who initiated autocratic power and renewed co-operation with the West. The first 'soviet' republic, Gilan, was established in the north of the country in 1919, only to be suppressed by military force under the leadership of Reza Pahlavi Khan, who then had himself crowned as Shah. The Second World War accord between the Western allies and the Soviet Union almost superseded a century and a half of arm's-length management of Iran's affairs, when the temporary allies intervened directly to oust German forces from Iranian territory – and to adjust Iranian government by replacing Reza Shah with his son, Muhammed. The latter was to remain shah until the revolution of 1979. His growing military forces were used against further outbreaks of post-war, 'soviet' secessionism (in Azerbaijan and Kurdistan), and then against the populist government of Mussaddiq's Tudeh Party, which, having built up a mass base among the urban poor during the Second World War, had (with Soviet strategic support) temporarily nationalized foreign oil assets. Thus, in 1953, it was Muhammed Reza Shah who mounted a coup against popular government.

The Pahlavi Shahs favoured centralized, top–down modernization and used the traditional institutions such as the Shari'a legal code to support their own oppressive dictatorship. Over the course of the twentieth century, on the strength of Iran's oil, the Shah gradually reformed the agricultural sector and built an economy of big industries firmly controlled by the monarchy's powers over national trading concessions. This was a sort of co-operative emulation of the modern world. Western governments were willing to pay the regime's price in return for co-operation, anti-communism and firm control of potentially more awkward internal political forces. Substantial sectors of Iranian society itself, trained up and supported by this Iranian 'modern' society, were prepared to tolerate the absence of political expression. Other, traditional sectors, among the peasantry and the bazaars, were left untouched, or worse off, by this modernization. The high-point of the centralized modernizing strategy was reached in the 1970s, when the Shah, egged on by the advantageous conditions following the 1973 oil crisis, took to rehearsing the success of what he termed his 'White Revolution'. The Shah had embarked upon that dangerous phase which de Tocqueville identified, persuasion after oppression. But the social, economic and industrial change had also thrown peasantry off the land into urban centres, to join a swelling industrial working class, while his centralized, coercive regime had itself proved wasteful and inneffective in the strategic planning task it had taken on. Guided too much by fear of military coup, the Shah had even broken up the command structure of Iran's privileged, up-to-date armed forces, which he would in due course be unable to call upon to protect his state (Roberts 1996). Foreign capital, together with the global oil price, soon let him down. By 1978, global modernization pressures had cornered the Iranian regime, which was unable either to complete the ostentatious programme of its own version of 'modernization' or to contain the popular resistance in the towns that its reforms had nurtured.

Iran had long exhibited a relative freedom in relation to global modernizing forces (Foran 1992). During the twentieth century, the relationship had been a mix of emulation and co-operation. The pattern had been for the state to encourage modernization on terms that exploited, as best it could, Iran's position between Western and Eastern European modernities: the state had imported modernization in a form basically agreeable to the Western version, but driving a bargain which maximized its own power and wealth. The last Shah merely represented the *ne plus ultra* of that attempt to carve a unique position in the semi-periphery (Foran 1992, p. 417). In the 1979 revolution, there emerged from within the surviving vestiges of Iran's earlier, pre-modern society a number of quite original forces for popular resistance. These represent a quantum extension of the room to manoeuvre possible in revolutionary confrontations on the global boundaries between the twentieth century's competing forms of modernization. For they underwrote ideologically the redirection of a non-Western state on to a distinct historical course that could in no way be described as communism.

In particular, Iran's other-worldly, Shi'a version of Islam adapted well to utopian aspirations among a disorientated, oppressed urban workforce and others marginalized by top–down modernization (Halliday 1988). Shi'ite belief included a notion of future history (namely, that the missing Imam will reappear) which framed utopian expectations, rather as Puritan messianic biblical faith had done in sixteenth-century England. For years, the émigré resistance leadership under Ayatollah Khomeini had run an infiltration campaign using methods both modern (dissemination to an illiterate population by cassette tape) and traditional (the gerontocratic authority of the 'Imam' Khomeini himself; the surviving social networks around the bazaar, which the Shah's bloated secret police were unable to suppress). In the historical situation of Iran, which had maintained both territorial integrity and ethnic distinctiveness *vis-à-vis* the wider Islamic-Arab diaspora, these ideological forces of religious belief could supply the power of a mass national resistance. This ran quite counter to both Western and communist assumptions about the demise of religion in the modern world.

Before 1979 there had been no really persuasive demonstration of the revolutionary power of Islam. Various modernizers in the Islamic world had put forward a case for Islam as a society capable of organizing industrialization without social disruption.[2] 'Arab' nationalism had briefly held the international stage in the figure of President Nasser of Egypt, who had successfully overturned a weak monarchy and, like the Shah, exploited Cold War rivalry to promote industrial build-up. But its transnational constructions – such as the Arab League, or the Egyptian–Syrian United Arab Republic (of 1958–61) – remained weak and riven by inter-state suspicions. By the 1970s, strategic developments had fractured this version between the claims of different states: Syria, Iraq, Egypt (Ajami 1992). It was the Iranian revolution that first succeeded in using Islam as such to weld a large population around common religious belief and overturn an existing, native political order.

Some readers may be surprised to find Islam identified as a new form of modernization. But that is what it had become by the 1970s: a complex of ideological currents able to formulate comprehensive, future-oriented prescriptions for social organization, which had adopted currents coming from elsewhere in the modern world – notably cultural authenticity and nation-statehood – and attempted to plot a new historical course in response to contemporary conditions. Iran's anti-Westernizing revolution established Islam's most visible institutional base. It also brought out the extent to which this tradition could, in a thoroughly modern way, confront established power. From this point, it has played a crucial role in other 'modernizing' resistance on the boundaries between the West and the Communist Bloc – notably in Afghanistan – and duly attracted the hostility of both Western liberal and Soviet socialist contenders for the title of modernity. It continues to generate legitimations for revolutionary action in the Islamic part of the world (e.g. El-Affendi 1991); though whether it will, in the longer term, prove intellectually flexible enough to embrace the demands of contemporary living is another question (Al-Azmeh 1993).[3]

If we turn to the case of Afghanistan we can indeed sense the limits to the potential of an anti-Westernizing revolution within the Islamic border territory of the old Cold War confrontation between modernities. Like Iran, only from a little later, the Afghan state had had modernization imposed upon it by the British Empire, which, after the second British war of invasion in 1880, began to train up and equip the military forces of a client state. In the twentieth century, government in Afghanistan developed overwhelmingly in that form, living by the grant of concessions for extractive industries in exchange for foreign military, financial and technical support. Its power remained highly personalized (assassination being the most common way to leave office) and poorly rooted in the countryside, where warlords and mullahs sustained a clan-based order. Until 1978, modernization was primarily Western, but also superficial and confined to elites in Kabul. Outside that area, traditional power structures and values remained firmly in place.

That balance was broken only when Left elements of the military, known as the *Khalq*, assassinated the long-standing leader General Mohammad Daoud, and undertook a programme of 'socialist' reforms which were soon revealed to be beyond their political and financial resources. Confronted by the habitual hostility of clan-leaders and mullahs, and lacking the support it had counted on from a debt-stricken peasantry, a faction of the *Khalq* in turn took the customary Afghan route to make up for a lack of internal political strength: it assassinated the leader and sought foreign help, from the USA. Whereas Iran had been able to exploit the rivalry between the Cold War states, Afghanistan looks much more like their victim. Rather than see the USA extend its influence right on her southern border, the USSR intervened with the co-operation of a different, left-wing *Khalq* faction. Both sides in the ensuing 'revolutionary' conflict were managed, and funded, largely by foreign governments.

The claims of transnationally organized Islam entered a revolutionary situation here for the first time – though profound internal divisions had to be put aside to achieve such action. Conservative Arab Gulf regimes put up the money for anti-Soviet *mujahedin* fighters to be schooled in Pakistan, indoctrinated with Iranian enthusiasm and armed with American weapons. But, by the time of writing (mid-1998) it appears that there never had been a sufficient combination of internal social forces to take Afghanistan *as a whole* in any direction other than chaos (Rubin 1995). The withdrawal of the defeated Soviet forces in 1989 merely allowed inter-Islamic and inter-warlord rivalries to take over a costly conflict and sustain the as yet unresolvable imbalance. Even the ideological unity of anti-Western Islam has developed cracks, as Pakistan and Sunni Saudi Arabia sustain the Taliban in their current military ascendancy while Shi'a Iran discreetly makes common cause with Russia in channelling resources to the Taliban's opponents in the north of the country.

It may be that the Islamic Taliban forces in Afghanistan will in due course succeed in subduing the remaining warlord resistance in the north. If that happens, it will still remain to be seen whether a second post-revolutionary Islamic regime can establish its ideological and economic base and survive in the modern world between the old boundary of Eastern and Western modernizations. Apart from in Iran, there is no clear evidence as to whether Islamic modernity has a global future. It has made great progress, in the form of a fundamentalist mass movement of protest against Westernized society, in a string of Islamic countries from Turkey and Palestine to Algeria and Morocco. But Islam in power exhibits an opaqueness to popular inspection which may, in the context of a cash-rich Middle East oil market, make it too vulnerable to cosy, corrupting arrangements among elites. There are signs that even the Iranian revolution may fall victim to that tendency which will undermine its popular legitimation and rigidify its economic management.

Post-Soviet reversion: pro-Westernizing revolutions

To a considerable extent, the appearance of pro-Westernizing revolutions in East–Central Europe is the story of the *reversal* of post-revolutionary Soviet society. It cannot, of course, be described as the *abolition* of 1917; for that would imply that the Soviet Union itself has reverted to the *status quo ante*, undoing all the effects of the reorganization of production, property, class, and political *mores* that was developed between 1920 and 1980. Even in its collapse, the Soviet period impacts on history.[4] After so long a period of distinctive development, we cannot expect that the core of the old Soviet territory will even now follow the historical course of the classic, Western modernized societies. Steven Fish's 1995 study of post-Soviet civil society indicates as much. Neither can Central and East European areas, though more marginal to the Soviet experience, simply slip into the again-dominant model from the West. Looked at more widely, the Soviet experience was the twentieth century's longest-surviving, deliberate experiment in a mode of modernizing development adapted from, but opposed to, the prior, Western one. In the pro-Westernizing revolutions of the end of the century, we are dealing with rejection of a rejection of a *version* of modernity. So, the specific possibilities inherent in the pro-Westernizing revolution of the late twentieth century can only be understood in terms of the century-long episode begun by the rejection of 1917.

What have been reversed since 1989, though not to the *status quo ante*, are the ideology, the values and, most of all, the *separation* of the territory that was embraced by Soviet state communism. Both ideology and separation were founded on a particular, but by no means perverse understanding of one big fact about world history at the start of the twentieth century: namely, the predominance of a dangerous self-defeating competition between imperialist Western European nation-states. Given the destruction in the inter-state conflicts in 1914–18, not to mention the consequences of that conflict for Russia (which was not even engaged in the colonial competition), the post-First World War situation could perfectly well be interpreted as it was in Russia. In itself, isolationism (turning away, to Russia's own, substantial physical, human and cultural resources) would have been a tempting option for any Russian – just as it was for the majority of Americans until at least the early 1940s (Lipset 1996). European modernity had run into the buffers by 1914–18, and many people, right across the world, thought that it could not survive.

Isolationism could take many forms, of course. The form with the greatest numerical backing in Russia in 1917 would undoubtedly have been local order developed by the peasantry,[5] unschooled in the notion of national-state order and embittered by their recent brush with its effects at the front. Evidently, no revolutionary seizure of the state could come from that quarter. Among potential state leaders, in 1917 those of a more bourgeois-liberal modernizing tendency *were* inclined to accept the continuance of the alliance that lay behind Russia's involvement in the war. This did more than anything to hamper them, and delegitimize them in the eyes of the country over which they sought to establish rule. But, in any case, as Weber observed at the time (Weber 1995) and others since (Figes 1996, p. 811), there was no socio-political nexus on which a liberal bourgeois regime could be established. So, in the circumstances of the time, it was radical anti-war Marxists who alone came to power and could hold it. As Hobsbawm (1997, p. 250) says, 'the centralized Leninist structure of the Bolshevik Party, an institution constructed for disciplined action and therefore *de facto* for state-building, was essential. . . . [I]f not the Bolsheviks, then nobody.'[6] Russia's isolation followed from that fact – or, rather, it followed from that fact plus the non-occurrence of the general disaster for European states which was a premise behind the Bolsheviks' chosen manner of ruling. The Bolsheviks were emboldened to seize power and insist upon their own wartime line (independence from the strategies of Russia's European allies) because they did not expect those ally states – for all their strength and modernity – to survive imminent revolutions. The feeling of expectation was forcefully recorded by Victor Serge in the late 1920s (Serge 1992, pp. 373–6).[7] That expectation was given authority in 1916 by Lenin's *Imperialism: the Highest Form of Capitalism*; but it had, in any case, considerable commonsense appeal under the circumstances of the war, and for many years afterwards.

Autarchy was initially a short-term political gamble; subsequently the keystone of the whole Soviet structure. To rule in isolation meant to rule by new methods, within the limits of Russia's own resources, to achieve the modernization made all the more necessary to the Russian state by military defeat and all-too-evident backwardness by comparison with hostile states to the West. True, Lenin's first approach at centralized autarchic party rule, 'War Communism' (which, ironically, was based on emulation of the German war-time administration) was soon superseded by a different, relatively market-orientated strategy, the 'New Economic Policy'. But that could only be a stop-gap to overcome failure and assuage popular resistance (Aves 1996, pp. 146–61, Figes 1996, p. 770). The resources available to the new regime in political personnel and social loyalty meant that, if the new Russia was to be alone, some version of a centralized top–down command economy – Stalinism, or something else – was more or less bound to emerge. Dramatic action was needed to persuade and/or suppress peasantry and proletariat.[8] Hastily assembled state power, in the form of an expanded Bolshevik Party, was the most easily available, and (at the time) rational-seeming, resource to lead Russia forward. Moreover, it had the apparent virtue of by-passing the contemporary irrationalities of European modernization. Once established, this ill-trained and easily corruptible body of functionaries developed a momentum of its own (Figes 1996, pp. 682–96). From autarchy and the Party-monopoly, the other elements of the Soviet economic and social system would follow (Waller 1993).

In this way, the Soviet state system settled down to a solitary competition with the Western forms of modernity, in which, it has to be admitted, it scored notable victories.[9] To hold on to power over an economically sustainable country, the Soviet leaders understood that they had to emulate Western modernity in a distinctive way. So the system put forward a new, deliberately pursued modernity as organizing principle, challenge and political legitimation of the entire state. To commit Russia's uneducated masses to this effort – and, what was to be the same thing, to loyalty to the regime – they were mobilized from above in an ill-directed rush, politically fuelled by unrealistic optimism combined with crude suspicion and jealousy of the better-off and the old order (Figes 1996, pp. 771–2, Zeman 1991, pp. 129–37). There is no question that this was a strategy of competitive emulation of modernity elsewhere. 'We are fifty to one hundred years behind the advanced countries. We must cover that distance in ten years,' declared Stalin (Figes 1996, p. 814). 'Either we do this, or they will crush us.' The grandest, most megalomaniac, yet also most inspiring of the Soviet Union's undertakings in forced emulation of modernity, the new Siberian steel city of Magnetogorsk, was accordingly based on the model of Gary, Indiana, USA (Kotkin 1995). It is no wonder, then, that the 1917 revolution revived the notion of an all-conquering power in collective human agency (as I discussed it in chapter 2). The idea was integral to the survival of the Soviet state in isolation; and it was in some measure confirmed by the extent of changes wrought – albeit bloodily – across the Soviet Bloc.

A great range of theorization has been brought to bear on the demise of Soviet modernization (Holmes 1997, pp. 24–61; see also Csaba 1994). Whatever account is adopted, however, it is clear that a system so crucially, and consciously, grounded in its own version of modernization was bound to falter if modernizing change was seen to fail – and to do so with a peculiar degree of open ideological and political disruption. Thus the rejection of Soviet-style autarchic modernization came about initially by virtue of its reaching its own inherent limits, and was rapidly carried over into an open ideological, and international, challenge. One, logical limit (anticipated by early theoretical critiques – e.g. Mises 1947) was the sheer volume of information needed to manage economic activity comprehensively from the centre: this was reckoned by one commentator at 10^{12} units of information per year (Flaherty 1991, p. 130). In order to cope, the Soviet system developed a crude fixation with gross output, unaccompanied by an ability to regulate efficiency, quality or actual demand. Surplus could be used neither to satisfy consumption demands properly nor to invest in improvement (Ticktin 1992). But whatever the structural basis for the setback, a long decline did set in: whereas in the 1950s the Soviet Union had been able to proclaim annual growth rates of 10–14 per cent, by the mid-1970s these shrank to below 4 per cent (Lane 1996, p. 153). By the 1960s, experiments in modifying the central direction of production were already being undertaken in Czechoslovakia, the USSR and Yugoslavia – but to little avail.

Military failure in Afghanistan was an immediate source of external pressure on the Soviet state – a classic one in terms of Skocpol's theorization. The conflict had first arisen from a challenge to the Soviet Union on its unstable, Cold War border. Defeat struck a system which had placed considerable reliance on military strength – the more so as economic success ebbed away. What is more, military defeat on the ground, against technically less advanced rebels, came at a time when the basis of Soviet military power was deliberately being challenged. Under the guise of the Star Wars Project, the USA was using the weapon of the West's relative technological lead to gain an edge on the East. Finally, as Waller shows, the ramifications of the defeat undermined the shared interests of the Soviet military-industrial complex, which had been a crucial nexus of political and administrative support (Waller 1993). Despite the optimism it evinced at the time (Bloomfield 1989), the contemporaneous appearance of a policy of renewal, perestroika, actually betrayed a wider, and more explicit, ideological crisis. Parts of the upper echelons of government, seeking to shift the political basis of support for the state, were to succeed in undermining its elite legitimacy without managing to engage alternative solidarity and commitment from other potential supporters (Lane 1997, pp. 152–76). Central state officials around Gorbachev recognized (as others had before them) that progressive decline relative to the West could not be allowed to continue, and identified a disparate range of potential agents of change which they hoped to weld into an effective body for radical economic and social reform. In the event, the conservative elements already on the inside were able to block and harry the leadership too effectively, whilst the reformers on the outside either chose to remain there, or found no alternative to doing so. As Lane puts it, 'Modernization led to the collapse of social solidarity under the traditional type of Communist party leadership' (p. 195). The 1917 marriage of state and Party, having become barren some time before, turned mutually destructive.

The spillover from economic to ideological challenge which resulted in the collapse of 1991 is well illustrated in the thinking of a noted Russian academic rebel and supporter of reform: Tatyana Zaslavskaya.[10] Zaslavskaya mercilessly analysed the way in which the Soviet system failed to generate efficiency or plenty. Particularly preoccupied by the misallocation of resources which I referred to earlier, she is prepared to advocate a considerable extension of 'economic' modes of labour measurement and income allocation (as against 'administrative' ones) in order to encourage and reward greater efficiency and a more socially useful deployment of labour (Zaslavskaya 1990, pp. 118–32). She openly draws the conclusion that such measures imply a recasting of the egalitarian concepts of social justice traditionally operative in the Soviet system, approvingly quoting the view expressed in 1986 in the dissident literary journal *Literaturnaya gazeta* that: 'Justice consists in everybody receiving not the same amount but a different amount justly.'[11] For her, this implies that quality, quantity, scarcity, productivity and private (co-operative) employment should all be taken into account in the wages system, and resultant differentials recognized as 'a natural phenomenon and one that is useful to society' (p. 131). She was likewise prepared to see 'economic' allocation of housing and other freely available welfare resources, in order to attract finance and labour into these chronically under-supplied sectors (pp. 147–52).

Zaslavskaya did, however, balk at the 'social consequences' of introducing the same allocation for retail goods. In other words, she hoped to confine these major departures from the legitimizing principles contained in the explicit norms of the Soviet system, so as to leave the politically most sensitive areas untouched. When she turns to the question of the political basis of support for the changes she is advocating, one can see the reason for her hesitation. Potential supporters are, she acknowledges, scattered across a wide range of middle-level and non-state positions (pp. 181–93); the predominant political mood is 'social pessimism'. This, more than anything, was the most striking feature of the collapses in both the Soviet Union and Eastern Europe: whatever were the forces for change, they were rarely mustered by any particular political or ideological position for long enough or in sufficiently coherent form. Eastern Bloc states had found themselves under heavy pressure to change in order to match their legit-imizing claims about socio-economic progress, or to meet the pressures from the external environment – including widespread popular awareness of the greater material progress of the West. But their socio-political environment impeded any drawing together of united internal forces to conduct or support change. Holmes (1997, pp. 15–21) accordingly identifies fourteen features of 'post-Communist' society, of which a good half (e.g. instability, insecurity, rejection of teleology, ideological vacuum, cynicism towards politics) betoken an absence of endogenous coherence.

Hence, these revolutions to reject an alternative modernity have so often led to subservience to the newly dominant, Western form. Cases differed, of course (East and Pontin 1997). Insiders in the administration sometimes resisted, as in the Soviet Union, where conservatives had the strength briefly to rebel at Gorbachev's strategy, but immediately fell apart making way for the final break-up of the Union. But it was rare for the elites so integral to the Soviet version of modernization to put up a fight for their own system. Romania, where communists appear to have used a 'revolu-tion' as a pretext to purge their ageing autocratic leader, is the exception. But it is one that proves the rule, in so far as the new communists in power there duly embarked upon a show of Westernizing reforms. Reformers from within the Communist Party in Hungary, where market forms had developed furthest over the decades before 1990, took a lead in 1988, repositioning the communist elite early on (and renaming the Party the 'Hungarian *Socialist* Party'). Such seems to have been the loss of power in the entire model of economic and social modernity that the state/party insiders of the Soviet Bloc had been brought up with. Not infrequently, as Callinicos argues (1991, pp. 50–66), the insiders themselves deserted the state, embracing Western market principles and privatization for the sake of what they themselves could take with them as they left. Suspicious circumstances over subsequent privatizations (e.g. in Slovakia, Hungary and Poland) bear out this impression.

Frequently, there were moments in these revolutions when new, broadly based social movements held the stage. They often proffered renewed versions of older Western European values: democratic freedoms com-bined with economic welfare. But these movements were quickly swept aside: New Forum in East Germany by the Federal German political and economic takeover; Civic Forum in Czechoslovakia by a political split after the defeat of the communists, which left its right-wing liberal portion (the Civic Democracy Party) alone in power; Solidarity in Poland by internal splits and its own former leader, Lech Walesa, thus making way for the return of cleaned-up former communists (the Democratic Left Alliance); the Bulgarian United Democratic Front by monarchists to one side and reformed communists to the other. In short, various distinctive reforming programmes surfaced from the internal crisis brought on by the pressures for change building up within these societies; but the economic and political results diverge starkly from those programmes. The principal feature of the outcomes in the different East European states has been more privatized and liberalized economies or more unreformed, state-managed ones. After the upheaval, a variety of political groupings took the initiative and participated in power: nationalists, ranging from cultural revivalists (especially in the Baltic states) to neo-fascists (e.g. in Croatia, Romania or Hungary), populists (such as Yeltsin), technocrats and economic liberals (significant almost everywhere) and, strikingly, re-styled communists. The high-minded democratic, republican values of a Havel found little real purchase in the early-1990s Central European order of privatization, for-eign investment, debt rescheduling, integration into Western European institutions, and holding on to power.

In these revolutions, as I argued in chapter 1, long-term exogenous forces are very much to the fore. The Soviet centre had confronted the competition of the West as the leader and model of its type of moderniza-tion, put up a long struggle, but eventually lost. Once it was clear that the Soviets could no longer exemplify and defend their system, the other states in the bloc came under enhanced pressure. The subsequent reappearance of communist political elites in effective, elected parties of government signifies, as much as anything, how these revolutions rejected the Soviet model of modernization, but lacked their own alternative. The rejection of the Soviet Union's somewhat unintended autarchic alternative to Western modernity left no substantial alternative in its wake. This negation of a negation implied no strong *positive* direction of change with a firmly grounded body of support which could face out the renewed moderniz-ing pressures from the world system in the late twentieth century. Hence, the actual direction of social and economic change has been towards sub-servience to the Western economic norms and power. Yet, given the strategic misfit between the economic structure of the former Eastern states and the West, that has had dramatically harsh consequences for these post-revolutionary societies. Unlike the smaller economies of Western Europe, such as the Netherlands or Denmark, which have found their own, comfort-able niches in the zone of modernity where they are located, the ex-communist economies have had only dislocated internal production systems and poorly equipped rivals to the strongest of Western European or US capitalism (Gowan 1995, Haynes 1992). They have also, throughout the period of their decline and restructuring, had to live with the burdens, and disciplines, of indebtedness to globally dominant Western financial institutions.[12]

My account of late-twentieth-century pro-Westernizing revolutions has tended to stress their *lack* of autonomy and historical originality. That throws into ironic light the imagery around the revolutions of 1989 onwards (N. Parker 1994), which set them back in the classic, post-Enlightenment revolutionary narrative of the conscious, rational human group ('We, the People', as Garton Ash (1990) puts it) taking over and

recasting society. These were revolutions with an initial display of collective human agency, quickly followed by the disciplines imposed through
global economic values, financial institutions and strategic formations.
The collective agency expressed at the height of the revolutions was
accordingly lost in an overall direction of change which resembles more
obviously a *reversion* to the structure of early-twentieth-century globally
organized finance than any distinct follow-up to the autarchic Eastern Bloc
experience. But the situation of Central and Eastern European societies
reverts to having to find a way to survive at the margins of global power.
Hence, these societies remain different from the West and have to do what
they can to exploit their marginality and difference. The bigger states
(Russia) and the oil-endowed ones (Kazakhstan) exploit their leverage as
one-time independents.[13] The smaller ones juggle the hopes of joining the
'mainstream' with a strategy of 'coalescence' to allow them to negotiate
from strength (Hartnell, forthcoming).

The scope at the margins: two exceptions?

No definite alternative model of modernity has emerged from this series of
breakdowns on the border between the old rival forms of the Cold War.
This is part of the broader picture at the end of the twentieth century –
easily confounded with a general 'globalization', which I shall discuss in
chapter 7. When the overt autarchy of the communist world collapsed, it
left countries without the power of core status in the global system more
exposed to the demands emanating from the core. As Tiruneh (1993,
p. 374) put it:

> the end of the cold war . . . ushered in the end of the state-system which had
> been governing the relations of the European states in the last several centu-
> ries and those of other continents since then. It has meant that poor states can
> no longer hide behind the skirts of such principles as the sovereign equality of
> states and non-interference . . . but, rather, toe the line of rich nuclear states
> willy-nilly. The development in the political sphere is in addition to the poor
> states' loss of their right of economic self-determination which has been
> increasingly the case since the West's assertion of structural adjustment in the
> last decade or so.

But that is not to say that the post-revolutionary political orders in the
Central and East European political systems had, or have, *no* scope deliberately to negotiate the future course of their societies within the larger
structures that call the tune. The very differences between the post-revolutionary career of the different societies – between, say, Lithuania and
Yugoslavia – illustrate that. Geographical position and the prospects for
economic integration are thus crucial background factors in any accommodation that these 'post-revolutionary' political orders may find with the

newly dominant Western model: witness the different support offered to Baltic and Balkan countries. It is clear that some Central European countries, once their dependence on external powers is admitted, are even able to *exploit* their marginal position to force concessions from dominant economic forces in the West. Thus Hungary and the Czech Republic, which offer both a security buffer to the West and a future Eastward jumping-off point for Western capitalist industry (Flockton, forthcoming), are given a fast track into NATO and the EU. But this is, as I say, a matter of *negotiating* with, rather than *setting aside*, the dominant exogenous forces and their model. Thus, a renewed significance for the position in between established forms of modernity: the margins, and how to exist on them, have acquired new historical potential.

Hence, we must look, finally, at two other special cases of twentieth-century revolution on the margins between existing modernities: Turkey in the first half of the century, and China in the second. It can be said of both that they exhibit a strong attachment to, or dependence upon, their territorial base and to the vestiges of their distinctive, inherited statehood. The Turkish revolution can, indeed, readily be interpreted as a top-down modernization following the post-First World War reassertion of a surviving element of the defeated Ottoman Empire (Trimberger 1978). Mustafa Kemal (afterwards 'Ataturk') initially established his position by using his command of the 9th Turkish Army to organize resistance to Greek seizure of parts of Turkish territory in the early 1920s and, more broadly, to represent the forces for a fightback against the settlement being imposed on Turkey after the war. The military remained the core of his governing personnel during his period of power and radical reform up to the end of the 1930s – and are, indeed, the greatest single power in Turkish political life to this day. With the abolition of the Caliphate, the centre-piece of the Ottoman claim to exercise political authority for trans-national Islam, the Turkish revolution chose as a model the secular, national, territorially integrated form of its victorious Western adversaries. Likewise, the new state adopted Western-style alphabet, education and legal framework for social life. Accordingly, industrialization and integration into the Western capitalist market developed rapidly in the post-Second World War period.

On the face of it, therefore, this revolution on the margins of Western European modernity looks like an attempt at *dissolving* the distinctiveness of the given society. Except that Turkey has self-consciously remained ethnically distinct, and has continued to exhibit the consequences of its past and its geographical position: authoritarian government, strong Islamic distinctiveness and political pressures (notably Kurdish secessionism) met with enormous coercion on the part of the state. That has been matched on the 'Western' side by Turkey's unspoken exclusion from Europe. This is prompted politically by the parallel belief that Turkey is different and hard-headedly by the judgement that the cost to the European Union of completing Turkey's modernization is too high, given that it has no strategic alternative to its present position. These factors certainly do not amount to a separate, Turkish line of post-revolutionary modernity; but, rather, to a path forced somewhat unwillingly upon revolutionaries originally intent on merely joining the dominant strand of modernity. By exploiting its well-established pre-existing governmental integrity as a state, the Turkish revolution was able to hold the state together during what was plainly a crisis, defeat in war, brought about by exogenous pressures from more modern neighbours. It has since found its marginal position disadvantageous and difficult to live with in various ways.

One cannot be at all so categorical about the case of China. In short, the Chinese revolution exhibits features of various of the categories and instances that I have considered up to now. Like Turkey, it was directed at a long-established imperial state – a uniquely long-established one, indeed – whose territorial extent it has more or less preserved. Like Turkey, the post-revolutionary power was centred on an army. But it was not the reformed army of the old empire; for in China the state's own modernizing army, Chiang Kai-shek's nationalists, *lost* to a 'People's Liberation Army' which was always intended to have a distinctive rural base, peasant origins and explicit role in the leadership and re-education of traditional society (Mao Zedong 1927).

Like Russia's revolution, the Chinese followed a period of imperial decline, including a period of unconvincing, top–down liberal reforms, initiated by the monarchy itself in 1906 (under Empress Ci Xi). But this period ended, in 1911–12, not as in Russia with the indisputable victory of a new centralized movement, but with the *division* of the country between two regimes, and subsequently a number of areas under the power of separate warlords. Reunification, when it came, was indeed under the 'Communist Party of China', which is what prompted my earlier classification of this as a 'communist' revolution. Yet, the party organization was already part-Leninist party, part-militia: a fact which emerged forcefully after 1967, when the Cultural Revolution undid the position of the party bureaucracy but left the People's Liberation Army in a unique position that it still holds in China today. Whilst some (the Western media certainly) see an incipient crisis of legitimacy in China's revolution like that of the Soviet Bloc (Ding 1994), there are plenty of reasons to hold that the distinctiveness of the 'Chinese way' has provided the post-revolutionary state with the means to survive into the long-term future (MacKerras et al. 1994). Furthermore, as Lane observes (1996, pp. 97–8), the peasant mass of Chinese society was never embraced, as Russian and East European masses had been, by the state's social security net, so that its withdrawal in the 1980s, for the sake of competitive, capitalist modes of economic allocation, was never likely to meet with the resistance that it confronted in, say, Poland. In the present state of things, with Chinese society still in the throes of massive, deliberate economic and social change, even the temporal limits of China's 'revolutionary' experience are hard to determine.

Perhaps someone thinking through, as I am, the scope and implications of theoretical models of socio-political change should not be overly troubled to find that a political order embracing one quarter of the world's population is *sui generis*. Generalizations are intended, after all, for the mass of cases, not the one that is bound to be without parallel. We could also take fuller measure of China's *distinctive* spatio-temporal position. Thanks to its being the prime target of Japan's late, competitive colonization of Asia, China's reunification under a revolutionary regime could (as I argued in chapter 1) be regarded as a kind of national liberation revolution. That is to say, it emerged from combining 'nationalist' forces against a colonial power. But still it is special. The Japanese colonists hardly had time to impact on the social order, or restructure, as European empires had done, the administration of the territory they held. Instead, they were soon reduced to impotence not by revolutionary resistance but by military defeat in a global war happening elsewhere. That is why, after 1945, this seeming 'national liberation' struggle was aimed against a *native* Chinese government, albeit one tacitly backed by the Cold War leader of the Western world.

There are, furthermore, broader reasons why China's revolution and its after-effects might have a special spatio-historical classification. Nowhere else in the history of the world had political and cultural unification been able to arise so early or over so extensive a territory. This meant that China was a world centre of commerce and production for at least two millennia, and a model of civil order in Europe itself once it became known. Even well into the nineteenth century, Chinese textiles survived in their home market, and Chinese growth kept pace with Japan's until the 1930s (Waites 1995, p. 28). Those facts alone could account for China's survival as a single territory in spite of the pressure of the colonizing European empires. Add to that the late-nineteenth-century appearance, in Japan, of a far-Eastern colonizing rival and alternative model to European modernization. Eastern models of top–down authoritarian modernization have indeed long been an influence in the direction of change adopted in China. It was Japan's *Meiji* revolution which produced the imperial military-industrial power that subjected China to its uniquely brief colonization. Furthermore, just as the *Meiji* reforms were appreciated by Chinese modernizers at the turn of the century, so the rapid industrial expansion of Far Eastern economies such as Singapore, Taiwan, South Korea or Malaysia in the 1980s reassured the Chinese post-revolutionary state that economic growth on the basis of imported foreign capital could be managed from above without Western-style political democratization (Holmes 1997, p. 118). In this, the current version of the old People's Liberation Army, now a major trading enterprise in the Chinese economy, has a key strategic role.[14]

So far, Tiananmen Square notwithstanding, the Chinese state has won its gamble with authoritarian, 'Eastern' modernization. In sum, there are much stronger reasons than in the case of Turkey to see China participating in the overall direction of historical change as the basis of an amended model of modernization. In the case of China, long-standing and exceptional territorial integrity is found in a global location where distinctive forms of modernization are establishing themselves. China's revolution now looks able to partake of, indeed influence the form of, an 'Asian' version of modernity.

I take this survey of how the models of revolutionary change work out at the margins to imply the following. It has always been exceptional for a revolution to establish its own distinctive version of, and answer to, modernity. In the past, primarily with the French paradigm, a revolution near the centre of the world system has had the best chance of shifting the pre-existing direction of modernity. Other things being equal, a revolution on the margins of the system is at a serious disadvantage in any attempt to impact on or counter the system. Whether that is in fact possible depends upon, *inter alia*, the territorial integrity and the geo-political position of the state, and upon, the coherence of the revolution's political and ideological resources. Political systems on the margins which are large and coherent, notably Russia, can sustain competitor modernizations outside the system; but in the twentieth century that attempt has been expensive and, in the end, temporary. Political systems that find a niche *between* alternative modernizations can also exploit that position to find leeway in relation to the pressure of the rippling impact of modernity. Little Cuba falls within this category – just. China, however, by combining size/territorial integrity with a favourable marginal position, seems to hold all the cards that permit a revolution to cut against the grain of global modernization. With Russian experience in mind, however, we ought not to say that China will be unique, self-directed and autonomous. Rather, the signs are that China's revolution will carry more weight *within* the nature of the modernized world as a whole, depending on how eventually it rejoins the mainstream.

Part II
Why Revolutions Matter

5

Revolutions and Historical Change: 'the Revolutionary Narrative'

The broader effects of revolutions and their global narrative

The first half of this book has used historical investigation and sociological analysis to examine revolutions as processes accessible for objective study. That has itself suggested that revolutions have to be understood according to a number of distinct causalities which themselves overlap and evolve. There is an *internal* dynamic to revolutionary contests, which has itself altered as, for example, different social groupings, state forms and ideologies have appeared within revolutions. There is an *inter-state* dynamic, which the revolutionary political order challenges, is accepted into and/or is reshaped by. There is a broader *spatio-temporal* framework, the spreading ripple of modernization, which modulates the given revolution's occurrence and impact.

This second half is concerned not just with causal explanations of revolutions, treating them as objective processes. It consciously mixes the analytical/nomothetic with the interpretative/hermeneutic. That is to say, in order to understand revolutions and their place in human history, we must address the *meanings* that revolutions embrace as well as the factors that operate to shape them. Indeed, as the reader will see, I do not think that, in the final analysis, these two modes of addressing the topic can be separated. Revolutions occur, and have the impact that they do, not a little because those who participate and those who react to them do so according to the meaning that they ascribe to 'revolution' or to a particular 'revolution'. 'The revolutionary narrative' is a concept intended to get a hold on this level of explanation.

Even in the analyses of the first part of the book, it was evident that 'revolution' was a concept liable to break apart in use. There were two kinds of reason for this. Each revolution consisted of sequences of events happening at different levels: institutional breakdown within the circuits of power; unthought-out local action against some specific grievance; migrations and other changes of allegiance between the groupings of the wider society; parallel social movements abroad; inter-state responses to the perceived opportunity or threat; the intrusion of more advanced socio-economic systems bringing challenge or dependency; etc. Each of these sequences suggests a distinct version of the 'revolutionary' event. The second kind of reason for our difficulty arises from the movement of history. With the passage of time, each 'revolution' occurs in a setting that has changed since the last, as the French Revolution, for example, confronted a Great Britain recently bruised by the loss of power implied by the American Revolution and, accordingly, inclined to reinterpret and give a new role to its own 'Glorious Revolution'. That British response produced, in the form of Burke's *Reflections on the French Revolution* and the whole body of 'conservative' politics that it inaugurated, a long-standing counterdrive to France's revolution across many countries of Northern Europe and even in France itself. My concept of a 'ripple of moderniza-tion', operating through different levels (i.e. military, ideological etc. forms of power), was introduced to try, *inter alia*, to capture the movement of history that gives rise to this second difficulty. The analytical discussion of the first part poses a problem, then: how are we to capture any common notion of 'revolution', or – if that proves impossible – to define terms by which we may move between the levels and the historical moments of given revolutions?

This problem is actually made not harder but easier by including an inter-pretative/hermeneutic approach. For the interactions between levels we referred to above often occur via the *interpretations* put upon the 'revolu-tionary' confrontations of others. Interpretation and counter-interpretation are, indeed, the stuff of much politics in revolutions as elsewhere. Count Egmont's 1565 mission to Philip II, for example, was seen by the Dutch nobility as a polite reminder of their established rights, by Philip as a personal visit from a respected adviser, and by the urban icon-breakers of 1566 as a chance to demand religious freedoms. The interactions between these different interpretations began the Dutch Revolt (van Gelderen 1992, pp. 37–8). Thus, we will often find that the reactions between the levels are a matter of action, *interpretation* and reaction, which is precisely what the interpretative/hermeneutic approach enables us to capture.

We can extrapolate from this and other interactions across the range of revolutions an overarching concept of 'the revolutionary narrative' which I will use to consider revolutions across different places and historical moments. 'The revolutionary narrative' is the *form* within which the events and actions that constitute one revolution or another are interpreted and acted upon. It frames the elements that determine and interpret any given revolution, including its relationship with other historical events. These elements are: the potential for irreversible change in the direction of some end-state profoundly different from the given present; the possibility of power to initiate or control such change; the expectation that one or more agents exist with power and intentions as to the future; and an overarching frame of historical time which provides both normative and predictive indicators for the anticipated future. These last are primarily positive: reassurance that the end-state will be better than the present, justification for action to produce it, and so forth.[1] But the narrative form also allows for negative versions: apprehension about the potential future and condemnation of action intended to bring it about.

I take a 'narrative' to be an ordered sequence of events and actions located in its own time-span. Narrative, that is to say, stretches events and actions out across time, linking one state with other, later ones. A narrative possesses an internal coherence which lends a certain kind of necessity to the sequence of states that it organizes. The sequence is so embedded in time by the narrative that it seems the events and actions it embraces could not have happened otherwise. While a narrative may embrace causal relations and regularities, by virtue of its nature as narrative it has two assets in the interpretation of human experience which causality lacks. Because a narrative does not require that situations are repeated, it does not require evidence of causality, or the possibility of repetition, in order to lend coherence to events. Secondly, narrative readily includes human roles, hopes and experiences. I will return to this idea also in the next section, leaning on the thought of Paul Ricoeur.

The revolutionary narrative straddles the analytical/interpretative distinction: those who participate and those who react to a revolutionary process will do so on the basis of differing content that can be embraced within the *form* of the revolutionary narrative. Various socio-political actors will, for example, ascribe to the initial revolutionary events a capacity to produce some specific future condition and to certain specific groups or individuals an intention to produce it. Such interpretations will inform those actors' actions, with their attendant consequences. Under the umbrella of 'the revolutionary narrative', different specific narrations can be formulated for the same revolutionary events or comparable ones. Each such narration specifies end-states, determining powers, agents of change, justifications of change etc. – different contents inserted into the general form of 'the revolutionary narrative'. These elements can be mapped loosely on to the different elements of explanation that I specified in chapter 2 – subject to the different rules of admissibility which distinguish narrative from explanation. Thus, actors' interpretations enter into relation with the pre-revolutionary conditions which can be accounted for analytically. For different narrations will attract the support of some and the opposition of others, providing terms of exchange between the different levels and moments in a revolutionary upheaval.

This abstract description of 'the revolutionary narrative' can be illustrated by an example of how one specific narration, Marxism-Leninism, fused with and competed against others at a given historical moment. Looking back, twenty years after his first edition, on the career of the idea of revolution which his book charts, Dunn (1989, pp. 245ff) observes how two components of Marxism-Leninism made it a peculiarly exportable ideology during three decades following the Second World War, as colonial power receded under its own weight and pressure from the US/global system. In my terms, Marxist-Leninist ideology constituted a revolutionary narration: the defeat of imperialist capitalism and global spread of classless socialism were the end-states that would be achieved by the party of liberation leading the masses. Lenin's concept of 'imperialism' and its end suggested that colonizing power was doomed to give way to a greater equality among peoples, while the role of the 'professional revolutionary' could be taken on by the nascent, Western-trained elites of the colonized areas. The formative potential of the professional revolutionary could be applied to the creation of a national entity which could at once emulate and confront the metropolitan nation which drew its origins from an earlier, liberal-nationalist moment. What is more, minority opposition to colonial power was neatly situated and amplified by the *counter*-narration of revolution espoused at the time by US-led Western states. These took all revolutionary contention as instances of the *same* worldwide movement, more or less manipulated from Moscow, to reverse the historic success of liberal-democracy and the global free market.

Three major narrations appear together in this instance: the nineteenth-century national-republican one that invented European *nation*-statehood; the internationalist, nineteenth-century socialist riposte to that; and liberal 'modernizing' twentieth-century rationalism, centred on the USA. Each exhibits the same revolutionary narrative form – the prospect or threat of irreversible change, the power of certain agents to advance or prevent such change, and notions of the irreversible end-state to which such change was directed. Each of them has, of course, been associated with a particular phase and version of the spreading ripple of modernization. Indeed, they all share a certain underlying form that expresses assumptions in modernization: change is (or ought to be) irreversible and results in human agents taking command of their world for human material benefit. The contents of the different narrations transpose this form between one narration and another: nineteenth-century human progress has, for example, to be captured for the benefit of exploited human beings from monopoly by the few, protected by the now sham national interest of European nations; nationalism in pursuit of national self-expression becomes anti-colonialism; anti-colonial contention is inserted into a powerful, deliberate, worldwide conspiracy against established achievements in human freedom and welfare. Each of these contents includes an agent and a final goal, though they differ as to what these are. The shared form of the different revolutionary

narrations actually enhances the cogency and force of the different ideologies they are associated with. The aspirations of modernization have
been adopted from Europe, and translated into other terms to account for
both anti-colonialism and the Cold War riposte to anti-colonialism.

Dunn, whose writing is always ironically sensitive to the human condition, makes one other comment on the force of Marxism-Leninism: it
epitomized 'a metaphor of the recapture of control by the virtuous over
inimical destiny' (1989, p. 255). Just as I have generalized Dunn's observations by making Marxism-Leninism an instance of my broader concept of
the revolutionary narrative, so will I return to this idea of revolution as the
struggle of the virtuous in the face of forced change. For the power of the
revolutionary narrative is, in my view, enhanced by its capacity to encom-
pass the hope that change can be channelled by the combined power of the
'virtuous' or their equivalent. The next section deals more widely with the
force of the revolutionary narrative in a modern world facing historical
change. The remainder of the chapter then defends the logical coherence of
collective agency as it figures in the revolutionary narrative.

Narratives and historical change

The affinity I pointed out above between assumptions in modernization and
the underlying form of the revolutionary narrative is no accident. The
revolutionary narrative and its hermeneutic power are not merely contingent developments of revolutions themselves. Rather, the context created
by modernization provides an interpretative need which the revolutionary
narrative is adapted to supply. Across the length of Part I, we met worldwide modernization as a source of pressures which challenged, or threatened, societies with transition, even while it implied the possibility of
originality and invention. *Some* of the societies under these pressures
would experience revolution. But, regardless whether a revolution actually
occurs, the revolutionary narrative speaks to the condition of societies
experiencing pressures from worldwide modernization. By specifying end-
states, determining powers and agents of change, offering justifications and
providing a time-frame for change, the narrative holds together the contrary pulls of the experience of modernizing pressures. It maps out the
direction of change, but specifies also the grounds for it, and who will
manage it. It can take the incoming pressures towards modernization and
integrate them under the control of members of the existing society experiencing their intrusion. That is, I suggest, the underlying reason why the
narrative has appeared and has acquired the force it has in the behaviour of
human groups. That capacity has a great deal to do with its character as
narrative, as well as its character as *revolutionary*.

I want now to consider the power of narrative over human beings' grasp
of their time-bound world. These are phenomenological considerations;

that is to say, attempts to abstract the underlying structures of 'phenomena', a term that embraces anything that a conscious being can assimilate
as a representation of the objective world. The phenomenologist's purpose
is to find any more or less universally present forms which we, conscious
human beings, are bound to pass through to understand our world. Of
particular concern to my discussion are any underlying forms whereby the
human consciousness is able to appreciate change and events in historical
time. After the phenomenological observations, I will return to what makes
the revolutionary narrative *revolutionary*. If persuasive, the phenomenological considerations will account for the power of the narrative generated
within and around revolutions. The phenomenology then substantially
reinforces the place of my 'revolutionary narrative' in explaining the career
of revolution. It also has the virtue of approaching revolutionary actions
and perceptions from the reverse side to the topics of Part I. Instead of
seeing revolutionary narrations as an ideological *effect* of 'real' revolutions
which spreads (through, say, widespread use of ideology by states and
political groupings as instruments of their goals), we can consider narrations and ideologies from the point of the humans' susceptibility to construct their world in terms of narrative. My discussion thus passes from the
nomothetic explanation of revolutions, which predominated in Part I, to the
human creation of meaning, the hermeneutics of revolution.

The purpose of stripping away, *à la* phenomenology, features of our
particular experiences of the world is to be left with general features that
make particular experiences graspable. The crucial core of phenomenological findings usually turns out to be an analysis of how conscious beings
can unearth a degree of unity in the diversity which they experience as the
objective world. The unity of time occupies a particular place in that
problem, and has been a special focus of attention in twentieth-century
phenomenological thought. Time's unity is peculiarly difficult to discover.
First, at any particular point in time, the vast portion of events in time is not
present to us. Secondly, the passage of time can itself make sense only
against some marker of change, which will naturally counteract unity: time
requires change, that is to say, but a greater extent or pace of change
challenges that very unity of time within which events are to be temporally
located. Given that tension, we could expect the phenomenal mechanisms
of our understanding of time to be working hard when people find themselves in the midst of partly forced, one-way change. Prima facie, mechanisms for holding time together would be crucial to any widespread
approach to interpreting time and the changes which people are living. The
revolutionary narrative, I believe, contains the phenomenological mechanisms for the unification of time under circumstances of one-way change.

One aspect of the modern world directly supports this expectation. It is
the irreversibility of some historical change under conditions of modernity
which gives rise to models of *one-way* historical change (Adam 1990).
This notion appeared implicitly under the topic of progress in chapter 2.

But even before that concept emerged, from the time of the Reformation in fact, there occurred what Koselleck (1985) refers to as the modern age's early 'temporalization' of history: replacing the world held to be constant, until it met its cataclysmic millennium, with one in which change could properly occur *sub specie aeternitatis*. This was also the moment when the term 'revolution' itself descended from the heavens to the sub-lunar world of politics (Hill 1990). With the Enlightenment, 'temporalization' was reinforced. Sequences which might previously have been repeatable, or even reversible, fade out of the picture; change is admitted at all levels of understanding. For its part, in the era of 1789, 'revolution' too becomes irreversible instead of circular.

To accommodate to this, Enlightenment and post-Enlightenment thinking constructed models which frame change, such that some events or actions cause different results in a later stage from those which they produce in an earlier one. For example, the better harvests arising from fortunate weather which, in one historical phase, will strengthen the relative position of the peasantry, in a later period enhance the power of rentiers. Such variation in causal connections cuts across the most evident feature of causal regularities in human social experience – their consistency across time – and entrenches the passage of historical time. Post-Enlightenment thought characteristically offers a sequential understanding of history where a diachronic scheme frames, but also belies, the synchrony of causal relations. If, in modern experience, even the uniform relations underpinning the world are themselves subject to change in time, we should expect that fact to put a high premium on phenomenological categories that can reunify time. If time is to be grasped as unified, such categories become more than ever necessary in the logic of human consciousness. The affinity between the revolutionary change and post-Enlightenment ideas of progress rests, I suggest, upon the fact that, phenomenologically speaking, the two are doing the same job: imparting a unity to time in spite of irreversible change which breaks into the repetition of familiar patterns.

The greatest recent exploration of how the passage of time can be grasped phenomenologically is to be found in the work of Paul Ricoeur, in particular his *Time and Narrative* (1984–6).[2] Ricoeur's distinctive approach brings to the phenomenological problem of the coherence of time a concept of narrative as a phenomenal structure for consciousness – a necessary form through which human beings grasp the temporality in life and in society. Over the course of its three volumes, *Time and Narrative* explains how narrative in fiction and historical writing pursues and accommodates various *aporias* (edges of understanding) in respect of time. These include time's paradoxical apparent unity, and the relation between sequences of time as experienced or measured from different perspectives. Ricoeur is especially conscious of the way this latter impinges upon human beings as responsible actors in their world: the past, fixed and unalterable though little known; the present, accessible but fleeting; the future unknowable and open to alteration. His investigation explores the way that, even if these *aporias* of time cannot be definitively resolved by logic, the hermeneutics of time can accommodate them, such that conscious human beings can pursue their lives within time.

According to Ricoeur, the human consciousness deals with the *aporias* through *mimetic* resources which are most evidently deployed in narration (Ricoeur 1984–6, vol. 1, pp. 52–77) – hence the book's title. Mimesis casts the time-bound world of experience in three versions, depending upon the relation that the consciousness has to it. The future world is 'prefigured': as subject to change, to the effects of our and others' action and to the processes of time. In addressing the past, mimesis 'refigures' it into a structured narrative located within a temporal reality which opens out on to future change and action. Finally, mimesis extends the present beyond the immediate moment: 'configuring' it in narrative so that it has a place linking it into the passage of time and incorporating change and continuity, including our own role in them. Ricoeur pursues an analysis of first fictional and then historical narrative forms. But his approach does not maintain an absolute barrier between these different literary forms, or between the way that narrative shapes forms of writing and the way it structures the phenomenological consciousness of human existence. In volume 3 of *Time and Narrative*, he accordingly broadens discussion to accommodate the intersections and parallels between fiction and history, and includes in the latter not only history as represented and studied, but also history as lived. '[N]ot only recounted history,' he writes (vol. 3, p. 6), '. . . but also history as made and undergone by human beings.' Ultimately, then, Ricoeur's account is intended to license an analysis such as I intend: of how narrativity embraces the tensions of *living* time bound within history.

In Ricoeur's analysis, the poetics of narrative dissolves the various paradoxes within the continuity of historical time by 'the invention of a *third time*', bridging objectively measured time and time as experienced. 'Third time' is sustained by the intra-subjective understanding of the community (vol. 3, pp. 245–9). In this 'third time', an *evolving* 'narrative identity' can be attributed to persons living through temporal processes: a fluid identity which is sustained in spite of the movement of time – with its outcomes of actions, its passages from cause to effect, to the following effect, and so on. Their narrative identity entails the presumption that participants may survive through time; that they must possess various capacities to be authors of some actions; that they must acknowledge the associated obligations to accept responsibility for past actions (which are identified as belonging to them in their given identity); and that they will accordingly experience an impulse to act in some directions rather than others.[3] In spite of the fact that identity is unfixed, the intra-subjectivity of the human community sustains the narrative identity of human subjects over time.

Ricoeur is propounding a hermeneutics of narrativity: a mechanism of interpretation which will underpin the identity of participants who exist through the changes occurring across time. He rejects Hegel's construction of any consciousness that can own the final totality of *all* historical time (the 'Absolute Spirit'), on the grounds that this would be to abolish history and change altogether (Ricoeur 1984–6, vol. 3, ch. 9). The narrative identity of human agents possesses merely an open-ended total*izing* potential, a capacity which underwrites their unity provisionally, so as to draw together in time their action and its outcomes.[4] In short, Ricoeur's historical 'third time' is peopled by intelligent beings with a continuous, but changing, existence. Their self-awareness consciously requires them to look back; to recognize their own present existence, their continuity, their capacity for action and their responsibility; and to anticipate the future in ordered, continuous but open-ended temporal sequences. That is the insight from Ricoeur's analysis that I wish to take up in order to account for the power of the 'revolutionary narrative'.

Ricoeur shows why humans' consciousness should persistently structure as narrative the changing but time-bound world of their lived existence. To be able to live within a 'temporalized' world calls for a sense of being susceptible to change: an awareness of the irreversible givens and regularities of the past, combined with a grasp of possibilities in the future and the power of action to affect them. The revolutionary narrative possesses those features too. It interprets the patterns of the past so as to turn susceptibility to change into the possibility of future improvement and identifies human beings as collective agents of such progress. Marx himself provided a *locus classicus* expressing precisely those aspects of the revolutionary narrative in his epigram (in *The Eighteenth Brumaire of Louis Napoleon*) that: 'Man makes history, but he does not make it under circumstances of his own choosing.' The remark hardly constitutes an analysis, but it expresses incisively the paradoxical fashion in which human beings can conceive their position, in between what Ricoeur would call the 'refigured' world of the past and the 'prefigured' future. Ricoeur's analysis thus brings to my explanation of the revolutionary narrative an account of how the elements in it derive from the deeper phenomenological needs and the function of narrative in resolving them. Where radical change is a possibility, the revolutionary narrative thus offers human understanding an invaluable orientation.

The revolutionary narrative is, however, more than merely one useful hermeneutic tool in the eternal repertoire of human consciousness. The prospect of one-way change is a specific feature of modernity: an epoch, as Therborn puts it (1995, p. 4), 'turned to the future'. And for modern human beings, as Marshall Berman has demonstrated, this has often been a tragic challenge, which Marx's works explore (Berman 1983, pp. 38–129). Modernity poses the future as an unknown necessity to be strived for; time becomes a one-way street towards a rational future completeness. We have observed in Part I how the external, global pressures of modernity were conveyed primarily through the state. On my reading of their history, revolutions are echoes of, and responses to, the spreading ripple of modernization pressures. Modernization bears down upon modern human beings with an altered temporality: irreversible; directed towards an ideal state which appears as an alien import; an ever-ungraspable order of how a society ought to be.[5] Conversely, the existing 'traditional' social order, marked as it is for breakdown, loses its legitimacy. In short, the pressure of modernity, which the revolutionary narrative has phenomenologically to accommodate, posits together: irreversibility, necessity, alienation of the inherited order and its values, and disruption breaking loose from human control. This combination underpins what Zigmunt Bauman calls modernity's *horror vacui* (1992, p. xvii).

On the other hand, as Agnes Heller observes (1993, p. 34), in reflecting on history and the moderns, 'story-telling makes sense, it renders meaning – but it does not necessarily sublate contingency. The experience of purposefulness without purpose, attributed by Kant to the perception of beauty, is by no means characteristic of our experience of history.' I would go further. It is precisely the quality of narrative that it imparts a sense of has-to-be to the contingency of passing time. But the revolutionary narrative does more: it *embraces* the necessary passage of time towards the future as the fulfilment of the will of agents who have taken the alien force of modernization in hand. The revolutionary narrative enables humans confronted with the necessity, risk and/or possibility of change to enfold that prospect in a narrative of *willed* change, towards *a better future*, under the direction of, as Dunn says, 'the virtuous'. Thus, the revolutionary narrative has a quite specific function for the modern consciousness of human beings: it enables people to translate the threat of change into a possibility of deliberate improvement. And this is never more so than when modernity and its drive for change are (as was discussed in Part I) pressing in upon a society and its received ways. That is to say, the revolutionary narrative will have force for *all* those who experience the nature of modernity and its demands for change; but it will be especially powerful in the situation where revolutions are, in fact, most likely to occur: where the ripple of modernity impinges upon a given socio-political order.

In one way, I am adapting the original terms of Ricoeur's analysis. For Ricoeur, a complex of interactions between different conscious human beings and 'the same' agent over time assumes the seemingly continuous existence of the latter. In *Time and Narrative*, a single, stable interpreting society is taken as a premise: Ricoeur is concerned with narrative hermeneutics rather than with the intra-subjective communicative framework within which interpretation as narrative takes place. My interest, however, is in situations of revolutionary change, where human consciousness operates with anything but stable community. The *philosophical* possibility of this has been suggested by Calvin Schrag, whose analysis of narrative embeds it in the intra-subjectivity of communicative practice. His perspective on the question of narrativity prompts Schrag to see how narrative thinking 'articulates patterns and lines of continuity in human experience and transforms stories into cohesive and powerful social instruments' (1992, p. 93).

There is, then, no reason to suppose that the narrative hermeneutics developed by Ricoeur and his like should not operate *a fortiori* where the interpreting society is *not* stable. In conditions of forced, irreversible historical change even to the point of revolution – as the big, global timescales of modernity meet and disrupt the lived time of ordinary human beings – human consciousness would surely be more than ever reliant upon narrativity and its 'third time'. For under such conditions, the continuous existence of the community is *harder* to guarantee and calls for greater hermeneutic resources. Ricoeur's 'third time' could only become more important, therefore: for, in it, even though present actions contribute to radically altered future states, the narrative identities formed in the present are capable of surviving into the unknown future. In precisely those conditions where revolutionary change might occur, then, phenomenological thinking indicates that we would find the same *forms* of narrative identity as Ricoeur has outlined.

The revolutionary narrative and its collective identities

If we do indeed, employing the manner of Ricoeur, trace hermeneutics in the phenomenology of consciousness under circumstances of radical change, the identities in the narrative will pose particular difficulty. We would expect those beings who are identified in human consciousness for revolutionary circumstances to fit into the same narrative *form* as any others: a recognition of the past as a given; participants' awareness of their own continuous, if fluid identity with an open prospect of the future; their sense of power and responsibility, as agents, for future outcomes; a perception of the present as a turning point where the agent stands between past and future. But what species of human subjects can a narrative of radical change suppose who would straddle the present moment and the radically different future and function between one and the other? The particular difficulty of the revolutionary narrative as a narrative is that the beings who can sustain identity in conditions of irreversible, radical change are bound to be special among human agents. This, ostensibly philosophical, problem needs to be brought out and resolved in order to sustain the case for the real impact of the revolutionary narrative upon real humans' perceptions and actions. A theoretically unacceptable concept is less likely to carry weight in use.

We evidently have to extend the notion of identities formed in narrative *à la* Ricoeur, setting aside in particular his emphasis on the single mortal individual so as to consider a bigger variety of possible human actors. The terms of analysis require identities with the same narrative forms: continuity over time; conscious, evolving identity; direction and power to act towards the future. Individual human beings are unlikely to fulfil those requirements in conditions of radical change. The changes envisaged most probably exceed the compass of individuals' lives – not solely because the disruption they entail can be dangerous for the survival of those individuals. The changes that occur, or are brought about by any agents of change, are on a scale beyond the capacities we can easily attribute to individual human beings (though heroes, great leaders, historic individuals, men of destiny, etc. might be put forward as exceptions to this stricture – albeit not very convincing ones). These considerations lead us to look for narrative identities at a supra-individual level. Assuming, in the modern manner, that we consider only secular, non-transcendent beings, it is most probably various human *groups* that will fill the bill: large groupings that seem more likely to survive over time and are better able to exercise leverage upon the most general features of society. Such supra-individual entities in the revolutionary narrative I call 'collective agents of change'.

An early historical case of a group which was well aware that it constituted just such a collective entity illustrates how a collective agent of change may be formed in response to conditions which we can recognize as those of modernity. Walzer's *The Revolution of the Saints* (1966) is a study of the English Puritan clergy and their followers. It describes a group of men who had been initially excluded from the society of their day (self-educated outside the established church and its institutions, literally banished for their beliefs during the reign of Mary Tudor, subjected to harassment by the authorities after their return), but whose ministering and public pronouncements were gradually accepted by an educated Protestant public and their political representatives. The Puritan belief system *instilled* uncertainty; for it held it right for man to be 'unsettled' in this earthly life. But it also provided the clergy and their followers with reassurance, moral self-discipline, and a strategy for survival where the old certainties of traditional norms were being undermined. Puritanism served this expanding group as 'an ideology of transition' (Walzer 1966, p. 312). Indeed, Walzer argues that it was a functional response to the situation of breakdown that they sensed around them: [6]

> [g]iven the breakdown of the old order, it is predictable that some Englishmen would make that reasonable choice [of sainthood]. . . . [I]ndividual men experienced at once a new and exhilarating sense of freedom and mobility and an acute anxiety and fearfulness, both of which may be summed up in the Puritan notion of 'unsettledness'. . . . In this society the activity of the organized 'people' was as necessary to social discipline as was popular passivity in the traditional world. The old order was imagined to be natural and eternal, but it is in the nature of the new to be regularly renewed. It is the product of art and will, of human doing. (1966, pp. 310 and 311)

The career of the revolutionary narrative is littered with putative human groupings for which such attributes and status have been claimed: enlightened humans everywhere, the rising classes of commercial society, the proletariat, the international labour movement, the progressive nation (France, the people of the United States, etc.), oppressed colonial peoples of the world, and so on. Each of those might indeed fulfil the preconditions for the role of actor in a narrative under revolutionary conditions: for they are large entities that could plausibly survive through time and effect profound change. They are not transcendent beings (though they may or may not be held to have God on their side). Other groupings are to be found in the modern world which possess the attributes to fulfil a role in the narrative under conditions of change. Some are conservative or *anti-*'revolutionary': the national family, international finance, the Aryan race, the international Jewish conspiracy, and so on. Even though not all of them are associated with change, they are all, I suggest, 'collective agents', susceptible to narrative identity in the sense outlined above. Each of those putative groupings has had a more or less persuasive claim, from the standpoint of different contemporaries or later reflection, to exist and to possess agency in the narrative of history. At some time or other, they have all been summoned by participants and/or observers of radical historical change to fill the role that the phenomenology of human consciousness of history seems to require from a narrative identity; namely, continuity of existence, power to effect change, and so on. In short, they are suitable for accommodating the prospect of historical change.

I anticipate a number of objections to this account of how human consciousness will assemble collective agents in a narrative to embrace radical or revolutionary change. The most obvious objection, flagged in my selection above, is that belief in such collective identities may license horrendous political acts. 'The Jewish conspiracy' is a case in point. The Kulaks would be another: a grouping, like the Jews, defined by others and then made the object of an extermination campaign on the grounds of the historical role attributed to them – to corrupt in the spirit of the *Volk*, to obstruct the path to socialism or whatever it may be. The claim behind that objection is indeed true. However, my phenomenological account concerns the necessary *form* of collective identities and how they come to have a place in the narratives of history. The analysis does not show, and is not intended to show, that the identities adopted must be well grounded in empirical realities. Nor does it exclude those identities that are foisted upon a group by others with hate in their hearts. Conversely, there is no reason why any collective identities formulated for the hermeneutics of history should not be challenged from the point of view of empirical inaccuracy or moral distaste. The Jewish conspiracy was a fiction and the counter-revolutionary intent of the Kulaks a cloak for dictatorial cruelty by the state. My analysis concerns only the phenomenological *form* that narratives will take under conditions of profound change. It is not a defence of all particular contents inserted into that form.

Two other, logical objections seem to require a more elaborate response, however. First, collective agents may be logically so difficult to identify that they are more likely to cripple the narrative of historic change than sustain it. Secondly, what I am calling collective 'agents' may so rarely succeed in realizing their intentions that they hardly qualify as *agents* in the first place. If these objections are valid, what could be the hermeneutic force of collective agents? I will consider the question of collective identity here, deferring the problem of intentions and outcomes to the next section. Against both points, the burden of my answer is that, even if they are not entirely satisfactory, collective agents are needed.

I hardly need to dispute the fact that collective agents of change are difficult to identify. It gives rise to perpetual travails for those thinking in terms of the revolutionary narrative, which are the very topic of this part of the book. As the direction and centre of modernization divide and shift in the twentieth century, previously accepted collective agents of change totter and dissolve. But the difficulty of formulating their identity has to be balanced against the experiential need to think in terms of them. I have set out above why there is a phenomenological need for agents in a narrative of change. Nonetheless, I cannot avoid some argument for the relative merits of a bias I have installed into the Ricoeur narrative form: that is, the preference for collective over individual agents to star in the narrative. Of course, I am not disputing the ontological status of the individual *per se*. But my preference goes against the grain of our prevalent Western individualist view of human life and society. Yet, obvious as individualism may seem, if we consider under different headings this choice of collective over individual agency, the balance is by no means obviously in favour of the individual.

The most obvious hermeneutic merit of the collective agents is their more plausible claim to possess enough power to effect change at the historical level. Indeed, the case looks unanswerable if we ask what capacity individuals would enjoy to achieve even their individual purposes in the absence of the means which the collective puts at their disposal. That consideration has always inspired collectivism in both social philosophy and epistemology. As Alex Callinicos has argued (1987, esp. pp. 35–8), individuals living a social existence have to operate through a structure which exceeds their individual existence if they are to obtain most of the objectives which they can formulate for themselves as individuals.[7] It is true that individual acts might be thought to contribute to historical change merely by aggregation. But if grouped solely on an additive basis, they lose all the intentionality required for agency, and hence fail to qualify for the necessary role in a narrative of change. If I see myself acting as an individual alone, I can have no idea of effecting any historic change; if I act with the action of others in mind, then I depend upon that collective level of human existence which embraces them and myself. No individual 'agents' can act with an intention to produce historical change, therefore, without some presumption as to how their individual acts belong with the collective.

The case for the cogency of collective agents looks much harder to sustain when it comes to their continuous identity. The physical criteria of individual identity are straightforward by comparison with the efforts called for to identify the boundaries of a grouping whose individual members are often difficult to enumerate and who perpetually come and go. Of all types of group, social classes display those features most strongly, since many individuals may belong to more than one, or apparently to none of the available range, or they may pass from one to another. This problem has long been an obstacle to class-based accounts of society, as of revolution, and there is a substantial literature about it.[8] But other collective identities – nations, families, movements, etc. – give signs of comparable problems, shown not least by the very routines and rituals that they seem to need to *sustain* their collective identity. Nor is the contrast between identity in individuals and in collectives as obvious as might at first appear. David Hume pointed out long ago how the physical constituents and appearance of the given individual are in reality subject to constant change – giving rise to a long-standing presumption among philosophers that individuals need to have spatio-temporal *continuity* first in order for a unified identity to be added.[9] The *psychological* make-up of the individual human being is plainly every bit as variable and discontinuous as the physical, whilst more difficult to embrace in spatio-temporal continuity. So there is no easy continuity to underpin the identity of an *individual* human entity any more than a *collective* one. In real life, the identity of the human individual is actually not grounded in the continuity of his or her component parts.

Rather, many features which underpin individual identity are overlaid on a constant shifting of grounds (Glover 1988). Identifying features are often derived from the individual's relationship to a larger, putatively more stable entity: links to other members of the family, specific training or professional activity, employment, place of abode, past actions, and so on. If relational criteria are to have priority in affirming the identity of the individual, however, the collective agent certainly has as good a claim to a determinate identity as the individual. A given individual may be identified as a mother, a friend, an influence upon certain others, a leader, the author of this letter or that decision, etc. Just so may a given collective agent (the peasantry of a region, say) be identified as those who occupy that particular land, feed that society, retain the ancient culture of that people, supply the opposition to commercial enclosure, and so on. Awkward as it can be, the collective agent's identity is not so uncertain as to disqualify human consciousness from appealing to it where other phenomenological requirements are satisfied by doing so. True, neither the identity of individual agents nor that of collective agents is easy to establish and sustain. But that does not prevent both from being construed as identities in Ricoeur's sense of a narrative: that is to say, assigned a determinate place within a sequence in which putative agents engage in relations with other objects and where people acknowledge certain outcomes attributed to them. Prima facie, then, it is not decisively harder to establish a continuous identity that is collective than one that is individual. The identities of both specific individual and collective agents are established and sustained by relational and narrative features such as those above. All cases are subject to a degree of uncertainty and change.

On the face of it, the choice of the collective agent as a narrative category seems directly to confront methodological individualism: the theorists' claim that all social facts have ultimately to be accounted for by facts about individuals. Given the size of the debate this has provoked, it is fortunate that my aim here is not to address the question of which, collective or individual, is *ultimately* decisive. I have merely to put the case for the essential usefulness of the collective in a hermeneutic account of historical change in revolutionary narrative. That does not imply that the collective is determinant, ultimately or provisionally, *vis-à-vis* the individual. It leaves it open to us, for example, to see collective structures, in Giddens's terms, as both 'medium and outcome' for individuals' actions. Structures may *constrain* individuals in their choice of courses of action, yet they also *enable* individuals to take action and are themselves the constantly renewed, or amended, outcome of individuals' actions (Giddens 1984). On the other hand, if pressed too far, the concept of the individual quickly runs out of steam in understanding social experience. Martin Hollis, a commentator basically sympathetic to methodological individualism, tests individualist accounts of rational human behaviour over the whole gamut of complexity (Hollis 1987). Were a person to think solely in individualist terms, Hollis concludes, he or she would soon be crippled in rationally calculating the outcomes (and hence benefits) of any particular course of action: the range of possibilities is simply too enormous. Without expectations which place individuals in definite social roles and make working assumptions about what behaviour is normal for that role, individual rational calculation would never be completed (Hollis 1987 – esp. ch. 10).[10] Hence, social roles ascribed to individuals and groups emerge as unavoidable components of an *understanding* of social behaviour.

The collective agent has a special *merit* over the individual in narrative forms to embrace the conditions I am considering here. The collective is both more necessary and more difficult where consciousness has to grasp behaviour under conditions holding the possibility of radical change. The collective agent is more *necessary* because the outcomes of action are irreversible and distant. The route to outcomes is more complex than in the normal, synchronic conditions where some given action repeatedly prompts similar responses and a foreseeable result. Where the world is liable to change radically, individuals' calculations to decide their course of action would be more complex by far than in the familiar territory of ordinary life. The social role of others and what that suggests as to their likely course of action would therefore be vital to orientation. This gives Hollis's argument still greater force. Suppose a crisis is in the offing and an individual must decide on some action, such as to withhold payment of taxes, which could play a part in events. The individual will have to make numerous assumptions about the behaviour of other individuals *as groups*. He or she may properly assume, for example, that property-owners will act as a group, according to their shared interests and customary views; that is, they will, say, withhold payment of taxes, and that this widespread action may then force reform upon the state. The individual's action could not be formulated, and hence intentional, without the notion of such groups in his or her appreciation of the situation.

Yet, in the circumstances we have in mind, thinking in terms of groups is also more *difficult*. These assumptions about the behaviour of groups have to be made concurrently with the awareness that any given individual may not conform to the pattern expected for his or her group. As Olson's theory of individual rational decision stresses to a fault (Olson 1965), members of any group may have a specific motive for *not* complying with assumptions about group behaviour. If I lie low and leave it to others to take the risks of the tax revolt, the outcome will be the same and I will still enjoy whatever benefits result in the long run. The motivation to 'free ride' on the efforts of others is at its greatest where each individual can place reliance on a larger group whilst the anticipated benefits are a great distance away. Yet the rational temptation to hold back from the group action does not alter the logical necessity, under these circumstances, to *conceive* others as a group in the first place, and to think of them as more or less predictable collective agents.

The fact that assumptions can be mistaken, actions misconceived or expectations disappointed does not remove the necessity for making certain kinds of assumptions in the first place. It may alter the terms in which one acts upon assumptions – encouraging an individual to keep open a way to backtrack, for example, or to seek assurances as to the behaviour of others.[11] But, in the end, as Hollis's account reminds us, imperfect views of the social world (such as Weberian 'ideal types') are adopted not because they are believed to *match* reality in any straightforward sense, but because they *guide choices* that have to be made somehow or other: 'social actions are solutions to problems of choice, which come close enough to ideal-type thinking to be thereby understood' (Hollis 1987, p. 185).[12] It is on such terms that collective identity will figure in the revolutionary narrative and in the human understanding of a world which experiences profound, irreversible change.

We can sum up our discussion of the priority of collective identities for the revolutionary narrative in these conclusions. Yes, there are drawbacks and impediments to perceiving social reality in terms of collective agents. Yet the difficulties – doubts as to the effectiveness of groups, their shifting identity, uncertainty about any predictive characterizations – can equally be found in individual agents. Furthermore, in circumstances of radical historical change, individual agency is plainly inadequate and collective agents must therefore hold a prime place in the narrative understanding needed to lend coherence to human experience. Hence the key place assigned to collective agents in the revolutionary narrative.

Collective intention

By comparison with individuals, what I am calling collective 'agents' seem rarely to succeed in realizing their intentions. This is especially the case in the uncertain circumstances of revolutionary upheaval. Prima facie, this would diminish the status of collective agents *as agents*. This is the problem of *intentions* in collective agents, which I deliberately deferred earlier. It introduces consciousness into the question of identity and hence into the formation of the revolutionary narrative.

Unlike the roles in my 'revolutionary narrative', the question of consciousness is widely discussed in relation to revolutions. Notably, revolutionaries themselves have had intermittently to come back to a view of shared consciousness as a precondition and/or outcome of revolution. The turn of the century debates on 'revisionism', initiated by Bernstein's wish to promote a consciously political Marxism for the German Social Democratic Party, brings out the parameters of the problem. Bernstein felt the need to abandon the expectation of a cataclysmic revolutionary transition, since that put the future beyond the range of what could be anticipated and formulated in an explicit, politically negotiable programme. For his opponents, to do as he recommended would simply license the continuation of established (bourgeois-liberal) society: clear, conscious intention would have been bought only at the cost of tolerating most of the given economic structure. Georges Sorel tried to straddle the tension between free consciousness and the given order in various, almost chimerical positions about working-class beliefs. He rejected both the claims to a 'scientific' status for socialism, and the established late-nineteenth-century socialist 'legend' of the Paris Commune (Sorel 1898). But, at the same time, he recognized the force of 'revolutionary myths' expressed in newer, syndicalist forms of working-class activity, such as the general strike (Sorel 1908a), which he hoped would recover some of the 'symbolic value' he found in Marx's writing on revolutionary change (Sorel 1908b). To some extent, Lenin's disciplined revolutionary party can be seen as a mechanism to organize the working class to act on radical Sorelian myths (Paquot 1982, p. 10). Finally, at the theoretical opposite end of the scale from Bernstein, represented by Lukàcs (discussed in chapter 2), one could turn a unique, and uniquely effective, collective consciousness into the grounds for the revolutionary class's unprecedented, transcendent place in historical transformation (Lukàcs 1971).

Conversely, 'structuralist' accounts of revolution have done their utmost to avoid altogether reliance upon, or even reference to, consciousness, which they regard as impossible to establish and/or devoid of explanatory value. Skocpol's thesis represents a sociological version of this case against consciousness. I shall return to those claims in chapter 6, after discussing why it is perfectly feasible to include collective agents' consciousness and intentions in the revolutionary narrative. My general line of argument resembles that of the previous section. The apparent difficulties of dealing with consciousness and intention in collective agents must be viewed in comparison with analogous, sometimes more serious, drawbacks in the case of the individual: if these difficulties are not crucially harder to accommodate for collective than for individual actors, then we cannot balk at accepting the place of collective consciousness in human beings' understanding of the historical possibilities of change that they are living in.

Let us look at *individual* intentional action. Understanding it calls upon an apparently quite unmanageable battery of both prior objective conditions and what we might call the subjective 'mental furniture' of the individual consciousness. Any act is based upon a complex interaction between the facts of the agent's situation and his or her appreciation of them. The agent's interpretation of the given situation already includes an assessment of the objective balance between those causal outcomes of the present which are, by the present point in time, inevitable and those which may be prevented, encouraged or confidently brought about. In short, no agent can view the world in terms of a single modality, such as what is present and certain, from which further clear outcomes follow with certainty. Any agent must hold in mind a welter of certainties, probabilities and possibilities. So the individual agent's numerous prognoses of possible future states – ranging from confident expectations to not-daring-to-hope – are bound rapidly to enter the picture.

The picture does not yet include the agent's *wishes* for the future, which would themselves range from mild preferences to hopeless desires. None of these are given in a simple sense. Rather, they are built up in a complex relationship with perceptions of reality and whatever certainties and possibilities that suggests. The smoker may formulate a wish to give up smoking in terms of past failures, future stresses and discomforts, social settings, the attitudes or responses of others, and so forth. Conscious action somehow emerges from a number of such apparently insuperable barriers to be comprehensible for both agents and observers. Each additional input into the mental furniture that contributes to action seems to make interpretation, decision and action itself harder. Hence, the temptation to leave consciousness out of the picture altogether. Both interpreters and agents themselves fall victim to this temptation – hence, the agent who excuses himself or

herself by saying 'I just didn't think' or the observer who excludes consciousness as simply not amenable to analysis.

Now let us compare a judgement on *collective* intention. Having completed her analysis of three 'old régimes' which collapsed under the pressure of inter-state rivalry, internal disunity and peasant rebellion, Skocpol
pauses before going on to the second half of the book and an account of the
outcomes of the revolutions (1979, ch. 4).[13] Her aim is not only to justify
the 'focus on state-building' which is the dominant feature of the book, but
also to defend her more general anti-voluntarism. Given what I have said
about the underlying cogency of the 'revolutionary narrative' – including
the place it accords to the agency of collective entities such as classes,
nations, parties, etc. – the anti-voluntarist construction that Skocpol puts
upon her analysis conflicts with my account. I want therefore to dispute the
way she uses her findings to undermine the notion of collective agents' will
and intentions.

Skocpol's argument here has three stages. First, following de
Tocqueville, she points out that 'the changes that social revolutions make
in the structure and functioning of states' are more striking than the
changes in social relations (1979, p. 164). Secondly, in an echo of Burke
(though more immediately attributable to Alfred Cobban), she draws attention to the class backgrounds of revolutionary leaders, who usually do
not hale from the classes whose interests they have claimed to advance.
Finally, she focuses (pp. 170–1) on the gap between outcomes and the
objectives proclaimed by revolutionary ideologies.

> it cannot be argued . . . that the cognitive content of the ideologies in any
> sense provides a predictive key to either the outcomes of the Revolutions or
> the activities of the revolutionaries who built the state organizations that
> consolidated the Revolutions. . . .
>   In short, ideologically oriented leaderships in revolutionary crises have
> been greatly limited by existing structural conditions and severely buffeted
> by the rapidly changing currents of revolutions. Thus they have typically
> ended up accomplishing very different tasks and furthering the consolidation
> of quite different kinds of new regimes from those they originally (and
> perhaps ever) ideologically intended. . . . Revolutionary crises are not total
> breakdowns in history that suddenly make anything at all possible if only
> envisaged by wilful revolutionaries!

The broad weight of Skocpol's evidence supports this view of her
chosen revolutions well enough. It is difficult to say how the actions of
participants can be based on an objective apprehension of reality. As
moments of extreme disorder and change within the social system, revolutions present a peculiarly strong case for the general scientific stricture
against putting participants' knowledge on a par with that of later 'objective' analysts. In revolutions, that is to say, anticipations of the future are
very frequently wildly wrong.[14] That is no doubt why Skocpol highlights –

the better to discard them – what the revolutionaries' ideologies have to say about the future course of events. But is that grounds for the general anti-voluntarism she espouses? Only if one operates with a simple binary division between acting within the reality of the world and knowing about it. As Skocpol indeed seems to be doing when she observes: 'that which political leaderships in revolutionary crises are above all *doing*' is 'claim-ing and struggling to maintain state power' (1979, p. 165). If they do not achieve what they think or say they are aiming to, this implies, then revolutionaries are doing something quite different, of which they are most probably unaware.[15] Hence the irrelevance of the revolutionaries' will. We need to question this claim on two grounds.

First, in the realm of human activity, on what grounds can it be said that such-and-such is what people are doing *above all*? Such claims depend upon certain elements of the situation and of the actors' behaviour being picked out and accorded a special objective status.[16] Whilst it may be the business of the structural analysis to build and use *models* of inter-state rivalry, worldwide modernization, state-building etc., such structures can-not show what people are doing 'above all'. It is far more plausible to suppose that the historical actors really are *intending* to do some things, but *succeeding* in doing something else. The form taken by their 'success' is no doubt partly attributable to those structures which the analyst identifies and within which the participants are taking their action. But that is not grounds for side-lining *ex hypothesi* the agents' conscious intentions. Outcomes *are* related to intentions, even though they do not simply match them.

That leads us to the second, broader consideration: how does the 'real' world include what the human participants *think* is going on? There is an extreme position enclosed within anti-voluntarism to the effect that partici-pants' ideas have no place in the real world studied by the social sciences. It is the notion of 'intentional action' that forms a bridge between the world and what participants think. Intention is not about *predicting* outcomes. It does the work of holding together a dense cluster of conscious factors in action in a world that will not easily fall in with the wishes of the agent. It signifies that action is grounded in an ordered summation of diverse mental furniture. The concept of intention simplifies the interpretative situation for actors and observers alike, by organizing and privileging parts of the mental furniture behind action. 'Acting with an intention,' is, in Donald Davidson's words, 'action . . . caused in the right way by attitudes and beliefs that rationalize it' (Davidson 1980, p. 87). The concept of 'inten-tion' makes it viable to consider the actions as intentional *wholes*, in spite of the complexities referred to above. Some possible elements of the agent's consciousness are, for example, viewed as too trivial, irrelevant or uncertain to be worth worrying about. The range of mental furniture is narrowed by the concept of intention, and the whole is organized into a hierarchy of strong reasons, weak reasons, mistaken reasons, the effects of a passing mood, misperception, force of habit, or whatever. All of that constitutes a coherent picture of the actions of individuals, capable of embracing expectations, preferences, self-awareness, and so on.

Though clearly not a straightforward picture of the actions of ourselves and others, this *is* a viable one. If, given the notion of intention, both agents and observers choose not to disregard consciousness in spite of the numerous uncertainties, that is because, as a result of the very complexity, consciousness and intention contribute indispensable dimensions to understanding any action that is undertaken. To decide upon present action, or to describe and account for past action, without taking account of conscious intention would seem impossible. Even though notions of agents' conscious intention are subject to manifold uncertainties, they help us in various ways: to predict, to choose, to justify, to interpret. Even though we might, in any particular instance, fail to find a valid conscious intention guiding action, we cannot avoid the search for one.

I can now address the problem of intentions in *collective* agents. Prima facie, the above remarks, with all their strictures on the complexity of intentions in any given case, apply equally to the action of groups and to that of individuals. Hence, consciousness and intention are necessary (even if often frustrated) categories for interpreting the actions of both individuals and collectives. In some ways, in fact, it is both more necessary and easier to find consciousness and intention for group than for individual action. The need for members of a group to communicate and to share beliefs or motives for action is plainly greater, so that motives and intentions are more likely to be explicitly articulated and accessible to hermeneutic scrutiny. But the limitations with regard to groups are also serious. As sub-groups and individuals embrace or drift away from the 'common' intention of the larger group, the tensions between different levels of intention are more evident than for the individual agent. This problem has in itself fed a substantial literature in the social psychology of revolution from Durkheim to Lewis Coser (1956), to Charles Tilly (1978) and all those influenced by him (Rule 1989, ch. 6).

Yet the conscious intentions of agents, individual or collective, emerge from these observations as vital for undertaking action, for understanding, self-understanding and explanation. Conscious intentions are an essential element in our understanding. They contribute to, but do not necessarily determine, action. But they are subject to error and to falsification, and are perpetually frustrated in their intended outcome. They remain poor predictors of action and even poorer predictors of outcomes. Though not unique to collective agents, the risk of not holding to an agreed *collective* purpose is greater than for individual purposes; hence the hazards on the path to realization are more serious. So intentions are more obviously limited as predictors of outcomes for collective action than for individuals. But to approach intention (as Skocpol does) in pursuit of predictions for final outcomes of action manifests, from the start, a misconception as to both its weight in action and its nature. If intentions are primarily ordered assemblages of the reasons for action, they are neither the sole, nor the best, place to look in order to predict outcomes. Whilst it is true that intentions must themselves *anticipate* outcomes, such anticipation precedes the entire sequence of events which will begin with the intentional action and necessarily ignores numerous other causes that will contribute to the eventual outcome. It is, then, in the nature of intentions to contribute far more to the decision, description and explanation of an action than to its outcome.[17]

This summary account of the character and status of consciousness and intention in human agents indicates how mistaken it would be to exclude intention from either individual or collective agency. But it also cautions us against placing too much weight on intentions in either collective or individual agents. We should certainly not demand that intentions are usually – or *ever* – realized in full in final outcomes. Outcomes often entail the defeat of the intentions, or (more usually) an unsatisfactory compromise with outside forces of one kind or another – a compromise which those who earlier formulated intentions may or may not be willing to admit. This reflection on the nature and scope of intentionality in human action casts light upon the difficulties that will be generated by the necessary inclusion of collective agents within the revolutionary narrative. But it offers no reason to *remove* intentions from the normal understanding of action, be it individual or collective. Since there are analogous difficulties about intention at the individual and the collective level, there is no reason to exclude collective intention from the account we give of revolutions and their narrative.

Conclusion

The aim of this chapter has been to isolate and explain a narrative form which subtends the understanding of revolution. The discussion has often been abstract, because the purpose was not only to describe a form but also to show that it was sufficiently viable in theory to be adopted for use by real human beings. The 'revolutionary narrative' is found in various specific narrations at different times and places, covering one or more specific revolutionary confrontations. It comprises the potential for irreversible change in the direction of some end-state profoundly different from the given present; the possibility of power to initiate or control such change; the expectation that one or more agents exist with such power and intentions as to the future; and an overarching frame of historical time which provides both normative and predictive indicators for the anticipated future. It partakes of the phenomenological force of narrative (in Ricoeur's sense) in general. More particularly, it enables human beings confronted with the modern necessity, risk and/or possibility of change to enfold the prospect in a narrative of *willed* change, towards *a better future*, under the direction of 'the virtuous'. Thus, the revolutionary narrative has a quite

specific function for the modern consciousness of human beings: to translate the *threat* of change into a possibility of deliberate *improvement*.

True, when it comes to the identity of collective agents, intentions and
outcomes, the ingredients of the revolutionary narrative present formidable
problems of conceptualization. But, I have argued, these are usually no
greater than analogous difficulties with regard to individual identity etc.,
and are certainly not impediments to the hermeneutic use of the revolutionary narrative by all those subject to the uncertainties of historical change –
or by us who try to understand them. The revolutionary narrative is, I
conclude, a coherent and powerful form with which modern humans may
often comprehend social experience.

6

The Revolutionary Narrative in History

The preceding chapter identified and defended the 'revolutionary narrative' as a firmly rooted impulse in the human understanding of historical change in the modern world. This chapter traces more carefully the career of the revolutionary narrative *in* history, preparatory to a consideration of what its impact may be in the future. The revolutionary narrative is a needed construct of modern consciousness. Initially, I will consider some instances where the revolutionary narrative is adapted to take a hold on reality and so enter into history and impact upon it. I want to argue that the revolutionary narrative, in its various manifestations, should be considered as an autonomous form of thought, with its own currency and hence historical impacts. My approach entails a 'reading' of any given narration for its rendering of the central figures of the revolutionary narrative – potential change, an identifiable agent for change, a time-frame – and for what it conveys to social actors who may assimilate its meanings. As I will show in the remainder of the chapter, the interaction between the different versions of the revolutionary narrative and other historical circumstances is itself complex and subject to distortions and inversions. Some of these are the consequence of the very structure of the narrative itself.

Revolutionary narrations

It is my contention that the narrations of those contemplating or involved in revolution will do the phenomenological job of narrative in general. That is to say, they will construct fluid but ordered time-frames, which 'configure' the real world, attributing to participants certain capacities to change, to initiate action and to affect things. Within these time-frames participants are accorded an identity continuing over unified time and change. These narrative constructions are never definitive, of course. They are confronted with rival narrations, with which they contend for a purchase on events and on the actions of those involved. They struggle to adapt to, and achieve, a successful impact upon an environment which includes forces and events beyond present human expectations or intentions. I offer some examples of narrations of revolution which have impacted upon the actions of historical actors and the actual out-turn of events: in particular, those found in Philippe Buonarroti's *Conspiracy for Equality*, the work of Alexander Herzen, and Lenin's *State and Revolution*.

Buonarroti's *mémoire* retells revolutionary deeds from long before, which had cost him his liberty and his home. He had been a member of the group in Paris which, under Babeuf, had planned in 1796 to provoke a popular insurrection with a view to reviving the radical 'revolutionary' government overturned in 1794. In the event, the conspirators were betrayed and arrested; two of them, including Babeuf, were executed, whilst Buonarroti and others were deported. But Buonarroti returned to France in the 1820s, under the revived monarchy, and became the doyen of Paris revolutionary circles. He published his account of the conspiracy in 1828, thirty-two years after the events. Buonarroti proclaims that his book will 'at last' reveal the truth of the democratic party by giving 'an exact account of our intentions', which the powers of reaction have long suppressed (Buonarroti 1957, 'avant-propos', pp. 19–21). In practice, he talks little of intentions, however, but instead constructs a narrative history of the moral and communitarian salvation of France itself under the radical Jacobin government, and of its reversal. He places himself, Babeuf and their associates into that story as the surviving elements of revolutionary moral purity in a world since recaptured by 'egoism'.

The narration manages, then, to identify Buonarroti himself as a special repository in the collective memory of French society's capacity for moral transformation. Instead of a history of the conspiracy and its defeat, we find an epic of the struggle of good against evil, with Babeuf and the others holding the torch for the former. On the face of it, this ought to have been an account of *failure*. The conspirators aimed for a particular outcome; thirty years later that outcome was further away than ever. But the narration creates a quite altered reality: the heroic, if impotent purity of a secret good perpetually defeated, though never quite suppressed. This is hardly the way the conspirators would have construed things before they were arrested. In the terms I expounded earlier, Buonarroti's narration configures the world so that it contains a distant possibility to return in time to the moment of revolutionary transformation. The conspirators are endowed with an irrepressible purity, which can be summoned anew to return to potential readers a capacity to promote revolutionary transformation in the future.

If we regard this narration as a factual statement about events in the 1790s, it comes out as simply false. Babeuf and his co-conspirators remained hapless victims of forces that were too strong or efficient for them. In terms of structural analysis, these would be, for example, the forces rebuilding the centralized French state. But, since it is a *narration*, we can go beyond the unrevealing terms of its all-or-nothing truthfulness. We can take it in its own terms, as narrative to be conveyed between one human consciousness and another. In these terms, we can integrate Buonarroti's *narration* into the processes in play in French, and indeed European, history, where it successfully keyed into his readers' need to configure their own present. For the striking thing about Buonarroti's work is the possibilities for a future movement which it *created* out of failure. Buonarroti associated conspiratorial organization and lonely dedication with the historical possibility of radical social transformation. In this way, he founded the tradition of secretive, independently motivated revolutionaries who would push forward along the historical path they believed had been marked out in 1789, but frustrated thereafter. This narration and its 'Babouviste' inspiration underwrote the nineteenth-century revolutionary tradition (Hayward 1991, pp. 222–65) and then its 'Leninized' version in the twentieth century: the professional revolutionary and the party *nomenklatura*. The narrative can be seen in its own right in the real world of time and change, though more in its own *future* than in the past it purports to recount.[1]

Alexander Herzen's influence was also literary and intellectual. He might be regarded as the London equivalent of Buonarroti in Paris – though his revolutionary credentials are weaker, since he had undergone merely a brief internal exile in Russia after an involvement in Left Hegelian student politics, and his impact was much assisted by his money. He also bears comparison with the Polish émigré groups in Paris after 1848, who out of their exile developed a discourse of the suffering migrant people, which had perhaps all too strong a resonance with the romantic taste around them.[2] Herzen's Free Russian Press in London was a channel for the self-expression of Russian radicals of all sorts. The press also carried the influential output of his own self-expression, his multi-volume *My Life and Thoughts* and his pamphlet *The Russian People and Socialism*. Herzen brings a personal nostalgia for the life of the Russian countryside to the indignity of defeat, turning it into a claim for the distinctive, radical role of Russian society in the future progress of Europe as a whole. In his writing, the insurmountably large *problem* of Russia's rural peasant village thus became a pure source of resistance and hence of future progress:

> The commune has saved the Russian people from Mongol barbarism and imperial civilization, from Europeanized landlords and the German bureaucracy. The communal system, though, has shattered, has withstood the interference of the authorities; it has successfully survived to see the development of socialism in Europe . . .
>
> [H]ow fortunate it is for the Russian people to have remained outside all

political movements, outside European civilization, which would undoubt-
edly have undermined the commune, and which today has reached in social-
ism the negation of itself. . . .
  Russia will never be a Protestant country.
  Russian will never be *juste milieu.*
  . . . We perhaps ask for too much and get nothing. . . .
  Perhaps [Russia] will perish.
  But in that case Europe too will perish.[3]

Herzen's version of what was special and revolutionary in Russian society
led the way towards Bakunin's communal anarchism and the Russian
populism of the 1870s, bequeathing to Plekhanov, who founded the Marxist movement in Russia, a sense of the long game that must be Russia's
progress towards socialism against which Lenin was to react (Lichtheim
1970, pp. 119ff).

For its part, *State and Revolution* appears a strangely theoretical text to
publish two months before taking the lead in one of the biggest revolutionary actions of the century. It consists of extensive commentary on Engels's
works of political economy and on Marx's commentaries on earlier revolutions (1848 and 1871). In these, Lenin defends the claim that Marx and
Engels held 'completely identical' views of the modern state; namely, that it
was primarily an instrument used by the dominant class of society for the
coercive repression of the rest and would 'wither away' once the dictatorship of the proletariat had destroyed the social power of the bourgeoisie.
Once the exegesis is completed, Lenin moves on to a polemical attack on
the views of Menshevik rivals and various Western European 'revisionists'.
No narration, let alone a *narrative strategy*, is immediately apparent here.

Yet, within the pamphlet's manner of argument, there is a narration
nonetheless. In the preface, Lenin claims that

> the relation of the socialist proletarian revolution to the state acquires not
> only practical political significance, but also the importance of a most urgent
> problem of the day, the problem of explaining to the masses what they will
> have to do in the very near future to free themselves from the yoke of
> capitalism. (1918, preface to the first edition)

So Lenin sees perfectly well how this writing contains a narration for his
own revolutionary political activity. It narrates the progress of the clear,
unified insight bequeathed by Marx and Engels, and how it can be taken up
and completed by the working class. To execute his own role in that
narration, Lenin has to lay claim to the truth of a unified revolutionary
tradition of thought, explain it to the masses, and identify it in their eyes
with his own movement and tactics. In other words, the narration of *State
and Revolution* is *configuring* a time-frame in which Lenin's party can
move the masses to be agents of an altered future: freeing themselves and
causing the state to be superseded.

Again, we could have simply said that *State and Revolution* was 'mistaken' (mistaken about the nature of the state and what was to come), or simply that it was 'dishonest' (Lenin lying to the masses about his 'real' intentions). But this would be to suppress the narrative processes contained in the text and its readership. By virtue of the phenomenological possibilities of narrative, that inserts the text into the objective out-turn of a historical reality. Lenin's 'narration' enfolds a strategy to deal with political and historical forces which, interacting with other structures and other narratives (such as those of the opponents of the Russian Revolution), contributed powerfully to seventy or more years of the history of Russia – and the world. It held the Party and the USSR together until undermined by its own inheritors trying, in the 1980s, to deal with the effects of its autarchic inheritance. Furthermore, it translated well into the commitment needed by Third World revolutionaries and national liberation leaders, and subsequently into the manner in which they sought to govern.

I now want to consider what these instances can teach us about the impact of the revolutionary narrative within history and its place in accounts of revolution. Having, in chapter 5, identified the revolutionary narrative as a component of modern consciousness, my aim is to make a breach in the *exclusion* of consciousness from our understanding of revolution and historical change. For all their strengths, structuralist accounts of revolution should not prevent us from including conscious human intentionality, fed by narrative constructs in the lived world, in our understanding of the history of revolutions in the modern age. Framed and transmitted within the revolutionary narrative, narrative consciousness acquires an effective historical existence and significant historical impacts.

The revolutionary narrative as ideological currency

Of course, a social scientist may prefer to side-line consciousness, or incorporate it as a mere conduit in the causal processes. The whole picture of society and social change would then be accounted for in terms of supervening structures which are more straightforwardly coherent than human consciousness and easier to identify in different times and places. Participants' ideas about the world and what they are doing in it would then appear as at worst mistakes or at best devices: erroneous beliefs related to reality, if at all, because they may promote effects in the real world (such as somewhat benighted revolutionary action). People may *think* they are creating democracy; but above all they are falling in with the structures, and their ideas have little to do with it. The result is coherent, proof against the vagaries of consciousness, and readily defensible from empirical attack.

The alternative, to incorporate consciousness in the form of a reading of the revolutionary consciousness, is most conveniently approached via the the position directed against Theda Skocpol in an essay by William Sewell (reprinted in Skocpol 1994, pp. 169–98). Sewell argues, as I did in chapter 5, that a structural approach such as Skocpol's is wrong to write off the explanatory value of ideologies simply because 'ideological blueprints' do not correspond to revolutionary outcomes. His proposal is to construct an alternative 'conceptual framework' by 'defining ideology in structural terms and by de-reifying class, state and international structures' (p. 173) – that is, the structures prioritized by Skocpol. This strategy has the virtue of delineating revolutionary discourse *per se*, apart from its proponents and followers (insisting, as Sewell puts it, 'on the anonymity of the ideological dynamic') so that it becomes possible to trace a separate history of the discourse and its effects. Accordingly, Sewell refers us to the way that, in the case of the French revolutionaries, the ideology was 'constitutive of the social order', and how elements of it (such as nationalism) went on to have separate careers. In replying (Skocpol 1994, pp. 199–209), Skocpol restates the suspicion that 'sociologists and political scientists are not well served by supposing that sets of ideas are "constitutive of the social order"' (p. 204). Yet, she seems to concede the possibility that ideologies, or at least the weight of ideology, might be included in a structural model as Sewell suggests.

However, the terms on which this concession has been made, and the weakness of Sewell's way of formulating the proposal, are almost suggested by the terminology of Skocpol's assent. 'Epochal and transnational intellectual formations', she writes (p. 207), 'probably do independently affect the scope of transformations that revolutionary politicians attempt.' The problem is that to include ideology 'in structural terms' retains the greatest drawback of the structural approach in dealing with participants' ideas and consciousness. Participants' ideas must belong in some sense to the real world that social and human scientists study. But we have to avoid incorporating them at the cost of occluding their primary ostensible function; namely, to represent and interpret the world. Even on the modified structural account proposed by Sewell, ideas still appear as *mere* error: functional in the world, but shorn of their role of representing it.[4] Even though it can be applied with consistency, this is at best an unenlightening approach.

In commenting on participants' ideas as representations of the real world, we would like to be able to say more about them than that they were correct (or more likely *in*correct). We need to find the bridge between ideas and objective reality, between saying that they reflect reality and saying that they fail to do so, and should count as error. We need, as I put it earlier, to include consciousness 'on its own terms': to conceptualize ideas belonging to the world other than by being a passive mirror or a function of it. But recourse to the hermeneutic mode of thinking allows us to insert subjective consciousness itself into the real world in other ways than by merely reflecting it. Transposed into the shared world of human social life, the subjective can establish itself as an 'objective' reality. Meanings, though ostensibly subjective, come to possess objective weight through the shared life of humans in society. Consciousness might be integrated with the objective, 'real' world of structures in any or all of three relevant ways. As the internally structured basis of intentional action, meaning defines the range of possible actions the agent may take, and their meaning. But it is also a structured basis for *others'* interpretations of agents' action – and of their range of action in response. Finally, external constraints are imported *into* consciousness as 'objective' parameters of action. In sum, there is a continual, negotiable interplay between consciousness and the 'objective' world, in which each changes, and is changed by the other through interpretation, action and anticipation.

Suppose, then, that we conceptualize participants' consciousness in this way, as both subjective and objective. It would comprise an *active* putative understanding, integrated within the structures of the social world. That would preserve the coherence of structural explanation while at the same time broadening its interpretative base. It could comprehend the processes within consciousness: of interpretation, anticipation and motivation *vis-à-vis* objective realities. In terms of the theory of narrative expounded earlier, a narrative consciousness would be 'configuring' past objective reality and 'prefiguring' the world of future possibility. The revolutionary narrative I set out in chapter 5 would do this by filling out the central figures: the potential for change/improvement/utopia, the identity of agents for change, and a time-frame for the potential to be realized. This is a way to incorporate consciousness into historical structures in what I have called consciousness's 'own terms'.

If the specific character and mode of operation for consciousness are recognized in the form of the revolutionary narrative, we can anticipate certain aspects of that narrative. Operating in a distinct fashion, the revolutionary narrative may perfectly well produce effects outwith those of revolutions themselves. The findings of Part I regarding the long-term effect of spreading ripples of modernity may not apply, or may apply differently to the revolutionary narrative. Whereas the politico-economic constructions of actual revolutions may be overwhelmed over time by the force of the core system, the same may not necessarily happen to the revolutionary narrative in human consciousness. Whereas revolutions themselves are constrained by their occurrence at the periphery, the revolutionary narrative may operate 'counter-systemically' (to put the point in Worlds Systems language). These postulates are, indeed, partly confirmed in the history of the revolutionary narrative in Europe.

The movements of the revolutionary narrative in Europe

As Eric Hobsbawm has written:

> the French Revolution came to serve a number of purposes. For those who
> wanted to transform society, it provided an inspiration, a rhetoric and a

vocabulary. For those who did not need or want to make revolution, the first two of these uses were less important . . ., although a major part of the political vocabulary of all western nineteenth-century states derived from the Revolution. (1990, p. 36)

His point presents, in other language, the force of narration about the French Revolution. The Revolution as remembered in the nineteenth century was a moment in the historical past with natural openings for reconfiguration in a possible future. If, in particular, the bourgeoisie were taken to be the heroes of 1789, the reaction of the mid-1790s left the way open to three new prospects: a resumption of bourgeois action, a fresh political self-immolation before a Napoleonic regime, or simply further compromise by the bourgeoisie with the existing state powers (Hobsbawm 1990, pp. 40–1). Both historical actors and time-frame were susceptible to reconstruction with a view to more or less open future prospects.

As I have argued elsewhere (N. Parker 1990, chs 4–5), we can find the narrative combinations that this suggests in politically informed French history-writing of the nineteenth century. Historical portrayals of the first half of the century are dominated by accounts placing the Revolution in a march to liberty stimulated by the long growth of the bourgeoisie. To a considerable degree, this can be seen as a narrational strategy intended to *insulate* the French present from its recent historical past: in the longer time-frame, a less dramatic progress was assured, led by a more shadowy entity than the threatening *sans-culotte* crowd or the massed weavers of Lyon. The route back from that particular, bourgeois abstraction lay through the alternative *romantic* abstraction of Michelet's *Peuple*, which ejected the bourgeoisie from their central role as revolutionary agent. Historians from de Staël to Michelet were juggling the roles in the revolutionary narrative, reconfiguring the possible future as they did so. In Michelet's case, the narrative strategy was intended not only to take back the revolution into the hands of the common people, but also explicitly to configure a radically more open future than his straighter bourgeois predecessors had in mind: 'Thierry saw a *narration* and Monsieur Guizot *an analysis*', he wrote in 1846 (Michelet 1974, p. 73). 'I have called it *resurrection.*'

Other accounts confirm the problems exhibited by the French in accommodating their own revolutionary history as narrative. Jack Hayward has drawn attention to this difficulty across the entire political spectrum. As a Constant or a de Tocqueville wrestled with the authoritarian or the centralizing tendencies revived in the post-revolutionary French *state* while Napoleon was at its head, so Proudhon and Blanqui attempted to claim back the revolutionary lead for some version of the lower classes. The first two represent an attempt to do without a unified revolutionary agent of progress, for fear that it may turn out to be the centralist 'Jacobin' French state. The latter two pursued radically different versions of a proletarian revolutionary agent outside the state, but with different views of the role of the state as a potential instrument of any revolutionary action. Proudhon preferred to side-line the state through anarchistic relationships between communities of the economically oppressed; whilst Blanqui hoped for a *Putsch* that would open up the state for the masses, as a body to take over and use (Hayward 1991, pp. 205–55). The two versions were put to the test through the presence of many Proudhonists and of Blanqui himself in the 1871 Commune, where both can be seen to have failed their supporters (Andrieu 1971). Both views had about them, indeed, nostalgia for the small fighting locality which left its mark on events in the 1790s and also evoked the localism in the community of warriors in the Ancient World (Hayward 1991, pp. 212 and 258).

And both perspectives were swallowed up in the mass movements of later years of the century, which were led by reconstructed Proudhonist and Blanquists. These had to deal with Hobsbawm's third possibility, a compromise with the existing state powers, which, as Hobsbawm points out (1990, p. 36), did not figure in the original story of the French Revolution and could not therefore be embraced in any narration envisaging a repetition: 'As the nineteenth century proceeded, the experience of the original revolution became increasingly remote from the actual circumstances in which revolutionaries found themselves' (1990, p. 46). Specifically, the short time-frame of the narrative in the original French Revolution, in which the people as a whole could rapidly reconstruct their society according to right and their collective will, could not be resituated. Originally invented, in my view, to shield the French from horror at their recent history, this long time-frame was by the end of the century a condition for any narrative configuration of the prospects of revolutionary change. Yet the stretchability of the time-frame gave to the revolutionary narrative an ability to survive and interpret the politics of opposition well into the twentieth century. That earlier sort of revolution was defeated by 1848, or 1871 at the latest, yet the revolutionary narrative survived in syndicalism as a force in the political consciousness.[5]

The narrative from the French Revolution has a *non*-French existence as well as a French one. There, the prospects of change, the time-frame, and most of all the leading instigators of change had each to be rejigged in order that the revolutionary narrative might take root. In Spain, Italy and the Netherlands, for example, the early movements of native progressives failed to achieve real conviction and then found themselves, in any case, side-lined by the imposition of the Napoleonic incarnation of revolution. This left their revolutionary narration without the prospect of realization in a specifiable time-span and without a local force for change to be its agent.

The need to recast the revolutionary narrative is not merely a function of political preferences. Defenders of the French Revolution shared narrative strategies with its opponents; and the attempts to rewrite the narrative for Spanish circumstances pre-dates the Napoleonic impositions. The epitome of enlightened Spanish constitutionalism, José Marchena, in exile in Bayonne in the early 1790s, joined the local Society of Friends of the Constitution and imbibed the progressives' taste for revolutionary debate on rhetoric. But his 1792 pamphlet, *A la nación española*, advocated above all liberalization from the 'superstitious' authority of the Inquisition. He believed that Spain was culturally backward and its people incurably prone to be duped. His formulations differentiated the direction of France from that needed in Spain, where mere 'renovation' would suffice.[6] And his reforming aspirations focused on the possibility that the *Cortes* could be reinstituted as it had been before the Bourbon monarchs had come to power in Spain at the beginning of the century. He hoped, it seems, for something more like the English compromise between monarch and reform: 'un gobierno justamente contrapesado'.[7] Thus, revolutionaries and counter-revolutionaries in Spain together ejected the people from their central role as actors in French revolutionary narration.[8]

Once Napoleon had taken matters directly into French hands, liberals were in an open quandary. On the one hand, this 'revolutionary' regime did more than the king and his reformers to effect revolutionary action and abolish Spain's feudal survivals. But, on the other hand, the French had imposed their own monarch and were deeply unpopular in fighting their Europe-wide war in Spain. One patriot expressed the narrative complex this required from revolutionaries: 'The Spaniard must now know that he is not struggling so gloriously against the aggressor in order to place his independence . . . once more at the mercy of a capricious court.'[9] The cause of patriotism called for a version of the revolutionary narrative, in which the act of radical transformation had to be an expression of a native collective will. To be seen to ape French principles became politically unacceptable (Hamnett 1989).

Overtaken by an alien revolutionary will in the present historical moment, Spanish progressives pressed forward with their native inspirations for reform and recast the time-frame for their action. In the absence of living sources of strength for the cause, constitutionalists such as Joaquín Villanueva reached for a more elevated, transcendental and properly Catholic basis: 'pure water from the angelic source' of Aquinas himself. Historians responded by trying 'to place the legitimate roots of the new political order into a solid historical past that antedated the absolute monarchy' (quoted Hamnett 1989, pp. 67 and 66). This strategy as regards the time-frame of liberty resembled that of the British and the French historians of the first half of the century. But revolutionary change remained without viable present, Spanish roots. The middle classes were pliant social climbers in the old regime and cautious rentiers living off the debts of the monarchy; the peasantry carried on with intermittent rebellion; the nobility had rallied to the 'patriot' cause of ejecting the French (Hamnett 1989): in this setting, the attempt to look back to an early Christian authority was incurably ambiguous as between the rights of property and the dignity of title or traditional authority. In short, Spanish admirers of the revolutionary achievements of France were unable to find in their own society the combination of agency and time-frame necessary for a persuasive version of the revolutionary narrative.

The Italian story is comparable, though the strategic situation was different. There the liberals of the 1790s achieved more, establishing their own republican regimes before the intervention of Napoleon. But they courted a vicious popular-conservative restoration in 1799, which left a legacy of isolated intelligentsia and hostility between bourgeoisie and peasantry.[10] Events in Italy had taken the classic course of earlier revolutions and failed to focus on government as such, becoming embroiled instead in the local rivalries fostered by the survival of older political boundaries dominated by the distant powers of Austria, Spain and latterly France. Over a century later, the historian Serrafino La Sorsa spoke of 1799 as 'terrible events in which the People showed what it was capable of, and with what insolence and audacity it knew how to impose itself on other classes . . . a dismal and savage event which had left an indelible mark upon the popular memory' (quoted in Broers 1989, p. 88). Italian revolutionary tradition could only move forward in enlightened educational programmes.[11] The character and persistence of similar reverses right up to 1848 *preserved* the narrative force of that Italian shadow of the French experience through the nineteenth century (Broers 1989). Revolutionary acts by romantic figures (Mazzini, Garibaldi) had to do service for the collective agency of the revolutionary narrative while political power was mopped up by an ambitious northern monarchy restored when the Congress of Vienna rearranged Europe to suit the triumphant monarchies: society was 'blocked'.

The peculiarity of the narrative in the Netherlands was that it did not depend exclusively upon the French source. On the contrary, Dutch publishing freedom was an important security for the ideas, publications and persons of French reformers as the Revolution approached.[12] The Dutch Patriot movement of the mid-1780s drew on the *native* republican tradition and imagery, deliberately fed with the more recent example of the Americans' success against the traditional enemy, Britain (Schama 1977, pp. 58ff). But, lacking the political strength to impose itself at home, the 'Batavian' patriot movement was launched in practice from the Paris of the early 1790s, and then reimported into the Netherlands with support from French arms. There the republican government formed in 1795 was soon isolated, both from wider political forces at home and from the confidence of the post-revolutionary French military, whose flirtation with conservatives encouraged the 1801 coup which modified the Batavian Republic's key unitarist principles. Then, during the first decade of the century the Napoleonic regime came to impose, as in Spain, first its own monarch from Bonaparte's family and then an increasingly passive (and expensive) role in Napoleon's grander war designs. In Schama's terms, the 'patriots' had been swallowed by their 'liberators' and the progress made in the Batavian episode was wiped from the Dutch collective memory.[13]

Britain was the country where the French Revolution narrative was most successfully rewritten and embedded in a lightly modified version of the pre-existing power structure. There is ample evidence that the conservative reaction of the 1790s was grounded in genuine loyalist sentiment among the middle and lower classes (Colley 1996, pp. 300–37, Dickinson 1989, pp. 103–25). Though the government certainly saw the propaganda potential of the 'Crown and Anchor' corresponding societies or the local volunteer defence forces, the movements as a whole had a dynamic of their own. They were, in the words of one group, 'deeply impressed with a lively sense of the blessings . . . as established at the glorious revolution of 1688'.[14] This was what distinguished the British experience: the greater possibility of naming some past event as the historic moment which had already brought the revolutionary narrative to a culmination. Linda Colley has argued, furthermore, that the British ruling elites successfully adopted even the posturings of the Revolution in France to sustain their own sociopolitical position (1996, pp. 155–207). Nelson's showiness was the *ne plus ultra* of this strategy. For Colley, the ruling class weathered a crisis both of legitimation and of *self*-legitimation through a 'cultural reconstruction' which associated them 'with patriotism and with the nation in a new self-conscious fashion' (p. 206) and imbued them with classical values of heroism and self-sacrifice. This transformation has much to compare with the neo-classical imagination fostered among the *French* revolutionary leadership (Parker 1990, pp. 83–92, Starobinski 1979).

English progressive radicals found themselves outflanked by these developments and, in the main, turned to chasing after as good an image (Rigby 1989). Mary Wollstonecraft's *Historical and Moral View of the Origin and Progress of the French Revolution and the Effect it has produced in Europe* (1794) had to distance the enlightened from developments in France whilst trying implicitly to claim a native capacity to achieve as good by calmer, better-informed intelligence: in France 'almost every precipitate event has been the consequence of a tenacity and littleness of mind on the political actors'.[15] The radicals could only join the consensus view that the settlement of 1688 constituted the only 'revolution' that was necessary, and hope (with some validity) that the liberal principles of that moment could be successfully extended in a more gradual reform movement to realize the full implications of the revolution that was already past.

If the revolutionary narrative made an ironically successful transfer from France to Britain, its analogous shift to Ireland was a more tragic and painful experience. There, the progressive republicans of the United Irishmen chose to *rely* on direct French military intervention. The failure of that left them exposed to wholesale coercion against the rural population and with no revolutionary agent other than minority militancy: 'The legacy of the French Revolution's impact on Ireland was a deeply polarized populace and the running sores of militantly sectarian republicanism and loyalism.'[16]

From the career of the revolutionary in Europe, we can say that the earlier postulates are substantiated. The *form* of the revolutionary narrative crystallized in France could indeed appear with a variety of situations, and with different collective *actors* playing the key roles in narrations that entailed different *periodizations*. These versions of the revolutionary narrative certainly appear and progress apart from the French (or any other) Revolution as such, and exhibit some autonomy from the spread of French, or other, power. On the other hand, their impact on the realities of power is not simply a matter of their cogency as narrative. That kept revolutionary aspirations alive in Italy, the Netherlands and Spain, but could not alone make up for the lack of a cohesive candidate for the role of collective actor in the revolutionary drama. Arguably, the force of the revolutionary narrative simply made those influenced by it into the dupes of other forces. (This, indeed, seems still more striking in Ireland or in Germany, until the latter temporarily took the lead in the late nineteenth century with a different, party-political narration built on the strength of the German Social Democratic Party.)

Conversely, the successful co-option of the revolutionary narrative by the British ruling class points to how it can be taken over by global patterns of power. A hegemon backed by financial and then industrial advance over its rivals, Britain could successfully cleave to, and even export, its view of the origins of revolutionary liberty. Where, on the other hand, power structures were already weakened, post-French revolutionary postures could contribute to their demise. Thus, even though the Spanish reformers were unable to confront the conservative state, revolutionary figures such as Bolivar in Venezuela or J. G. Rodriguez de Francia in Peru could lead distant parts of the ailing Spanish empire to break away. There we see too the syncretism that the form of the revolutionary narrative permitted: notions of claiming the rights of an ancient constitution, akin to the formulas of Montesquieu or the British conservatives, were applied to Indian communities in Mexico (Pagden 1989) and contributed to the earliest and longest-standing successes of revolutionary action in Mexico.

The revolutionary narrative displaced

The twentieth-century relocation of the central global instances of revolution must evidently imply that the displacement of narrative I have described above would change its terms in the twentieth century. Following military defeat and the general European depression of the 1870s and early 1880s, France definitively joins the European order of industrialized national economies operating under the liberal umbrella of international exchanges. True, France and its fellow European states were engaged in a competition – for raw material sources and protected areas of investment across the globe. But the *common* objectives of this competition imply a *shared* posture on the best direction of development across the globe, 84 per cent of which was under their direct control by 1914 (Huntington 1996, p. 51): to impose, with greater intrusiveness, European power and the European model of modernity. In short, the historical meaning of European societies in the period of late-nineteenth-century imperialism comes to be confined to the direction given by the dominant *European* centre to the globe as a whole. It is a pacified version of the revolutionary assertion of national identity that had been derived from the revolutionary narrative of the beginning of the century: national autonomy is confined to separate European national territories, extended by land grabbed in Africa and complemented by negotiated exchanges, the whole governed by British hegemony and the Gold Standard. By the end of the century, this version of the revolutionary narrative entails historical *continuity* rather than any radical, self-motivated transformation.

In the twentieth century, the revolutionary transformation of two great but peripheral societies, Russia and then China, was therefore bound to recast the terms for interpreting historical change and reconstitute the revolutionary narrative across different locations. As Hobsbawm puts it, the global politics of the bulk of the twentieth century 'can best be understood as a secular struggle by the forces of the old [European/Western] order against social revolution, believed to be embodied in, allied with, or dependent on the fortunes of the Soviet Union and international communism' (1994, p. 56). Even a sceptical voice such as that of François Furet, concedes the universal 'charm' of October 1917 for the entire century, originating in its place (for him a gratuitous place) in bringing peace in place of the First World War.[17] And the war, we should remember, was the self-destructive outcome of that late-nineteenth-century set-up, with its economic and imperialist rivalries between the European nation-states.

Yet, with the relocation of revolution to the margins, the elements of the revolutionary narrative – potential for change, agent and time-frame – enter into a more complex relation with the experience of revolution. The transposition of that experience takes place in a complicated fashion. As I argued in Part I, it was in the nature of the global system that the gap between the global centre of gravity and the potential location of revolution would be progressively greater. But this effect comes into play most forcefully in the twentieth century. In nineteenth-century Europe, we can see the narrative displaced lock, stock and barrel to other European countries: the point of interest is the manner in which a transfer takes place. But the twentieth century witnesses the *replication* of narrations, in which elements from one location are projected into their analogues from another. The prospects of change and agents of revolution seen in one place are often those from another location, shifted and reconstructed.

The most obvious instance of this was the Cold War domestic logic pursued by *opponents* of revolutionary change in Western countries. Both sides in power during the Cold War concurred that domestic oppositional forces in the West could be regarded as one with revolutionary agents on the Eastern side. In point of fact, Western oppositional forces never came near to making a revolutionary critical mass;[18] while, on the other side, communists in power freely ascribed epithets such as 'counter-revolutionary', 'bourgeois', 'CIA agent' etc. to a range of domestic opponents or politically inconvenient figures. Soviet strategy for most of the century treated socialist allies from the West primarily as useful advocates in their inter-state rivalries. 'Reds' from Moscow were thus being found 'under the bed' in the USA, while 'fraternal support' from oppositionists in the West was being taken to legitimize the Soviets (or sometimes Chinese) as the leaders of a 'world revolutionary movement' to which they belonged.

These effects can be examined more revealingly at the most peripheral and the most central locations for the revolutionary narrative: that is to say, in the Third World and in France. Leaving aside explanations of the cruder Cold War and 'Moscow gold' type, two lines of interpretation present themselves for the revolutionary narrative in the Third World: that a culture of revolution spread, or was spread between potential oppositionists; or that the notion of revolutionary change offered a pragmatically effective construction for the reality they or others experienced at the periphery of the global system. These two are not mutually incompatible. Post-war (or, indeed, Cold War) US structural-functionalism, for example, combined the two in the idea of an *undesirable* growth of revolutionary ideology in the course of the changes attendant on modernization. As Chalmers Johnson put it (1964, p. 10), revolution is 'one form of social change in response to the presence of dysfunction in the social system'. This implied the strategic importance of encouraging political institutions adapted to the social changes of modernization which would absorb the otherwise dysfunctional rising elites of at-risk developing societies (Huntington 1968).

Forrest Colburn's comparative analysis of twenty-two Third World states led by 'revolutionary' governments since the Second World War (Colburn 1994) represents a recent account in terms of my first 'line of interpretation': the more or less deliberate 'spread' of revolutionary culture. His principal intellectual target is in fact the kind of structural explanation, represented by Skocpol, which would render ideological influences irrelevant. His analysis concludes that a culture of revolution among intellectuals was a decisive independent factor in the *initial occurrence* of 'revolutionary' movements and governments. Typically, future leaders of Third World revolutionary governing groups had earlier passed through Western European higher education, particularly in Paris. Conversely, the prospects of *survival* of the twenty-two revolutionary regimes were not altered by their ideological affiliations. They fared no better than other governments in the countries in question: sooner or later all succumbed to the pressure of war, the international order, or a mix of high expectations,

low legitimacy and limited skill in government. As regards the factors that
operate *against* revolutionary regimes in the Third World, these findings
are entirely consistent with my account. For they amount to forces generated within the world system: pressure from core states; obstacles to
achieving freedom of action for a society in a peripheral position; the
political cost of raising hopes that this position could be altered. As regards
the original *appearance* of revolutionary ideologies, on the other hand,
Colburn himself seems perversely content to conclude that the common
revolutionary beliefs were present in the twenty-two states solely by virtue
of their transmission from person to person. This reasoning plainly fails to
include consciousness 'on its own terms'. That is to say, Colburn's account
includes revolutionary beliefs merely as factors like others identified in his
comparative work, paying no regard to what the beliefs actually say to
those who hold them.

Hence the need to introduce an alternative account of the apparent
pragmatic validity of revolutionary beliefs for those adopting them. The
burden of John Dunn's analysis of 'approaches to the ideological assessment and causal explanation of modern revolution' (1989, pp. 224ff),
which was originally published in 1972, is precisely that. For Dunn, revolutionary aspirations made pragmatic sense for the situation in which their
Third World believers found themselves. Whilst not disputing the necessity for there to be a breakdown of social control (i.e. the central emphasis
of structural accounts), Dunn wanted any account to include as well the
intentional 'project' of the politically active and the attraction followers in
the broader population would feel for their claims. For Third World insurgents in the heyday of its worldwide revolutionary hopes (when Dunn
was writing), the Marxist-Leninist idea represented a powerful teleology of
political practice and historical direction. In Dunn's ringing phrase, the
revolutionary ideology epitomized a 'metaphor of the recapture of control
by the virtuous over an inimical destiny' (p. 255). It asserted that a profess-
ionally organized group (especially, one might add, one whose members
enjoyed the benefits of First World education) could stimulate the just
energies of a Third World population and then manage the hoped-for social
transformation.

That was precisely the lesson which could easily be found in the narration going from Lenin's *What is be done?* to his successful seizure of
power and the subsequent changes to Russian society: the powerless on the
edge of the world system *could* obtain the power for change, through good
organization and shrewd exploitation of their position. It was a lesson
which official Soviet Marxism-Leninism was happy to package and convey. Even though, as Gérard Chaliand put it (1990, p. 23) looking back on
the period, a 'rather partial and simplistic explanation (as revolutionaries
would later discover), it was not without some degree of credibility'. And
under post-Second World War conditions of imperial decline and East–
West rivalry, the potential of such a political strategy in the Third World

must, indeed, have been very evident to the politically aware. Thus Dunn's and Chaliand's accounts read Third World revolutionary ambitions in their own terms, and show how they could offer a pragmatically effective construction of the reality experienced at the periphery of the global system. This accounts for the appearance of revolutionary narrative through its plausibility for the situation that those accepting it needed to interpret. It is not, of course, sufficient to account for the story not turning out as the revolutionary narrative anticipated. Reviewing the situation soon after the surge of national liberation struggles of the 1960s, Gérard Chaliand, still a sympathizer, observed how these revolutions' imported version of the Western 'mythology of the nation-state' had easily fallen victim to the ambiguity of their own nation-forming in the (post-Stalinist) figure of the national leader and to the persistence of social and structural forces tending towards 'parasitism' and bureaucracy (Chaliand 1977).

As we consider the displacement of the revolutionary narrative, we should note the transpositions which it had undergone. The Russian Revolution was itself the site of the first such displacement – as had been the Russian revolutionary thinking stemming from Herzen during the nineteenth century. In post-revolutionary Russia, disputed parallels were drawn with difficulty between their revolution and the French model (Williams 1996). Nothing prepared them for the intensity of civil war politics which engulfed their enterprise or the political forms it evoked (Figes 1996). Indeed the brief formulation (in 1794) of a rationale for 'revolutionary terror' seems only to have encouraged a Leninist/Stalinist habit of responding to setbacks with free use of state coercion on a scale hardly known in the French original. Likewise, nothing in the France–Russia parallel tempered the Russians' optimism with a realistic understanding of the extent and nature of the country's position by comparison with the latest, Western models of industrial society.

Continuing its self-identification with the regime of the French Revolution, the Soviet system readily claimed the distinction of picking up where France had left off – the more so in so far as the early revolutionaries had banked on the follow-up revolutions *in the European core* anticipated by socialist theory and by a century of expectation/apprehension on all sides. The revolutionaries' *mistake* in expecting a German revolution was covered by their learning to claim that *their* revolution was the very one expected elsewhere. In the transmission of revolutionary culture which Colburn examines, this account of things then passed *back through* the former European core, interpreted at one remove by the thinking of the French left and conveyed therefrom into the revolutionary ideas of the Western educated elites of the Third World. Thus, insurgent Third World leaders could give two meanings to their own revolutions: both a restatement of the principles from the core, European states, and the repossession *on the periphery* of the core states' strengths, to be directed against the core states themselves.

The 'return' of the European revolutionary narrative

Displacement of the revolutionary narrative has likewise affected perceptions at its original site. In Part I, I argued that, because of the proximity of revolutionary action to the core, European revolutions were most liable to give the impression that unified social action alone could take over and reform the society as a whole. The difficulties of this perception of historical process have been most evident back in France, for it is there that the revolutionary narrative displaced to other positions in the global system has had to be reassimilated to its original site, which has been transformed in turn by almost two centuries of restructuring. Commentary on these transfers can be found in a number of critical studies of the thinking of the left in France (Caute 1973, Furet 1995, Judt 1986, Khilnani 1993).

Much of the substance of such studies has been the embarrassments inherent in the left's self-identification with forces of revolution bigger than, and beyond, themselves and the Western/European situation. David Caute, for example, made great play with the way that enthusiasts for reform were so easily gulled on trips to the Soviet Union into believing that their hopes for socialist planning were being realized over there. Whilst there is no denying the accounts of individuals and what now seems their evident naivety, their reaction was, we should note, widespread in European society in the first half of the twentieth century. Elites everywhere looked for planned solutions to growing problems of urban society – between the wars, for example, London government, under a mix of liberals, Fabians and social democrats, took an interest in the schemes of both communist and fascist city planners. In short, susceptibility to believing in models from Soviet society belongs to a global phenomenon whereby change in the 'old' European world seemed to need to be regrounded on inevitably distorted perceptions of change in the periphery of the West. In France, as Hobsbawm's study of two centuries of claims and counterclaims to the revolutionary heritage (1990) reminds us, the key issue dividing the political spectrum had long been the question of who, or what social group, represented the driving force behind the nation as experienced in the Revolution. Such claims had never been confined to the political left: Thiers, Napoleon III, Pétain and General de Gaulle all made analogous claims about who could lead the French nation towards its historic destiny. The issue of politics was, in other words, where to find the agent of change in the revolutionary narrative. On my submission, the twentieth century sees versions of this search recast to adjust to the fact that the prime global motivator of revolutionary change is to be found *outside* the Western/European world.

Sartre is an easy object of derision in accounts of the difficulties of the French left. Yet, he demonstrates with penetration the complex created by the return of the revolutionary narrative to its home country. The intricacies of the *Critique of Dialectical Reason* (a text that I will return to in the appendix) provide ample illustration of the contemporary difficulties of defining the identity of the agent of change in that narrative. Sartre formulates the issue in terms of movement between a 'totalizing' historical subject and the anomic, 'serial', relationships of a modern society – by which he means, of course, the society of mass consumption and uniformity which he could see around him in France's post-war growth. He made clear in an interview at the time (Sartre 1970) his understanding of how collective action in the sense of the revolutionary narrative had been absorbed in the twentieth century by inward-looking party organization. Yet he looked gloomily at the prospect of the proletariat's role in the Soviet rendition of the narrative being realized in the modern West: when asked by his far-left interviewer if the working class were not the location of revolutionary consciousness, Sartre replied that he saw no prospect of the proletariat 'transcending' the limits of seriality, and that 'the working class can never express itself completely as an active political subject' (p. 237). Sartre may be taken either as a risible or a tragic figure, depending on how we understand the nature of the predicament that he worked within. In philosophical terms, that predicament arose from the particularly sharp individualism of his initial phenomenology, with its own roots in the exclusivist scientism of Husserl and Heidegger. In political and social terms, it arose from his being the single most prominent individual to seek for the revolutionary agent outside all the given political structures.

The structures on offer included, notably, the Gaullist state and the Communist Party. These two competed to identify themselves with the republican, revolutionary nation and with France's more recent self-assertion, in the wartime resistance to fascism. Not an easy choice, then: on one side, the state itself, on the other the *imported* voice of a highly statist revolutionary agent opposed to that state. There is a pathos inherent in this search, even if you are a world-famous literary figure. Yet Sartre's strategy can equally be seen as a sincere attempt to locate one of the original figures of the revolutionary narrative, the collective agent of revolution, after it had been transposed to the periphery, restructured in the disciplines of forced industrialization and Soviet 'democratic centralism' and then reimported from the dominant twentieth-century claimant to France's revolutionary heritage, the Soviet example. Khilnani's judgement on the outcome misses the point, then. He writes that Sartre had 'simply to place himself at the disposal of the masses: to convert himself into a tool for their authentic speech', and that this 'was a retreat into the most philistine and anti-intellectualist of positions' (1993, p. 82). Even if Sartre did make a fool of himself by hasty photo-calls and pronouncements before the media, he at least had the merit of realizing that the communists' version of the agent in the revolutionary narrative had been doctored before it was reimported and passed off as 'Made in France'.

The French left's take on the revolutionary narrative underwent a dramatic collapse in the 1980s. As Khilnani put it (1993, p. 3), 'Nowhere in the West was the collapse of the revolutionary identity of the Left more spectacular than in its original homeland, France.' Can the *demise* of revolutionary politics in France, like its earlier content, be understood in terms of the global transpositions of the revolutionary narrative? There is much to suggest that it should. For a start, the obvious facts of the disappearance of the autonomous Soviet model (or, for that matter, Deng Xiaoping's parallel switch of the Chinese model towards free-market principles) can certainly be accounted for, as I argued in Part I, within the movements of the global system. By the 1980s, the global structures which earlier had created the space for an autarchic communist counter-system had begun to swallow it up, through technological advance and indebtedness built on its inherent weaknesses. At a global level, then, the undermining of the left's reimported revolutionary narrative can be taken as one more step in the transformations of the narration produced in response to global movements.

But, closer to the ground too, the commentators' explanations of what happened to the revolutionary narrative in France combine to suggest a comparable response to global processes of one kind or another. François Furet, a former party member turned damning critic of the limitations of the French communists' 'Marxist' account of the French Revolution, gives testimony about decades of the 'illusion' of communism in the West. He sees the Soviet–French parallel as a fraudulent displacement from conditions where power is subject to principles of legality to those where, in the absence of all civil society, power was law-less, grounded solely in the personality of the leader (Furet 1995). For decades, Furet believes, dissenters in the West have believed in the fiction of one or another fusion of Bolshevism and liberal-democratic pluralism. The reimportation of the Russian narration into Western, French experience occluded the potential for various liberal forms of political life which had, for Furet, been contained within France's own revolutionary experience.[19]

The dramas of 1968 and after challenged the revolutionary narrative's modern French adherents. For the 1968 events failed to remove the right from power. Instead it initiated the disintegration of the 'revolutionary' left itself. Rather than any leap forward by the French nation, the 1970s find France, like other Western countries, caught up in the global recession brought on by the faltering of the world economy under post-war US patronage. Rather than any collective advance, France is trying desperately to hang on to the earlier welfare consensus between the 'social partners' and the state. It is the same old *external* motor, Germany, which leads the economic recovery; while France's own autarchic experiment in re-expansion (under the left as reconstructed by François Mitterrand) ends rapidly in a u-turn and open acknowledgement of France's subordination to the international free-market economy. In short, the experiences of the 1970s undermined the accepted notion of national economic sovereignty and the agency of the state (Khilnani 1993, pp. 116–23), while that of the 1980s undermined the accepted notion of national power altogether. The French public lost its confidence that their state could stand against external socio-economic forces (Hayward 1986). Mitterrand in power swung to behind-the-scenes supra-national deals in the EC, supported at home by a suspect network of elite cronies. Wherever it was in the 1980s, the politico-economic power behind the nation's direction was certainly not to be found in the nation united in a conscious, just transformation of its historical destiny.

As Hobsbawm (1990) concluded, two centuries after the Revolution, the right to act out the will of *the nation* is no longer the central issue of French political rivalries. Power over the future of society, I would add, had moved away from the framework suggested for it by republican, post-revolutionary, national terms. In the very capital of Europe's revolutionary history, the revolutionary narrative no longer seems viable because the power of an agent for the revolution cannot be mustered at the national level. In truth, the local existence of a revolutionary agent had looked questionable from the moment that revolutionary change moved to the periphery of the world system. But a hermeneutic bond of mutual need between revolutionary regimes there and advocates of change at the old European core had kept the belief alive that there was one revolutionary agent for world history – and, usually, that the communist movement was its voice. In France, the power of the autonomous nation seemed to be recalled by the French version of their wartime history. That is why Gaullism and the left competed for it, each with a version of how the French nation could remain a global actor. By the end of the 1980s the global scene had definitively detached the agent of change in the revolutionary narrative from an exclusively French national identity.

National identity and collective action in the returning revolutionary narrative

As Khilnani observed, just as the political left was *achieving* power, in its theoretizing the French intellectual left exhibited a distaste for *all* ideas of power (1993, ch. 5). A general flight by the left from the realities of power could be observed as some were assimilated in, and others fell out with, the Mitterrand regime. The fashion in sweeping denunciation of an omnipresent 'totalitarianism', led by the much-hyped French 'New Philosophers' of the early 1980s, was a glaring case of this distaste for power. Foucault and his intellectual heritage, in which power is generalized into the by-ways of the discourses of 'governmentality', is a subtler outcome; as is the mid-1980s appearance of the 'post-modernist' hopes for a liberated rewriting of values and identity freed of all inherited constraints.

Ever since the Revolution, the French conception has tended to channel democracy through the united will of the nation and the centralized French state that spoke for it, trusting the state's monopoly position in preference to the centrifugal processes in grass roots democracy.[20] It is, in any case, common enough to see left intellectuals in other countries – or indeed intellectual elites in general – fall out with one-time political associates now in power. Yet, we can also read this renewed anxiety about the locations of power as a more global phenomenon, arising from the repeated shift of the revolutionary narrative of change across the global space. Having been relocated to the periphery and then reflected back through the *former* global core, the agent of change in the revolutionary narrative, together with the power that agent claims, appears as an increasingly chimerical object of a continuing search. As the twentieth century closes, the European revolutionary agent, which had been here and then there across the globe, was now to be found nowhere. This dramatically recast the terms for understanding the possibility of deliberate social change. Reactions to the global situation of the late 1980s illustrate a continuing, but confused, sense that the bearers of social change must exist at some level or another. I will consider here those who responded by rediscovering the *national* entity occluded by earlier twentieth-century history. In the next chapter, we will consider others who sought to restate the identity of the revolutionary actor in a set of principles rather than a human subject.

Régis Debray makes a revealing witness of this search for the autonomous power defined in the revolutionary narrative, through the global movements and then return of the revolutionary narrative. Always a weather-vane of revolutionary thinking, he reacted early to the 1960s relocation to Central America of the focus of attention over revolution. His celebrated *Revolution in the Revolution* (1967) argued that, rather than revolutionary politics in the core, it would be Third World guerrilla insurrection against oppressive states ruling peasant society that would promote widespread revolution in non-Western countries.[21] His subsequent writings (Debray 1977, 1981) display the continual doubts of an integral member of the left French intellectual elite who has been sensitive to the potential for hypocrisy inherent in the European revolutionary's view of the world.[22] From the 1960s, he has exhibited a sense of the ambivalence involved when one is both fulfilling the role of metropolitan activist in a particular political situation and espousing the voice of a universal revolution going on elsewhere.

Latterly, after a spell on the edges of Mitterrand's government, Debray has emerged as a eulogist of de Gaulle's nationalism, praising de Gaulle's restraint in commandeering the power claimed for the nation and skill in sustaining a dematerialized idea of the nation's power as 'a vocation'. In short, Debray now finds that de Gaulle's elusive version of the national identity is better adapted to the contemporary world than the revolutionary narrative of his own left intellectual roots.

I will venture a hypothesis to explain the mystery of the repeating [*sic*] error that so often afflicts those who are lawfully wedded to truth. What curse could have driven such respected persons as François Furet to be a Stalinist in 1950, as Debray to be a Castroite in 1960, as Glucksman to be a Maoist in 1970? Was it the same one that, some time later, drove them (except the second, enlightened in the interim by Guarani Indians and a few miraculous punches in the teeth) to become the same thing the other way round? . . . We were simply wrong about the *subject*, the subject of history and of discourses on history. The places of subject, verb and object have been switched around. We made subjects – living entities, motive forces, active principles of development – out of things like Revolution and Democracy, with capital letters, which really are just predicate material. . . . A lot of countries have had a bourgeois economy and a working class. But the Bourgeoisie was no more a collective subject than the World Proletariat. Yes, there are democratic societies, as there are revolutionary situations. But democracy is not a social subject and revolution not an agent of history, to be embodied successively in this or that society or situation. There is something that existed before the 'democracy' condition, before the 'revolution' condition, and will survive them. Something older, more active, more durable, that for some time has been known by the vague name of 'nation'. . . . Defining a collective personality, distinguishing a nation from a tribe or some other type of collectivity, is not so straightforward. But it is not because the idea of nation is badly defined that the reality it designates is not a determining one.[23] (Debray, 1994, pp. 61–2)

Debray goes through an extraordinary, symptomatic process of thinking here. He bears testimony right enough to the left's search, in one place and another, for the identity of the agent of definitive revolutionary change. But he scorns various proposed candidates for the role, because they are, *inter alia*, *features* of a society rather than *actors* in their own right. Then, having thus rejected all the candidates he lists, he makes a move worthy of Michelet in his more ecstatic moments. He simply switches his gaze to a more elusive subject yet: the nation, undefined and undefinable, rooted in the mists of time, and (according to his argument) all the more immune to critical analysis for that. It is, of course, that sense of the nation which Debray's book finds most to praise in de Gaulle.

The recourse to a simply more obscure idea of the nation is, I would argue, symptomatic of a continuing need to locate the collective agent found in the revolutionary narrative. It is a need manifest across the spectrum of reactions to the chaotic developments of the years after 1989. Widely read, sincere, sympathetic and well-informed commentators, such as Timothy Garton Ash (1990), Misha Glenny (1993), Anatol Lieven (1993) or Michael Ignatieff (1994), understood the retreat of the Soviet 'revolution' as the release of historic nations – be they liberating or mutually destructive. History as the drama of nations reappeared in Central Europe – and, at the same time, in the public politics and the social theory of Western Europe. There was widespread public agonizing about the sufferings as the 'nations' newly emerged in Bosnia-Herzegovina sought to displace each other. Nationhood again acquired fundamental meaning in the West, even as its bloody manifestations erupted into the news. Anthony Smith (1995), the leading figure in the UK version of the 'nation' trend in social theory, considered that cosmopolitanism had misjudged nationalism in terms of nineteenth-century experience and modernist fallacies such as the universal value of economic interests. Notwithstanding the current difficulties of the national *state*, Smith claimed, the historically embedded national identity of the *ethnie* remains functional for modernity, and is not about to be superseded.[24]

But this trend does not so much demonstrate the ontological priority of nations as pose a new set of questions about the existence of the collective. Studies of the ex-Soviet Union have observed the impact of social wealth and institutional structures in *promoting* this 'reappearance' of the historical nations: 'Relative wealth comes closest to being a necessary condition . . . [A] relatively wealthy but small republic that is economically advancing is the most common profile of a politically mobilizing nation in our study (five out of ten case)' (Bremmer and Taras 1993, pp. 523 and 524).

Some (Roeder 1991) have even found revived nationalism to be *primarily* a device used by those seeking a network for self-advancement: 'The politicization of ethnicity and protest are goal-orientated behaviours – often focused on pursuit of socioeconomic goals.' As Mary Kaldor (1993) has argued, in Central Europe the idea could easily become little more than the means to sustain networks of armed tribute-takers. In short, the idea of the nation has resurfaced not as the *solution* to the problem of the collective identity formerly offered by the collective revolutionary agent, but as an *expression*, in a revived language, of the *renewed problem* of making the collectivity a motor for the direction of society. As Bertel Heurlin argued (in a different context) with the end of Cold War *ideological* rivalry, being for or against communist revolution, was no longer coherent: 'There seemed only one real solution to the disappearance of the superior legitimacy, to construct new units based on the generally accepted idea of a state system built on sovereignty'(1997, p. 18). The national state emerged from the French Revolution as 'the only identity formation successful on a world-historical scale' (Habermas 1987, p. 366). And, as Margaret Canovan has argued, the idea of nationhood serves a purpose in so far as the 'democratic discourse requires not only trust and common sympathies but the capacity to act as a collective people, to undertake commitments and to acquire obligations' (1996, p. 44). In the nineteenth-century revolutionary republicanism of a Michelet or a Mazzini, collective identity in the nation combined the collectivity's historical rootedness with its capacity for action in common; that is to say, the nation was a historically specific site for the role of agent adumbrated in the revolutionary narrative. By the end of the twentieth century, after the repeated displacements of that narrative, historical rootedness has been detached from the revolutionary agent, and redounds to the nation *simpliciter*, now reborn in more ambivalent and intangible form.

We have seen how the revolutionary narrative has been combined to sustain expectations of conscious social change within specific historical conditions at different times and places. We have been looking at the movement of the 'revolutionary narrative' across national boundaries from one national situation to another, up to the recent historic collapse of that way of thinking. The relocation and re-relocation of the narrative reached its *ad absurdum* extreme when narration imported back into European, particularly French, political thinking in the late twentieth century met the declining power of European states to manage change for themselves and the disappearance from the world stage of the major non-European states that had been claiming, more or less convincingly, to be able to manage their progress in a revolutionary direction.

The revolutionary narrative had supplied a particular structure of thinking to account for, and offer the prospect of, social transformation in any given national unit. Different national units had thus taken in turn the role of model for the rest of the world. But the spreading boundaries of the global system, pushing the incidence of revolution gradually further from the dominant core, made the narrative harder and harder to transfer across actual historical circumstances, until, in the twentieth century, the relocated figures of the narrative, especially the revolutionary agent, were read back through metropolitan experience, in a deceptive game of mirrors. The basis for this game disappeared with the ending of the major national revolutionary episodes beyond the core states.

So, in the new historical conditions, is there *any* empirical ground for the figures formulated in the revolutionary narrative: potential change, identifiable agency for change and a time-frame? We cannot address that question until we have seen how the revolutionary narrative functions in the bigger, global scene *per se*, the scene of international relations and 'global' institutions and values.

7

The Revolutionary Narrative at the End of the Twentieth Century

Locating the processes of the current global system

In the last chapter, I explored what had been happening in terms of the movement of the 'revolutionary narrative' across national boundaries from one situation to another, and the recent historical embarrassment of that way of thinking. During much of the twentieth century, 'revolutionary' states, with the tacit agreement of those opposed to them, proclaimed that they were potential leaders of global revolutionary historical progress. Even if it is no longer feasible to regard revolutions in discrete national states, according to the classic revolutionary narrative along the lines formulated around France, as potential starting points for worldwide revolutionary social change, that does not exhaust the ways in which the revolutionary narrative may be formulated in, and impact upon, politics and events.

Studies of the *worldwide* impact of revolutions over the course of the twentieth century have naturally been focused at the level of the international system of states. This is seen as a totality which threatens, is threatened by, or is modified as a result of revolutionary developments in particular places (Armstrong 1993, Calvert 1996, Chan and Williams 1994). In these terms, it is the confrontation between the state system as a whole and the 'local' reversal of power in the revolutionary state that is most visible, and raises first and foremost any questions of a challenge to the world system. Whatever the mood of the commentator, in such a confrontation of contending forces the system has always seemed to hold strong, if not untrumpable, cards. So the reverses of the 'revolutionary' Eastern Bloc states since 1989 could not but give to the idea that revolutions in particular states might overturn the global order a sad and dated air. Of themselves, however, these reverses do not alter the perception of a world system and its challengers.

I have argued that there was always a misunderstanding of the meaning of the different revolutions on the edge of world modernizing forces – though a misunderstanding that served a serious purpose for those holding to it. Now, to discover that a mistake is a mistake does not of itself alter the underlying situation which the mistake formerly misdescribed. That is to say, that to come to the view, at the end of the twentieth century, that revolutionary parts of the world never have been – and will not be in future – the motors of a new revolutionary direction of change, does not dispose of the question of what (if anything) was actually happening when it was widely (if mistakenly) believed that they could be. Furthermore, having answered that question, it would be sensible to ask if whatever was really happening before might in some form or other continue to happen in fact in the future.

To understand these possibilities, we have to look beyond the limits imposed by the revolutionary reversal of power in single states and its subsequent effects on other states. We need, that is, to consider the different ways in which parts of the world *as a whole* interact, and how revolutions fit into those interactions. From this vantage point, it emerges that, even without the classic expectations of the impact of the revolutionary reversal of real state power, the revolutionary narrative can continue to figure in the discursive dynamics of global and international processes. Thus even though the idea of a direct impact of revolutions in one nation and then others recedes worldwide, the revolutionary *narrative* can be expected to survive in contests over the form and the legitimation of political action.

Confirmation of the wisdom of this focus on legitimation at the world level can be had from a surprising source: US strategic debate over the West's triumph *vis-à-vis* the 'revolutionary' Soviet Bloc. It is no accident that Francis Fukuyama's celebrated response to the end of the Cold War emanated from a US foreign-policy consultancy. For a start, his claim (Fukuyama 1989) that, because liberal principles had emerged as undisputed winners of universal global assent, 'history' had come to end, itself belonged squarely to the language of the revolutionary narrative. The primacy of liberal-capitalism in revolutionary modern historical progress was anything but a new idea in that language[1] – having been advanced originally by the 'bourgeois' historians of the French Revolution (Hobsbawm 1990, N. Parker 1990). Fukuyama echoed the post-Second World-War, Americanized version of that, more subtly adumbrated by Hannah Arendt (1965). As he wrote later, 'The United States and other liberal-democracies . . . are the heirs of the bourgeois revolution started over four hundred years ago' (Fukuyama 1992, p. 283). Comments of this kind on the triumph of American liberal values had, moreover, been recently rehearsed, in respectively optimistic and pessimistic visions of society, from the likes of Daniel Bell and Herbert Marcuse (Ryan 1992). But what Fukuyama added, at the very moment of the global triumph of those US 'revolutionary' values, was an upbeat view of how politics (especially US global politics) could be practised in future on the world scale. In short, Fukuyama's reading of 1989 laid claim, for that moment, to the revolutionary narrative: the revolutionary story had a particular, liberal-democratic dénouement; the post-revolutionary freedom of peoples had arrived; and politics on the global level would be henceforth subject to it for ever.

In 1993 Chalmers Johnson, long an analyst of how Western policy worldwide might head off the socialist revolutionary potential in Third World modernization, appeared in *The National Interest*, the same forum as Fukuyama's piece, discussing US options in Asia now that the Cold War was over (Johnson 1993). The USA no longer need concern itself primarily with the anti-communism of Asian governments, Johnson pointed out. Since liberal-capitalism had carried the day, the USA could now act free of any argument about its underlying value. No further need for political compromise with the doings of allies in Asia, then. It would now be appropriate to press liberal-democracy's version of egalitarianism on to Asian power hierarchies. So the USA could pursue more self-interested policies – in particular seeking the economic advantages of open trade currently obstructed by the 'corrupt and isolationist party' of government in Japan. For Johnson, like Fukuyama, liberal-democratic modernization on the world scale had taken over the revolutionary narrative unchallenged. What these commentators recommend to the world's biggest power (now its only superpower) is a sort of *continuity* of posture *vis-à-vis* revolutionary risks. What has changed is the degree of confidence in the rationale and the level of operations needed for this. The defeat of the 'revolutionary' bloc entrenches, rather than alters, the underlying strength of the US support for liberal-democracy. Once national pockets of a rival revolution have lost their force against the Free World, the earlier principles of liberal progress can be pursued with ideologically undisputed world power.

If the impacts of revolution are to be sought outside the confines of a confrontation between states revolutionary and non-revolutionary, then we should look at aspects of the global set-up beyond the customary emphasis on power relations between sovereign states. There is no shortage of modes of thinking that point in that direction, ranging from the human rights jurisprudence of the seventeenth century (for which transcendent values should constrain every polity), to the theory of imperialism (which saw inter-state relations as the global impositions of capitalism), to recent neo-realism in international relations theory, such as that of Kenneth Waltz (which urged researchers to look at group dynamics beyond the limitations of formally autonomous sovereignties and their interactions). The present moment, with the ambiguous changes ascribed to 'globalization', can only reinforce the grounds for looking beyond state-to-state power relations to trace the effects of the revolutionary narrative. Two aspects of global relationships are highlighted afresh by end-of-century re-examinations of international politics: the reassertion of transnational economic processes and a recent weakening of national states' power in the face of all global interactions.

The first of these aspects is explored by Justin Rosenberg (1994) in a critique of international relations theory born out of the remnants of the theory of imperialism. Rosenberg shows how the formalities of sovereign-state relations can actually *complement* economic operations that exceed the limits of any single state's territory. According to Rosenberg, world-wide inter-state interactions as represented by formal sovereign-state re-lations have from the very start been a way of *limiting* political over economic power within the confines of individual national jurisdiction. This is exactly what is required to *free up* the economic actors of world-wide capitalism. And never more so than now, as global institutions such as the IMF, sanctioned by the club of states, place limits on the powers of formally sovereign states to interfere with the free global activities of capital. There is plenty of scope in this view for identifying trans-world processes that fall outside the formalities of the system of states: such processes are simply the natural obverse of the formal relations of sovereignty.

The new weakening of national-state power goes under names ranging from the new 'porosity' of state boundaries (Camilleri and Falk 1992), to the breaking down of its 'hard shell' (Moravcik 1993) as governments play for advantages in between external and internal pressures. The burden of these developments is usually not taken to be the root and branch wither-ing-away of state institutions. Rather, states have to accommodate to a new environment in which the 'state-centric' arena, where only states can be players, is joined by a 'multi-centric' one, that states, corporations, non-governmental organizations, civilian movements and private individuals can also join (Rosenau 1988). What has to be said, however, is that this is a major shift in the ontology presented by the worldwide processes that are of interest at this point in my argument: 'The anchoring of society to a particular place and the relationship of society to other places are undergo-ing qualitative change' (Camilleri and Falk 1992, p. 250). In other words, processes that transcend individual states' territorial power begin to take precedence over those that can be thought of primarily through the organ-ization of the individual state.

None of this at all implies that processes beyond inter-state power relations were altogether absent before the coming of globalization, merely that it was easier then for states to dominate them within their own territ-ories. That was not particularly effective, as Halliday points out (1994, p. 141) with reference to revolutionary *ideas*: 'The most important inter-national and internationalist impacts of revolutions lie not in the deliberate actions of states, but in the force of example.' Alongside the state-to-state interactions around revolutionary reversals of power, then, there have always been other interactions, not mediated by state organization; but at the end of the twentieth century these have acquired a new importance. That reasoning rather confirms the sense of my approach at this point: to consider world-level processes which may now provide channels for the revolutionary narrative, whilst expecting that these processes in fact *continue* what was happening before.

What world-level processes do these lines of thought indicate for our inquiry? Several areas suggest themselves: international economic and financial activity; population movements across borders; security operations other than those encompassed by national-states' purported defence of their borders; media of communication; 'new social movements' (i.e., for present purposes, those framed around action in more than one country); and the impact of cross-national values such as human rights, democracy and social progress. None of these is new – especially in the context of revolutionary politics, where, for example, international movements and international 'assistance' with the technology of countermeasures have long been commonplace. But there is reason to believe that this sort of thing has a new form and significance in the contemporary world.

If we examine the worldwide effects of revolutions in the twentieth century, up to and including the present moment, we will find, I suggest, the following articulations of the processes I have identified above:

- global trade, especially trades in basic raw materials, and trades such as narcotics which tend to escape agreed inter-state regulation;
- global finance, e.g. providing loans to support currencies or moving out of the currencies of national states threatened by revolution;
- military action other than by national-states forces in defence of borders, such as espionage/counter-insurgency, subversion against new or old regimes, or intermediation (where states use other states or armed groups as third parties against forces in a particular territory);
- the rebel civilian equivalent of that, i.e. forms of resistance to authority imported from one state territory to another;
- movements of refugees and/or militants and rebels to and from areas of conflict within a particular territory;
- communications, both private (e.g. between insurgent political groups) and public (e.g. representations of revolutionary events in the mass media);
- competition between ideological hegemonies, such as the claim to be more socially progressive, or freer than others.

The last four of these, in particular, have an evidently greater import under current conditions. For the porosity of borders enhances the scope for refugee movement (Wang 1993), and, in so far as it facilitates communication, for both ideological competition and the spread of new modes of resistance. As Bertel Heurlin puts it, where state boundaries are no longer primary, 'The unit that encompasses most knowledge and capabilities will be the unit which will penetrate the others' (1997, p. 7). But my argument is that these worldwide effects have been present *throughout* the twentieth century. We can therefore discover them at work in relation to the century's revolutionary outbreaks, and then postulate that they will continue, with increased importance, in the 'globalized' environment surrounding the national state henceforth.

Revolutions and the core in the twentieth century

How, other than by challenging (while largely failing to overturn) the established order of states, have revolutions impacted on the political and economic order during the twentieth century? We can see that they have done so in the international system from an international relations analysis such as that of David Armstrong. He can rightly insist on how little 'international society . . . deviates from the Westphalian conception' (Armstrong 1993, p. 78). But at the same time, he notes a number of changes in world-level *concepts* and *values* that are derived from particular revolutionary states – as the price for their integration into the group. In the last two centuries, France and the USA, with their conceptions of proper internal mechanisms of government, have both exacted such a price.

Yet these two are countries near to the origin of the European system, and, as I explained in Part I, are therefore more able to act on the overall character of the modernized world. They have themselves been natural members of the core elite of states and 'central' in the senses defined in chapter 3; that is, capable of representing a threat in the centres of power. But Armstrong recognizes as well the impact of the USSR, which remained an outsider, and even of other 'anti-Western' revolutions since the war. It does appear though, as we should expect, that the latter, more peripheral revolutionary states are more effectively constrained by the global powers than are the earlier, 'central' ones. These later worldwide responses to revolutions, the action and reaction of revolutionary outbreaks and core states, are made in order to counter the demonstration effect of the rebel without overtly conceding the revolutionary values. They are instances of what I have referred to above as 'competition between ideological hegemonies' and 'imported forms of resistance'. Thanks to that interplay, the Soviet claims to represent the international proletariat and to stand for post-Second World War national liberation contributed to new international norms, such as improved labour conditions and self-determination (Armstrong 1993, p. 155). Likewise, the imported forms of resistance could be seen at work strengthening the organizational cohesion of Western labour movements. The International Labour Organization, for example, which has established non-mandatory international standards for working conditions, was set up because of fears that the Soviet Union would manipulate the labour movement in the West (p. 156).

For Europe in the twentieth century, this demonstration effect, and the consequent effort to answer the rebel claims, have underpinned the very possibility of a social democratic compromise by liberal capital (Hobsbawm 1994). Not that the West has simply tried to *follow* the course 'demonstrated' by the revolution to the East. Between the wars, the Soviet presence in the conflict between hegemonies assisted a major Western ideological departure, towards fascism. Western countries' foreign-policy thinking was persuadable on the subject of Nazi Germany, in so far as it presented a means to counter the Soviet challenge; while fascist tendencies across Europe could present the Nazi example as an alternative to the communist strategy in facing the socio-economic crisis of the day (Polanyi 1957, p. 246). The same ideological competition made post-war foreign-policy thinking susceptible to social democratic humanism (Crosland 1956, p. 287). But that impact too was far from a one-way process: as the episode of 'Eurocommunism', in which several Western European communist parties sought to accommodate 1917 in more social-democratic clothes,[2] illustrated.

For Europe/the West the competition for ideological hegemony with the Soviet rebel was always complex because of the latter's plausible claim to come from common ideological stock: Judaeo-Christian, post-Enlightenment materialism etc. This can be easily seen in the two-way game that both West and East played in order to claim parts of the Third World for their own versions of progress. Each side acquired, and then would periodically slough off, Third World claimants to its version – for many were merely engaged in what Foltz (1990, p. 62) calls 'revolutionary posturing'. Likewise, many of the century's intellectual disputes about revolution and history, which I refer to over the length of this book, illustrate the point. A little-known, and particularly telling, instance can be found in the career of Eugen Rosenstock-Huessy. In 1938, in exile in the USA, he published an extraordinary, visionary compendium of European history, one of various efforts from the mainstream of the great European intellectual tradition to counter the inter-war direction of European politics towards Spengler's circular vision, materialism and/or fascism.

Rosenstock-Huessy engaged in a complex strategy to demonstrate that all Europe's modern national revolutions (in Germany, England, France and Russia) could be accommodated under the meanings of *pre*-modern ones which occurred earlier within the classical European Church. These revolutions invented universal values of community, allegiance and authority, which the modern revolutions can only express within their own limited territory. Rosenstock-Huessy's aim was to find the cultural basis for an accommodation between the contending revolutionary ideologies of Europe – including Russia – by showing that 'all four . . . [are] interdependent and . . . have created a system based on their permanent interplay'

(Rosenstock-Huessy 1993, p. 10). Such ideas were taken seriously: Rosenstock-Huessy ended his career in a respectable west-coast US college, enjoying the patronage of the liberal White House for his ideas on education for citizenship.

The same process of ideological competition went on, of course, through the communications network: cheap Soviet (and then Chinese) copies of the works of Marx, Stalin, Lenin, Mao etc.; the Liberty Press; Radio Free Europe; educational tours and so on. In the earlier part of the century, the 'Soviet-inspired' press maintained a serious challenge to the views of established authority. By the end of the Soviet period, the tables had been turned: the plenitude of Western media contributed quite seriously to the collapse of legitimacy (Lane 1996, p. 161).

Over the years, there were also some striking financial processes involving the Soviet revolution and its final outcome. The Soviet Union itself fell in early with the common assent to pegging currencies to the Gold Standard (Polanyi 1957, p. 25), and in the longer term it profited from its co-operative attitude in supplying gold (and also diamonds) to the world market. In the 1970s, on the other hand, the Soviet Bloc willingly became a convenient dumping ground for agricultural surpluses that would have undermined the US or European markets had they been released on to them. It then became an outlet for the Western banking system – a development which in the end proved more destructive than any other for the Soviet revolutionary island.

The 1960s and 1970s saw the appearance of new effects at the core from more recent revolutions than the Russian. Versions of Chinese and Cuban revolutionary experience were taken as models for imported forms of resistance (Cohn-Bendit 1968, Debray 1967) inspiring challenges from outside the established left parties (i.e. communist and social-democratic ones), even though the parallels between the West and the Third World were themselves quite unconvincing (Kiernan 1970). These had a particular part in the embarrassment meted out to the Gaullist regime in 1968 – without, of course, actually causing it to collapse. The USA, gambling on its ability to control its 'backyard' in Cuba, embroiled itself disastrously in the restoration of the pre-revolutionary regime. In terms of the competition over ideological hegemonies, the long-term effects were to drive the revolutionary regime into the Soviet camp, hand to it the legitimacy of national self-determination as the leader of the 'Non-aligned States' and create a long-term cause of tension between the USA itself and its Western allies. In terms of post-revolutionary movements of population, the effect of the USA's receiving those in flight from Castro's regime was to foster a permanent network of anti-Castro politics within US politics itself. For most countries in the world, Castro's Cuba, for all its faults, has pursued the course of revolutionary self-determination, and they can see little point in interfering with that. But, thanks to the strategic political position of its anti-Castro network of Cuban immigrants, the USA still cannot fall into line with its allies.

The case of Vietnam, however, is much the most striking. Thanks to the particular circumstances of Western involvement, the Vietnamese socialist revolutionaries imposed substantial long-term effects on the core states, especially the USA. In the early 1950s, Vietnamese resistance to the reimposition of French rule had contributed significantly to the political pressures that pulled the mat from beneath European defence integration. For it reinforced the French sense of the importance of its own republican military autonomy (Stirk 1997, p. 131).[3] In the 1960s and 1970s, Vietnam decisively undermined both the dominance of the USA in world affairs and the internal legitimacy of US political institutions. The public frustration of its military policy objectives and the costs to its exchequer worked against the USA's leadership in western military and financial affairs. And the increasing demands of a war against an enemy whose ostensible purpose was to *follow* the USA's own revolutionary ambition for self-determination, encouraged those who challenged the war domestically in their resistance and undermined the case for it in the corridors of power.

Recalling his decision to resign from the US government, in which he had been the principal architect of military intervention in Vietnam, Robert McNamara recently listed the lessons for the USA (McNamara 1995, pp. 321–3): to avoid judging friends and enemies 'in terms of our own experience', not to underestimate nationalism, not to overestimate military technology against 'highly motivated people's movements', to act 'internationally' etc. McNamara also registers (pp. 324–30) a *permanent* shift in US international-relations thinking at the time, towards 'post-Cold-War internationalism', which accepted certain areas – Third World conflicts arising from nationalism, inequality, political revolution or boundary disputes – where 'the US no longer has the power . . . to shape the world as we choose' (p. 324). The shift in US state-elite thinking which McNamara speaks for has also been studied systematically by Holsti and Rosenau (1984). They chart (chs 1 and 2) the growth at that time of the view that US involvement had serious consequences for its domestic order and that the country should henceforth tolerate a multi-polar world where the USA would use peaceful means and international institutions. They demonstrate, moreover, that these effects on domestic political consensus were long-term (at least within the limits of their own research), and that 'American leaders are [in the early 1980s] sharply divided on the thesis that events in Iran and Afghanistan can be traced to American impotence arising from the Vietnam War' (p. 239).

The USA experienced what has been called the 'Vietnam complex' in these various effects of revolution upon a core state. But that is not to say, of course, that revolutionary states simply scored a *victory over* the core state. This is evident from subsequent history. On the one hand, US/Western military intervention certainly did not cease; rather, in the case of Iran and Afghanistan, it was more likely to take the form of intermediation (through Iraq and Pakistan respectively). And when it did occur, as in

Somalia or the Gulf War, it was carefully managed as in international event, fit for public presentation in the mass media. By the 1990s, Vietnam for its part had been brought into line as a state among states (Abuza 1996) and was embroiled in the same global processes which had undermined the Soviet Bloc – debts of 17 billion dollars and no more support from the USSR (compounded by a US embargo inspired by intransigence to its old enemy). Advocates of newer civilian methods of US management of the periphery were arguing, successfully, for a final push to bring Vietnam into line with the late-twentieth-century economic disciplines (Vo 1990; see also Pike 1993).

In the late-twentieth-century environment, financial flows, more or less actively organized by the USA, have again become crucial processes in the global order (Bello 1994), duly mediating the impact of revolutions. For the revolutions of the 'Socialist' bloc, they have generally created *adverse* pressures. Vietnam in the 1990s is a further example of this. The instructive exception has been post-revolutionary China. The size of the Chinese state following its revolutionary reconstruction again makes it unique. Up to the present Western states and Western-sponsored managers of the financial world have indulged the Chinese state, on the understanding that it moves towards some limited conformity with liberal-market economic principles (MacKerras et al. 1994). The reason appears to be that, in an environment of Western economic downturn, a securely governed China represents too big an opportunity for Western capital to resist, notwithstanding the serious limits on profits imposed by established China's political power-holders (Higgins 1998).

As I have argued above (chapters 1 and 4), the Iranian revolution marked the beginning of a new type, the 'anti-Westernizing' revolution, which opened up opposition to both Western modernization and its 'Eastern' homologue. Its insertion into global processes is also distinctive. It piloted new, subversive uses of media of communication (Halliday 1988, Sreberny-Mohammadi 1990). It constituted Islamic fundamentalism as a serious new, transferable form of resistance and a figure in global patterns of power, which neighbouring states struggled to ward off (Entessar 1984), and US policy in its previously established terms was quite unable to comprehend (Sullivan 1980[4]) – though the post-Vietnam organization of the US media proved largely co-operative in the management of the public media (Dorman and Farhang 1986). These are versions of global effects of revolution, now articulated in a new fashion, where revolution stands *between* two forms of modernization, rather than on the edge of the one form. This fact enabled the international impacts of the Iranian revolution to undercut the established modes of international/global response. Even today, the core's response to fundamentalism is trapped, trying to rediscover the Cold War ideological confrontation under another name – as the success of Huntington's facile idea of an ever-present 'clash of civilizations' illustrates (Huntington 1996[5]). As Castells has argued, fundamentalism belongs to a new type of resistance to imposed forces, which is relatively unnattached to country (Castells 1997, pp. 12–27).

Revolutions and the core in the era of 'globalization'

Given the historic novelty of the Iranian case, we must take stock of twentieth-century experience before pursuing its implications through to the last years of the century and the future. Iran's was the first revolution of the last quarter of the century. Two major underlying shifts characterize this final period: the disappearance of the 'revolutionary' Soviet Bloc and 'globalization'. Though distinct in themselves, they coincide at the very least in that they are reshaping the global order: away from bipolarity and towards multi-polarity or seamlessness. Iran's revolution, placed outside the Cold War power blocs, belongs to this world.

As regards the disappearance of the 'revolutionary' bloc, my contention has already been adumbrated at length: the revolutionary challenge from the Soviet/Eastern Bloc was a phase in the gradual distancing of revolution from the global core; yet even if that overt confrontation between Western powers and the socialist revolution is abstracted out, a substantial residue of world-level impacts of revolution remains. As regards 'globalization', the argument of this chapter is that various processes which are now called 'global' have always been present to some degree, though they are now more in evidence as other processes centred on the nation-state recede. Under conditions of 'globalization', therefore, the world-level processes identified earlier in the chapter can be expected to continue, but with a different visibility. Some stipulative observations regarding 'globalization' are needed before the discussion can proceed.

However disputed, we can take the concept of 'globalization' to begin with the markedly increased presence of trans-regional, global processes in the organization of contemporary social and economic life. The processes referred to range from industrial design, production and marketing to media of communication, especially mass communication and information transfer; to the movement of short- and long-term finance; to the organization of public affairs. These are all versions of the world-level processes I identified above, in which effects of revolution had already been articulated earlier in the century. It is hard to evaluate the import of these processes' becoming 'global'. Even if, for example, the post-Second World War raft of international institutions and conventions (under US patronage) shows an impressive rate of increase, agreements and assemblies of this kind are nothing new. Even the level of international trade, as measured by the ratio of trade to GNP, is no higher today than it was before 1913 (Hirst and Thompson 1995). What makes this into 'globalization' is the contention that the predominant structuring of political and economic life across the globe can now only be formulated in terms of the *global* level. This is what writers such as Martin Albrow call 'globality': each state no more a 'separated entity', but instead 'a globally extended sphere of meaningful activities' (Albrow 1996, p. 64).

It is the *relationship* between the economic and the public-political processes that makes for the dispute about the meaning of globalization. The recent manifestations of 'globalization' shake the previous relationship between 'autonomous' economic processes and the overall, political organization of social life. In particular, the dominant *political* instance of recent centuries, the national state, appears no longer to be at the optimal level for the exercise of political power over the economic sphere. For some commentators (Bello 1994, Hirst and Thompson 1995, Kumar 1996, Youngs 1996), this concept of a 'new' situation smacks of a self-serving delusion: 'globalization' belongs to a discourse either of the same old forms of control by other means, or of self-interested acquiescence in inequalities produced in the world economy. Indeed, it is hard not to notice that a declaration of new 'global' principles such as Fukuyama's coincides not so much with the *supersession* of national-state form of power altogether as with the *accession* of one national state, the USA, to unchallenged dominance in it. Yet for others, there really is a sea change in globalization – amounting to nothing less than the end of 'state-centric' thinking (Albrow 1996, Camilleri and Falk 1992, pp. 246–51), which may even entail the end of hierarchical aspirations for top–down design of social life itself (Gray 1995).

Even if we suppose no more than an enhancement, and an increased awareness of world-level processes, just that altered *perception* of the relationship between state power and the global socio-economic order must impact on the meaning of the revolutionary narrative. For the classic form of the narrative fed off the classic idea of the state. It was because the state was an effective level of political organization from which to manage the life of society or transform it, that it was also a suitable target for revolution and self-conscious, collective historical change. So the very *impression* of globalization must skew the revolutionary narrative – as it did in France in the 1980s. If the state level is weakened, it will be asked, at what level *can* conscious social change be articulated? That assumes, of course, that the revolutionary narrative does survive. If the main consequence of globalization is that, for lack of a cogent agent of change, *no* conscious social change is possible, then the revolutionary narrative will be short of an essential component. This in effect is what a critic such as Rosenberg suspects to be the very purpose of the idea of globalization in the international system (1994, ch. 5).

Hence, I am led to anticipate that the end-of-century prevalence of effects referred to under the title of 'globalization' will indeed amend the articulation of the revolutionary narrative. But, conversely, like those effects themselves, this articulation may not be a new form in itself. I have argued that already in the twentieth century there were a number of worldwide processes supervening the system of inter-state relations. Similarly, I postulate that in an environment impressed by a new perception of 'globalization', effects from the revolutionary narrative will continue to generate impacts, and that these will transcend the collapse of revolutionary aspirations centred on the transformation of distinct national societies. This proposition can be tested in connection with two recent revolutionary movements: Nicaragua and the Zapatistas in Mexico.

The Sandinista movement of Nicaragua drew explicitly on a model of localized, participatory democracy inspired by rural, native experience rather than the Marxism-Leninism of the Cold War national liberation struggles (*Latin American Perspectives* 1990). It belongs, then, alongside Cuba and the Sendero Luminoso in Peru, to the long tradition of South American peasant resistance from the very margins of modernization. Likewise, the combination of US government countermeasures against the post-revolutionary state was familiar: military intermediation (arming the Contra guerrillas) and trade embargo.

What is distinctive is the international visibility of the Sandinista regime and of the efforts to reverse it. The regime itself successfully drew on a newly prominent international discourse of rights (Brown 1990) – notably by appealing for vindication to both the International Court in The Hague and to the UN Security Council. Post-revolutionary Nicaragua received effective diplomatic support, trade outlets and aid from states in Europe and the Third World that were not wholly aligned with the USA (Nillson 1991, Vanden and Prevost 1993, pp. 101–6). Rather than seeking isolation, the Sandinista leaders went out of their way to explain their regime as a distinctive kind of revolutionary democracy, specifically adopted for local conditions. This was also the first revolution which drew explicitly on the worldwide force of Christian Liberation Theology (Pottinger 1989), and encouraged its friends abroad to publicize the fact (Zwerling and Martin 1985). On the other side, in the media-drenched post-Vietnam environment, with 'post-Cold-War internationalism' still a force in US public policy thinking, the Reagan administration had to make special efforts to represent the new regime as hostile to liberty (Kenworthy 1988, Parry and Kornbluh 1988). The US government felt peculiarly vulnerable to global media and legitimation processes. Likewise, US strategic thinking addressed this as a 'post-Cold-War' revolution, to be seen in terms of 'low-intensity conflict', rather than state-to-state or alliance-to-alliance conflict (Krueger 1995, Molloy 1992).

These distinctive features do suggest a revolution for the world-level environment of the end of the century. In this environment, both revolution and opposition seek to find an economic, strategic and ideological place in the post-Cold War global arena, representing themselves as legitimate inheritors of elements of the revolutionary narrative such as self-determination or democracy. Whether this change in the articulation of the revolutionary narrative actually leaves revolutionary movements stronger than before is, of course, an altogether different matter. Other social forces, opposed to the Sandinistas, the coffee elites of Central America for example, could perfectly well pick up from the wider world a narrative, that of neo-liberalism and liberal-democracy, with which to update their defence of their national privileges (Paige 1997). Ultimately, the Sandinista revolutionaries themselves were so hamstrung by 'international' standards of democracy that they were unable to maintain the basis of their support amongst a population hit hard by US-prompted trade effects (Foran and Goodwin 1993, Vanden and Prevost 1993, pp. 143–50). In short, Nicaragua's revolution on the edge of global economic forces was just as exposed to modernization as others had been, and arguably less able to protect itself because it could not create a base for autarchy. Nicaragua signifies a struggle with forces of modernization intensified and recast in terms of 'global' processes of legitimation. To articulate a claim to the revolutionary narrative becomes more important, but it is still far from guaranteeing success for the revolutionaries.

It was their media flair and their very presence on the internet that marked the Zapatistas out as a very contemporary revolution (Castells 1997, pp. 79–81). By skilful timing, they exposed the weakness of the Mexican regime on the global media stage at its weakest moment (just as the launch of the North American Free Trade Association in January 1994 was supposed to prolong the flow of hot capital into the Mexican economy) and forced immediate concessions from the government. The possibility of a destabilizing social challenge has always been a major disincentive to capital. And mobile finance capital has always seen the benefit of using the most advanced media of communication to anticipate conditions in different countries. So globalization has naturally been much in evidence in the electronic acceleration of financial information. But it is more common for fear of instability to work *against* rebels – by, for example, justifying oppressive state countermeasures, as it did for Peru's 'Fujishock' in the early 1990s. Not so in the case of the Zapatistas. To add to the government's international discomfiture, the movement also exposed the corruption of the contemporaneous national electoral process and the abuses of 'international' standards of human rights in the treatment of Indian land (Wiener 1994). So the Zapatistas can be seen to have used contemporary global media and current global conditions *against* the prevailing social and political order (Cockburn 1994, Martinez Torres 1996).

The place of the Zapatista rebellion in realities of global power is, on the other hand, altogether familiar from earlier twentieth-century revolutions. Given the importance of the rebel area for Mexico's international oil and gas trade, the issue of strategic resources for core states would, in any case, have been a powerful incentive for international pressure to control the situation – compare Iran in the early 1950s, or, for that matter, Mexico at the end of the nineteenth century. On the other hand, there is evidence that the Zapatista movement was 'international' in another long-standing sense:

in that it brought together movements of Indians from different countries (Churchill 1995).

Does all that make the Zapatistas exemplary revolutionaries for the 'global' era (Cleaver 1994)? Only on the basis that they put the older wine of the revolutionary narrative – oppressed peasant communities rising up to obtain new living conditions – into the new bottle of global media and international standards of human rights. While they self-consciously operated in a new global *arena*, they did so only by evoking *older* revolutionary forces. First, their human rights claims had, of course, a long pedigree in European revolutionary gains from the past. Secondly, they started their revolution in what might almost be considered the classic Mexican manner: rural uprising against blatant electoral fixing in a presidential election. Finally, their explicit evocation of the name of Zapata reflects the extent to which they constituted their movement from the established, indeed constitutionally recognized, place of peasant villages in Mexican history. The threat of a flight of capital may have leveraged the impact of the rebellion; but without the long history of Indian communities, and their specific struggles against encroachment (Nash 1995), the story of takeover by a mass movement would have meant nothing on an apprehensive international scene. The Zapatista insurgency reasserts older forces for revolution, even though it does so on a new stage. Yet these older forces are in a genuinely new situation in Central America: the government's attempt to revoke the post-revolutionary constitutional rights of the village *ejidos* was prompted by the advance of the globalizing economy, as enshrined in the NAFTA agreement. The rural bulwark against modernization that the first Mexican revolution had established in the 1920s was crumbling as business and big money pressed down upon it again from the north. What the Zapatistas did was to find a new language to respond on a 'global' level to long-standing forces of modernization recently dressed afresh in the style of 'globalization'.

How then does revolutionary activity interact with the current world setting? It interacts, as before, with global processes such as I identified earlier: international trade, legally sanctioned or not;[6] military confrontation, direct and indirect; population movements; and competition for ideological hegemony. Yet it does so in a global environment in which the limits on the autonomy of the individual national state (the USA apart) are recognized, and the game must be played out both in and beyond national boundaries. Penetrating communications is after all a dimension of global conflict which US strategic thinking has already recognized (Rondfeldt 1995). In this context, however, the revolutionary narrative has a renewed import: it is the language in which the claims of forces for change in one part of the globe can be understood, and potentially sympathized with, in another. To formulate and convey one's movement as a recognizable narration of revolution has therefore become relatively more important than before, by comparison with the mustering and organization of forces on the ground. It will not, of course, *replace* the hard-headed, armed side of revolutionary contention. Nor does it, in all probability, mark a shift to a completely different *kind* of motivation in which spiritual, or 'post-materialist' values surface (L. Anderson 1990). Such values, integrated with plain material necessity, have long figured in rebel motivations (Popkin 1979, Thompson 1971) and continue to do so.

Looking for legitimizing narratives on the global scene

We have seen that, on the global scene, revolutions have long impacted beyond their immediate, claimed boundaries. Intra-global interactions which fall outside the scope of conventional inter-state relations convey these impacts even where the revolutionary upheaval itself remains formally confined to the boundaries of a given state. In those situations, it has often been important for political actors to defend their deeds in terms classically articulated in the revolutionary narrative: such as ideas of democracy, natural rights, social progress and national self-determination. Accordingly, as the global stage becomes a more explicit level of political action, the legitimation of actions on the transnational level will be an increasing concern. That, indeed, is the motive of Castells (1997), who resituates Touraine's sociology, born of the spirit of Sartre's revolutionary philosophy,[7] by locating social action in the identity formed in struggle by *trans-territorial* groups – ranging from Christian or Islamic fundamentalists to feminism – which resist the pressures of contemporary globalization.

Where does the revolutionary narrative stand in such transnational legitimations? Having long been a shared basis for conceptions of how freedom and autonomous social progress come about, it would be surprising if those aspects of the revolutionary narrative did not resurface in legitimations in supra-national political action. Peter Calvert, on the other hand, is surely naive to suggest that one, Western liberal-democratic articulation of the revolutionary narrative will in future be the common ground of perceptions worldwide: 'The myth of revolution has subtly changed. In the West, revolution is no longer seen as Soviet-inspired and therefore unwanted . . . The changes [which revolutions] bring were seen as desirable, even where they had been accompanied by a high level of violence' (1996, pp. 38–9). It is logical to suppose that the revolutionary narrative elevated to the post-Cold War, globalized level, will be subject to recasting and dispute, as it was before in moving from one location to another. Francis Fukuyama's 'end of history' thesis has to be seen in this context, where the autonomy of separate national states suddenly counts for little – be that because of globalization as such or because of unchallenged US dominance. The thesis answered to a renewed need, which we can see to be inherent in the late-twentieth-century world situation: for the legitimation of actions beyond the limits of the order of nation-states.

An idealist notion of history guided by principle was an alternative to nationalism (see chapter 6) as a response to the dissolution of the communist revolutionary agent. Against particularist nationalism talk, this approach tried to unearth a motor for the present or future of history in some emergent principles of human action. Williams et al. (1997) conclude that Fukuyama's reaction to the historic shock of the collapse of the communist revolution belongs more to the Kantian perspective in European philosophies of universal history than to any other. It may not be accidental, then, that Kant's own writings on history can be seen too as the response of an enthusiast for the Enlightened principles of a revolution (1789) who was uneasy about the human representatives of those principles and their specific actions (N. Parker 1990, pp. 164–7). What we might call Fukuyama's 'renewed liberal progressivism' postulated that the economic advancement available through integration in the world free-market economy would progressively wean peoples off ideologically inspired interventionism at home, and military adventures abroad. The principles of liberal-democracy among nations, following naturally from their liberal economics, would ensure that they settled disputes peacefully within the rules of the international market.[8] Conflict of the older, 'ideological' sort, along with 'History' in that sense, was coming to an end.

In its early, brief, triumphalist statement, under the full flood of communism's global collapse, Fukuyama's liberal progressivism was content to declare without further ado the universal adhesion to principles of liberal capitalism and democracy. Later works attempt to embed these formerly unquestioned principles more fully into a real human population, primarily that of the developed West. This proves to be an uncomfortable exercise for Fukuyama (McCarney 1993). Fukuyama (1992) suggested that two deep uncertainties have entered the earlier attempt: (i) can the pursuit of isolated self-interest in the now dominant market economy sustain any social fabric at all? and (ii) can we expect a *democratic* future simply because the free market is without a global challenger? Human beings are now said to require *two* kinds of motivation for their social behaviour: material advantage (which the technologically advanced, modern free market can provide superbly well), and *thymos*, that is, in practice, people's wish for 'recognition' by the group in which they live. It is plain that the motivation for political life is no necessary corollary of the material life of the consumer in the capitalist markets of the modern West. In short, it is proving hard to insert historically triumphant universal principle into the specific human groups proffered as its agents. In specifying more fully the society in which its liberal principles were articulated, Fukuyama's thought drifted away from the confident self-management of a Daniel Bell and more towards Marcuse's perception of the dull-wittedness of the market society. The trend to find it more and more difficult to identify united, globally victorious principles of human social life continued in Fukuyama's 1995 study of *Trust*. For there he finds that this essential cementing virtue of social life is in constant tension with the secular individualism of contemporary Western market society.

Of the various European reactions to the disappearance of the Sovietized version of the revolutionary narrative, that stemming from Critical Theory was perhaps strategically best placed to pick up the revolutionary narrative in terms of universal principles. For critical theorists had always rejected the Soviet version of the story of socialism, condemning its narrow instrumentalist ideas of social progress, too easily reducible to formulas for growth lacking any legitimation that could be more firmly rooted in the living values of the society. In the positive rendering of Habermas, Critical Theory had sought the well-springs of social action in a rational conjunction of interests, interlocking circles of communication and networks of expertise. Together these offered the hope that socialist political values could be linked to the heritage of social improvement through science as it had been bequeathed by the Enlightenment. For Habermas, 'the philosophical discourse of modernity' has always contained the potential for a space to be found between self-centred, individualistic values and the oppressive, instrumental pursuit of the interests of society as a whole.

> The double battlefront makes the rehabilitation of the concept of reason a doubly risky business. It has to protect itself on both flanks from getting caught in the traps of the kind of subject-centred thinking that failed to keep the unforced force of reason free both from the *totalitarian* characteristics of an *instrumental* reason that objectifies everything around it, itself included, and from the *totalizing* characteristics of an *inclusive* reason that incorporates everything and, as a unity, ultimately triumphs over every distinction. (Habermas 1987, p. 341)

Thus, Habermas's immediate response to 1989 was to claim back the revolutionary narrative from *Soviet* socialism. The Eastern European revolutions were, he argued, a 'rectification' of the long-standing Leninist misconception of mechanistic history and social progress. With the meaning of historical progress wrested from the hands of Soviet and East European ideologues, the Western European social democratic agenda could now recapture the historical meaning of socialism and revolutionary change. He envisages new socio-political formations mediating interests at the different levels of society: 'radical-democratic universalization of interests through institutions for the formation of public opinion and political will' (Habermas 1990, p. 21). In this renewed historical quest to articulate the same rational values that have long been potential in modernity, the leadership of Western European socialism was needed more than ever.

What this high-principled descendant of the European revolutionary narrative tends to obscure, albeit unwillingly, is the same that was elided by its Kantian forebear. It has little to say, that is, about *who* will figure in any renewed version of the revolutionary narrative, or in what space and time-frame such an agent can effect the self-conscious historic change which lies at the heart of the narrative's inspiration. As the founding father of the historical sociology of revolutions, Barrington Moore had argued in 1978 that many older non-Western resistance groups could lay claim to the universal value of 'justice'. More recently, the appearance of new ideas about 'international civil society', often more or less under the influence of Critical Theory, goes some way to redress the absence of specifiable agents of change. Held (1995) represents the trend well as he attempts to describe principles and possible institutional forms for a 'cosmopolitan model of democracy' and 'citizenship . . . extended, in principle, to membership in all cross-cutting political communities, from the local to the global' (p. 272). This conception would overlay the forms of democracy contained in the national narrative of Europe's revolutionary past, with politically active communities that transcended the individual state.

The future formation of collective agents

The chapters in this second part have gone some way to recover the *idea* of revolution from the futility which, according to the argument in Part I, increasingly burdened the immediate aims of revolutionary undertakings themselves. In the form of the revolutionary narrative, the *idea* has been shown to appear and to shape crucial interpretations of societies' experiences. Yet that finding has left us pointing in two directions. On the one hand, the revolutionary narrative has a unique capacity to give sense and direction to processes of historical change, lending it an appeal that is not likely to go away. On the other, in specific historical conditions the articulation of the revolutionary narrative could easily evince displacements of its elements and structure which rendered it as much misleading as effective. Versions and effects of the revolutionary narrative could be found to pop up in many places; but they were quite likely to *mis*represent present political players to themselves or to others, or to encourage reactions out of touch with the reality the revolutionary forces reacted against.

This is a matter of interactions between the world and human ideas about it. Indeed the whole architecture of this book has been intended to explore such interactions. In itself, the revolutionary narrative has a demonstrable capacity to embrace the problems of humans' confrontation with modernity; but in specific instances, for reasons that we have been able to identify after the event, the actors in the story lack the cogency or the position required for the role they should fulfil in the narrative. It appears, in short, that socio-political actors of various kinds will continue to formulate their historical moment in the form of the revolutionary narrative, without realizing the expectations inherent in the narrative itself. Conversely, worthwhile ideas of social progress might take up the torch of the revolutionary narrative yet appear aloof from the realities of the groupings to provide agency for change in the direction laid out. This essay cannot close without a prognosis for how narrative perceptions of history might actually be formed in the contemporary world. The more theoretical dimension of this issue is covered in the appendix on revolution and the understanding of history. Here a more impressionistic approach is appropriate.

We can easily see the *empirical difficulty* in the way. The existence of a plausible collective agent of change is the prime condition for a level of intentional historical change to be identifiable in historical processes. Where more or less stable agents entertain intentions to pursue change in the direction of some future state and, in addition, those agents are in a position to weigh on the out-turn of events, it is a cogent supposition that those same intentions will produce effects in the future – even effects approximating to the realization of the present intention. Hence the revolutionary narrative's feasibility has always depended crucially upon the putative existence of agents with intentions of the sort defined above. The conditions in which the classic nineteenth-century revolutionary narrative flowered were more or less propitious for expectations grounded in the effects upon whole societies of large collective agents, such as nations or classes. In other words, the credible presence of various effective agents of change underwrote conceptions of history in which revolutionary collective agents could hold a major role.

We may learn to look back at that period as an exception: a phase of history when putative active groups could readily be identified at the level of the 'whole society' of a nation-state. The present historical conditions may suggest the demise of the nation-state as that natural arena of the collective agent inherited in the revolutionary narrative. Future historical circumstances may not support nearly so easily the teleology of collective agents and their intentions in understanding historical change. Following his long, unhappy experience with national revolution in South America, there is, according to one commentator, a 'crisis of the sociopolitical model' which made the state a target for anti-authoritarian struggles guided by 'a global ideological project for society' (Garretón 1995, p. 466). In the 1980s the decline of the state as an autonomous arena for social change indeed appeared as a crucial element in the embarrassment of the revolutionary narrative in its 'home' country of France. There is a problem of parallax here: near to the global seat of the idea of nation, as of revolution, our view of the decline of the nation-state is often informed by a naive belief that in the past the nation-state was everywhere fully developed (Dunn 1995, pp. 10–11). Likewise, it is easy to ignore the reality that the national *identity* of the state's subjects has itself always demanded continual constructive activity, including a discourse that covered its own tracks (Bhabha 1990). We should be careful, then, not to be star-struck by the merely *relative* decline of a form of political organization that may, in practice, be adjusting and 'diversifying' its modes of action 'rather than dying' (Mann 1996a).

Yet if we are considering the possibilities for collective perceptions of history to be formed in the contemporary world, we need to look at the level and form in which collective agents with putative capacity for historical effects may take shape. The mere *appearance* of decline at the level of the nation-state would be an impediment to belief in historical agents of change at the state level. Indeed, arguably that is exactly the point of diminishing the *autonomous* power of the nation-state even while it still commands a crucial place in the authoritative co-ordination of the global capitalist economy. In this way, in a search for arenas where collective agents of the revolutionary historical narrative may be identified, we are led on to the ambivalent path of reviewing locations that are less propitious than national institutions and single national societies.

That path was dramatically pursued in the left post-structuralism of Ernesto Laclau and others. Laclau's *New Reflections on The Revolution of Our Time* (1990), for example, boldly discarded all received ideas of the active 'subject' of history in its grand narratives – on the grounds that they were echoes of a now closed era of Enlightenment, with its grandiose aspiration for a seamless rationalist unity in society. Laclau proposed that in future revolutionary 'subjects' would be constituted at points of breakdown in political discourses. Resistant groups will not, that is to say, give expression to any *pre-existing* identity of will or interests; they have to *be formed* by the continual, *failed* efforts to state 'the will of all' in the political discourse of whole societies. In so far as it made the discursive formation of the group identity into a continuous process, this view can be taken as a radical statement of 'identity' politics. Politics, as conscious, wilful expression of interests and pursuit of goals, gives way to the introvert politics of formulating the identities of the groups formerly *represented* in politics – and formulating them, what is more, from the preordained *failure* of representation. This is a radical reconstruction of the politics in the revolutionary narrative. Democratic power becomes a matter disputing any final, unified representation of the group. The meaning of democracy itself has become 'the ultimate impossibility of all representation . . . the very placing in question of the notion of ground' (Laclau 1990, p. 78).[9] This writes out the post-1789 republican European model altogether, by breaking the link between political action and any larger structuring of the group as an agent in history.

For Laclau, 'our age' is 'the age of democratic revolution' precisely because it is exploring the possibility of historical change without representation of any ultimate, stable closure (1990, p. 75). Given my long account of the career of the European revolutionary narrative, before acceding to so radically altered a version, I would ask what is really new in the situation that Laclau and others use as their point of departure. Peter Burke has, for example, traced back comparable 'identities of resistance' to earlier centuries (Burke 1992). For according to the account of things given in this book, representation, indeed a sort of constructive *mis*representation, of the place of revolutionary agents in the history of world modernization has been present from the very start alongside the rise of revolutionary movements.

The move from class conflict to the play of discourse had, indeed, been anticipated in France itself in interpretations of the classic case, 1789. The entire Furet *œuvre* can be thought of as an attempt to prioritize the *formative* role of Jacobin revolutionary discourse over that of interests or social groups as such (Furet 1981, 1996). Laclau's thinking also has its European/ French roots: in the debate on fascism and in a critical rejection of the extreme rational ambitions of Althusserian structuralism. For Laclau had argued in the 1970s that – *pace* structuralist principles – fascism had known how to turn an ideology *against* a class-formation.[10] Laclau concluded even then that 'what constitutes the unifying principle of an ideological discourse is the "subject" interpellated and thus constituted through this discourse' (1979, p. 101). Yet to show that discourse operates separately, or even against, the dynamic of social groups could never be to demonstrate the *ontological priority* of discourse over the politics of the group as a potential historical subject. In the contemporary world the representation of group identity with its pitfalls and inversions, which was from the very early days a complex and hazardous dimension of the revolutionary narrative (Ifversen 1996, Jaume 1989, N. Parker 1990), has just come to be seen as the difficult process it always was (Phillips 1995). But that is no reason to dispense with the notion that the collective agent has a palpable, even if troubled, existence.

A favoured recent case for explaining how the resistant group can be a product of politics itself has been the revolution in South Africa. For the ethnic formations promoted by the political discourse of South Africa were primary in the subsequent resistance (Norval 1996). When Laclau debates South Africa with Norval, then, he takes the opportunity to condemn the way that 'emancipatory discourses [starting with Jacobinism] tend to manifest themselves as total ideologies' and to commend his notion of 'democratic indeterminacy' as an alternative 'totalizing horizon for the social' (Laclau 1990, pp. 169–70). South Africa's relative political and economic weight make it crucial in the African continent (Castells 1998, pp. 122–7), and the visibly crucial role of the global level in its revolution are reasons to see the South African moment as paradigmatic for the end of the twentieth century. But they do not justify a radical reversal of the inherited position of the historical revolutionary subject. The history of the formation, transposition and reformulation of the revolutionary narrative shows that real social forces for change have *usually* been reflected in, and interacted with, their representation in the revolutionary narrative. According to my account, we have to expect the formation of revolutionary agents at the margins of the world system to be more fraught as the edges of the system push outwards. Even then we can discover signs of 'conventional' class formation in South Africa also (Drew 1992). Yet, the revolutionary narrative, with its constructively misleading aspects, was formulated near to the core of the expanding world system; as that system reaches the extremities of the globe, the situation of historical change will be more and more manifestly subordinate to exogenous forces and the revolutionary narrative will become harder to formulate. South Africa, and its complex of identity politics, present in peculiarly vivid form the paradoxical dynamic of European discourses when replayed at a margin (Tin 1998). South Africa, that is to say, is simply a unique case in the evolution of a global system that encourages unique cases by making the formation of the revolutionary subject increasingly complex.

We should hesitate, therefore, before jumping to conclusions about the priority of a new 'post-national' and discursive arena in place of the collective agent embodied in the European revolutionary narrative over more than two centuries. We should bear in mind that, to date, the increase of visible constraints upon the nation-state as a place of collective autonomy seems not so much to have removed that element of the revolutionary narrative as to have encouraged more insistent, if less realistic, assertions of it. That is to say, in practice, 'the nation', 'the ordinary people' etc. have been more insistently evoked even as their real capacity to function in the active role assigned to them has seemed to diminish. And why should that surprise us, given that the revolutionary narrative has *always* managed to override the counter-pressures and constitute some large collective agent as the basis of society's reconstruction? Even a thinker acutely aware of how vulnerable are the nation-state's claims to spatio-temporal identity acknowledges that states are 'exceptionally dense political practices' which have not so much disappeared as become places where democratic struggles show 'an increasing ration of cant to achievement' (Walker 1993, pp. 153–8).

A fundamental cogency remains, then, wrapped in the national/revolutionary narrative and its republican/national idea. The need to constitute a collective agent by effort and ingenuity has been a feature of the modern world from its earliest days, in so far as modernity itself counterposed the idea of the human subject to a highly differentiated human life experience (Habermas 1987). All in all, therefore, we should be very wary about deciding that the nature of the collective agent in history has dramatically *changed* as the twentieth century draws to a close. We might anticipate, on the other hand, that this constructive effort will be *replicated* at levels other than the nation-state. Not that this either is *entirely* new. Nineteenth-century intellectuals' movements that revived/constructed 'national' languages shared common *trans*national ideals about national roots, even where they generated, according to circumstances, *intra*-national movements for local autonomy (Hroch 1994). In quite different, yet parallel ways, then, Habermas's advocacy of a 'republican heritage transcending the limits of the nation-state' (1996, p. 293) and Castells's tireless pursuit of signs of transnational political subjects in scattered, dissident fundamentalisms or new political movements, point in the same direction: a time of 'informed bewilderment' (Castells 1998, p. 358), when the constructive force of the revolutionary narrative migrates and takes root weakly alongside its natural home at the level of the national-state. Rather than announce the definitive demise of the revolutionary narrative and its picture of historical change, we must keep in mind a proper assessment of the creative tension that existed from the start between that idea and the forces of the global system. The history of that tension suggests that the *form* of the revolutionary narrative remains unchanged, but that the *ground* on which it may have to be formulated is more complex than ever before. But – to parody the words attributed to Voltaire when asked, on his deathbed, to renounce the Devil – now is no time to be making an enemy of the inherited, revolutionary idea of collective intrusions into history.

Appendix: Revolutions and the Understanding of History

My last chapter followed up the whole architecture of the book with a largely empirical consideration of how human beings' ideas about revolution and change might interact with the world in future. This is also a theoretical question: a question, in short, about the fundamental character of history. Theorizations about history have long been formed under the impact of revolutions. So the theoretical issue deserves review after all that has been said about revolutions in these pages. In this appendix, then, I take up this more theoretical issue, away from my main text. I return to the nature of history and consider how human actions can be embedded in it. I intend to approach this issue from two sides: on the one hand, considering the requirements of a shared 'perception' of history; and, on the other, analysing some of the literature from which to glean the nature of history from a *philosophical* point of view. The aim of my discussion is to explore what circumstances are required for human beings to constitute an idea of historical form.

Perceptions of history

Though I earlier discussed why specific modern human beings should be attached to a specific narrative structure in addressing historical change, up to now I have not asked the simple question why people have a notion of history in the first place.[1] The answer must, it appears, refer to how the human group may experience time that is longer than that of a generation. Of past societies, we know that they have devoted their mythology, their astronomical knowledge, their genealogical record-keeping or their chronicling to establishing the link between the present generation or moment and a founding person or moment from the past. To do that is to position the present and, very possibly, justify its practices or dispositions. More often than not, it gives a sense to the present moment as continuation, or repetition, of the same as before – though when met in its messianic or apocalyptic counterpart, that continuity is put under the shadow of a final *dis*continuation.

Though we may assume that the appeal of those cultures of *continuity* is still to be with us, there are two well-acknowledged reasons why we must suppose that the notion of 'history' developed within European and then modern culture will differ from them. First, the European discourse of history-writing begins with texts infused with the notion of human action *impinging on* time, be it the society's efforts to survive or the honour paid to the historic individual. Secondly, modern people's experience of time is far from guaranteeing continuity in the form which mythology etc. offered it. Change has to be taken for granted, anticipated or warded off. Indeed, these two features opposed to continuity are easy to place back-to-back, since the human-action side holds out the possibility of actively promoting change, or preventing it or whatever. The combination is surely what gives the particular distinctiveness to the concept of 'history', as against chronicling and the rest. The likelihood of change would leave any human group whose grasp of time was confined to the stabilist cultures severely exposed to surprise or worse.

The degree of need for 'history' to take a hold on change may be seen from the consequences of excluding change. Lutz Niethammer's 1992 critique of the roots of the concept of *'posthistoire'* in the melancholia of frustrated aspirations supplies an illustration out of twentieth-century European, especially German, culture. Niethammer traces the 'posthistorical' rejection of history to figures as diverse as Ernst Jünger, the Spenglerian novelist, Max Weber, the sociologist of bureaucratic modernization, and Antoine Cournot, the nineteenth-century theorist of the stabilization of history with the arrival of liberal bourgeois society. The discursive inclinations he finds vary – from the 'defence of self-esteem against the flood of unmediated arbitrariness' on offer in post-history's homogenization of teeming cultural invention (Niethammer 1992, p. 28); to compliant asceticism in the idea of value-free science (pp. 30–7); to unconsoled apprehension of the mechanisms of human desire (expressed in the cultural fall-out of the Freudian concept of 'death-wish' – pp. 40ff). But in their combination, Niethammer identifies a mood unable to reply to the century's 'exterminism' (p. 58): the inability to respond with any will to pursue alternatives when confronted with technical and organizational capacities to wreak immeasurable human destruction.

Subjective disappointment can here turn outward and assume a higher intellectual 'profile' because it knows that large parts of its generation have gone beyond it in their sensibility. Most of the authors in question no longer see any chance that a great personality or a vanguard can change human relationships; but that is the viewpoint from which they see these relationships. They draw up no new perspectives for action, but bemoan the irrelevance of the old. (p. 58)

Without committing ourselves to the complete picture of contemporary culture given by Niethammer, we can follow his account of the discursive temptation that comes with claims to return to a fixed 'end' of history. The capacity to do ill is sufficient argument for society to equip itself to do just that; the arrival of the close of history surrenders, by compliance or quietism, to uncontrollable external forces.

In spite of his heady optimism, it can be seen that this snare lies in wait for a Fukuyama's posthistoricism too. If it is wedded to the universal acceptance of the rules and outcomes of the worldwide market, it will find itself (like Cournot – P. Anderson 1992, pp. 279–375) defending some very unpalatable real consequences of the anonymous processes of the market. If, on the other hand, the arena of mutual recognition (*thymos*) is to stand apart from the outcomes of global market processes, it must surely re-establish a space for group values and group demands: history will then have resumed. This, it may be said, is an ungracious line to take: the proponent of a successful end finds himself on a par with the world-weary musers on the failures of the past. And so it is. Yet both have tried to get away from the historical perception as it is thrust upon human beings in the modern era – ceaseless movement that must either be confronted or bowed down to.

Agnes Heller has demonstrated an additional complication in the modern reasons for needing history: the modern sense of history has become self-referential, not to say inward-looking (Heller 1993, ch. 6). This is so because secularization/demystification has undermined reference to a transcendent will that could legitimize the direction seen, or sought, in historical change. Hegel's version of the Absolute in history adapted Christianity to be an expression of rational Spirit in European/Western history: this voiced the modern worship of modernity's *own* sphere without losing the moorings of some Truth beyond. But we are not as Hegel: in the twentieth century, secularization has gone further and we find that the historically necessary unfolding of Truth for itself 'has no explanatory power' (Heller 1993, p. 194). We are left only with modernity as it is given: the force of fact without the value of truth. Heller's point would hold good even with the revival of fundamentalist religious claims to historical meaning, since they either meet others as incommensurable myths or interpret each other as alternative cultures.

One recourse, considered by Heller, is to mine the meaningfulness of *all* pasts, as historicism has done. But this moves too easily to another fixity: the blindly conservative worship of the past as past. Looked at by a historian rather than a philosopher, this may be viewed as more a risk than a certainty. Thus Raphael Samuel (arguably the equivalent in the UK of Lutz Niethammer's German oral history from below), commenting on 'resurrectionism' in Britain in recent years (Samuel 1994, pp. 139–68), notes 'a new version of the national past' where labour is dignified and which 'is not only more democratic . . . but also more feminine and domestic'. But he also sees that stabilist historicism may be waiting in the wings: 'People's history may also unwittingly have prepared the way for more Conservative appropriations of the national past. Its preference for the "human" document . . . has the effect of domesticating the subject matter of history, and making politics seem irrelevant – so much outside noise' (p. 163). Even though people may need history to take a hold on change, then, it is no straightforward matter to formulate versions of the past that manage to do that. The past has to be convincing yet not final, dignified without being a ground for uncritical nostalgia. Epigrammatically, we might say that history has to be *in us* without our being *confined in it*. That is to say, it has to provide a point of reference for us to measure the changes that we might be subjected to, or hope for.

But, in the light of my argument in chapter 5, it makes little sense to speak of humans subject to, or impacting on, history-level changes without admitting the greater propensity of the larger group rather than the individual to do that. Thus the question of 'perceptions' of history becomes that of 'shared perceptions' of 'collective' history. History as an object of perception has to include one or more group identities that have existed over time. History as it extends into the present has, likewise, to include some surviving group identities, which have existed over a time that includes the present. The latter will, of course, cover possible identities for groups capable of existing in the present. And that in turn will include identity for some potential 'us'. Thus, this 'shared perceptions' of 'collective' history has both an objective and a subjective side.

Yet the collective identities in the perception of history have not to be fixed, incontrovertible or nostalgic historical identities, which would unavoidably be left behind by the world of change which is the lot of modern human beings, devoid of values to negotiate with the realities of those changes. We should now ask, then, what does any human group need in order to have a collective perception of history? I suggest the answer: temporal order (or time-frame), membership, ownership and power. The temporal order follows from the nature of historical narrative itself – which was considered at length in chapter 5: history formulates events in an orderly, comprehensible sequence across time. The other elements above – membership, ownership of outcomes and power over them – derive from the condition of being a *collective* perception. To exhibit identity, a group has to have a membership which is the possessor of what identifies it. And it has to have some degree of power to counter the strictures that appeared above where history was seen as something completely outside of living present humanity.

In spite of my deliberately approaching the topic of perceptions of history from an existential rather than an epistemological point of view, this would be an unreal discussion if epistemology were ignored altogether. So we do have to consider where perceptions of history's claims to *knowledge* stand. But to do so with an eye to difficulties in the path that perceptions of history have to tread: between too complete an explanation and one that loses contact with a reality that must be in part objective to it – i.e. between attempting to envelop either too much of reality or too little.

A seminal essay by Raymond Aron from 1951, 'Three Forms of Historical Intelligibility', exposes the tensions here. The essay speaks from within the post-war mix: hope for social progress; disappointment with communism turned to Stalinism; fear of worldwide totalitarian convergence; and the belief in a dauntingly comprehensive social science. Not without relief, one can imagine, Aron notes that the claims made by specifically *historical* determinism are in fact much less comprehensive than the Lamarckian equivalent, where *all* events from the start of time are inextricably interlinked (Aron 1985, pp. 40–1). A sober overview of the actual products of social and historical study suggests, conversely, how these forms of knowledge will inevitably leave spaces in the skein of determinism: comparative analysis shows differences between cases as well as regularities; a historical account pursued at any given explanatory level leaves space for events that are contingent (at least in terms of that level); epistemological seizure of the whole is not an available goal (pp. 42–50). Yet it is precisely in these spaces that the group may find room to embed itself into history. For that is where human agents can insinuate into the determinisms of history what Aron calls their 'works': that is, 'a creation whose end is inherent in the creation itself' (p. 38). *Given* that history is *not* simply deterministic, that is to say, humans may find space in it for their handiwork – and, we may add, their identity as agents. This is not to say, however, that the scope of human beings' real creations can be limited to what they themselves intend or expect: as Aron goes on to say, the 'meaning [of works] is never limited to the one consciously or unconsciously given by its creator'.

Aron draws a parallel (pp. 45–8) with the history of science, where 'truth' can be seen as both the constant motive and the plausible final outcome of the story. On his submission, other human 'works' are comparable to the long scientific pursuit of truth, though less consistent in pursuit of their singular final goal. Half a century later, when the scientific pursuit of knowledge appears a far less unified project, we can reassess this comparison: scientific research looks like other human 'works' in aiming at what it *hopes* will be a consistent, unified outcome. But this adjustment can only reinforce Aron's conclusion that the claims of a group to 'seize the whole at any moment . . . should not be condemned', even though the basis of such claims 'cannot be defined empirically' (p. 50).[2] In sum, Aron's essay opens up a space left for human collective actions to claim a place even where determinism is applied to history.

More broadly, we can conclude, the group's perception of history is bound to experience a tension between the need to explain the sequence of history and the possibility of human intervention. This cuts both ways: determinism has to be qualified; and, at the same time, human power and responsibility have to be limited. In any completed, persuasive account of a historical episode, we have to acknowledge sizeable human *in*capacity in order to understand the place of humans within that episode. There must be some power on the part of some at least of the participants to influence events; but to claim supervening power for *any* is to deny the historical specificity of both events and participants. That is among the lessons of Geoffrey Hawthorn's (1991) study of counterfactual possibilities in three, quite different, historical situations: claims that any particular group of actors in the situation might have altered the final outcome by different behaviour always run into limitations imposed by both the causative levers of the situation and the knowledge and interests of actors. Hawthorn invokes the concept of historical 'understanding' to capture the required mental attitude:

> even if [a political actor] could have reflected . . . it does not follow that there is a determinate answer to the question of what he would have been right to decide. What someone might have considered depends on his particular interests, his ability and his will. . . . Understanding in this more usual sense . . . turns on . . . locating the actual space of the possibles. But the possibilities for politics . . . can never in any strong sense be known. To understand more about any politics is thus to be less certain about it. (1991, p. 122)

These observations regarding history as a species of explanatory knowledge suggest how qualified the knowledge side of a perception of history has to be. If knowledge presumes to account for everything, the human group cannot own a part; yet if, conversely, the regularities of causation were absent, then there could be no grasping history and no levers to exercise power in historical developments. The human group's possession of history is both exercised through, and limited by, that which renders history explicable. Aron observed the consequent irony: where the meaning of human works is articulated in history, it 'is never limited to the one consciously or unconsciously given by its creator'. There has to be a sense of possession without the indulgent inspiration of an overweening human finalism.

But if not an overweening one, then what kind of a finalism? In other words, if human actors cannot rely on the realization of their intentions, on what basis should they enter the historical game in the first place? Walter Benjamin's 'Theses on the Philosophy of History', a piece of writing from one of the century's deepest moments of historic despair, confronts the question in earnest.[3] Accordingly, Benjamin does not rely at all on empirically grounded historical optimism. Rather, since 'our image of happiness is thoroughly coloured by the time to which the course of our own existence has assigned us,' argues Benjamin (1973, pp. 255–6), that image 'is indissolubly bound up with the image of redemption'. In other words, an attachment to a better historical *alternative* is inherent in humans' understanding of happiness. Thus, he postulates a (rather eccentric version of) historical materialism founded on a 'constructive principle' for which 'the historical subject [is] a monad . . . a Messianic cessation of happening' (pp. 264–5).

If we are to strip away the Judaeo-Christian eschatology of that claim (as surely we must), we return, even at that point of minimum expectations, to a notion of historical progress. Indeed, Benjamin in the 'Theses' had not been able to avoid the concept of progress. For that is the blanket term covering *any* optimistic finalism, regardless of conditions and regardless of *which* group's work is at issue. But Benjamin saw how unreliable a friend the concept of progress could be. The social forces he could have expected to resist the political direction of Germany had been lulled (with the encouragement of the SPD) precisely by regarding progress in 'technological development as the fall in the stream' (p. 260). That is a version of progress which comes with *no* human 'work' at all. The concept of progress has, that is to say, to include some call for active human possession of the future. Likewise, it has, as Dominique Lecourt has argued, to contain routes for the rational human being to embark on the pursuit of the future. Without offering an 'absolute guarantee', progress has to provide 'the analysis of whatever is virtual within the real world, so as to subject those possibilities to the test of the Common Good, which must itself be perpetually reformulated'[4] (Lecourt 1997, pp. 104 and 106). This qualified finalism is close to what Anthony Giddens, struck rather by the chronic *un*certainty of the modern condition than by the imposition of impersonal *certainties*, has proposed under the title of 'utopian realism' (Giddens 1990, pp. 154ff). We will return below to progress as an idea within collective action.

The coherence of philosophies of history

I argued a little while ago that perceptions of history require, among other things, 'ownership' of some outcomes by some actor or actors, and 'power' of actors over given historical conditions. The so-called 'philosophies of history' epitomize the received effort to lend more than merely contingent validity to the link made, in perceptions of history, between ownership of outcomes and the power of agents. Hence, debates around the philosophy of history are the route on which to proceed with the problem of how human actions can be embedded in history. We can examine the logic underpinning these 'philosophies' so as to reach a judgement of the prospective *logical* force behind power over, and ownership of, outcomes in narrative perceptions of history, revolutionary or otherwise.

Philosophies of history are characteristically historical narratives that envisage a future radically distinct from the past and the present, yet not unconnected with it. Being modern historical narratives, they have not merely been theistic or messianic prophecies, claiming that the future state was the realization of structure or a plan located beyond the scope of the ordinarily known world (Heller 1993). Rather, they connect the future to the present by recombining two explanatory strategies, causality and intention, which modern thinking began by distinguishing. Each can in principle be grounded in the world as it is known: some present causative mechanisms may be expected to produce certain future effects; and some present intentions may be expected to be realized.

Philosophies of history combine the projection of the future with *both* these narrative strategies. That is to say, they assert that widespread *causative mechanisms* can be linked to the intentions of an identifiable consciousness, making the outcome of the causative mechanism at the same time the realization of the *intention*. Both causative mechanisms and intentions have a defensible place in the narrative conceptualization of change in the modern world. Each explanatory strategy has its merits. Causative mechanisms are easier to identify in present entities and events; though their very presentness means that they are more obviously eradicable in the future states they may themselves produce. If realized, intentions are easily associated with identities which survive into the future; but they are both harder to establish with certainty and more susceptible to disappointment at the hands of a world of contingency and unintended consequences.

So the combination of causality and intention is viable where it can be shown that the intentions may be running closely with the grain of the causative mechanisms. Clearly, such identification is especially cogent where some group or groups can plausibly claim to have had their intentions realized in history. Yet, even in the absence of such favourable circumstances, logically speaking, it is perfectly conceivable that intentions could run with the grain of causality in this way. Indeed, in order for their intentions to be realized, all agents must have a notion of arriving at just such a match between their purposes and causative mechanisms which are objective to them (Callinicos 1987). None of that entails that causal mechanisms and intentions *must* be in line – indeed, that is rather rare in human experience. But it does entail that alignment is logically possible.

Philosophies of history exhibit a marked tendency to state this logically *conceivable* connection as a logically *necessary* one. The difficulty in formulating them coherently is therefore to avoid making that sought-after, but rather infrequent, mechanism–intention link into a logical necessity of some kind. Philosophies of history are subject to a natural temptation to reduce the contingent risk that threatens the realization of all intentions. There are two obvious ways to do that: by ascribing to a conscious agent (and hence its intentions) a transcendent existence beyond the reach of contingency; and by asserting that change will cease once the intentions of the given agent are realized (which is normally said to be in the near future). From Hegel to the late-twentieth-century liberal triumphalism of Fukuyama, philosophies of history have given in more or less to those temptations, strengthening their assertions at the cost of overreaching the logical foundations of what they assert.

Hence the affinity linking philosophies of history to both transcendental subjects and the supposed end of history. Hence, also, the link found by some between merely formulating a philosophy of history and a totalitarian hunger for power (Popper 1957, Russell 1938). Those affinities are also at the root of a counter-tendency which rejects altogether the intentionality in any philosophy of history. But to do that is to reject the degree of logical coherence that *could* be properly ascribed to the tendency (which I argued for above) to construct narratives of intentional change in the future. To reject the intention side of the philosophy of history means to replace it with a purely causative version of historical change. That has been a marked tendency among Marxists, who have found themselves particularly exposed to unwelcome association with metaphysical, and latterly very implausible, claims about the capacity of an abstract historical subject to produce definitive, historical change.

Of the many, Alex Callinicos (1994) exemplifies this tendency most explicitly in relation to the philosophy of history. Callinicos identifies (1994, ch. 1, esp. p. 41) a treatment of history which he calls 'theories of history', a type of historical overview which both 'surveys' known history and applies common causal explanatory principles across the breadth of it. He distinguishes such 'theories' of history from the 'philosophies of history' which deal – in his view, improperly – in the *meaning* of history as well as its *causal* explanation. He then goes on to argue (esp. ch. 4) that a theory of history in his preferred terms, using only common *causal* analyses, can envisage various future trajectories for change: avoiding Eurocentric blinkers, weighing up possibilities in relation to known historical studies, and attributing a progressive character to some as against others. To sustain this insistence on the causative understanding of history, Callinicos must reject, or severely limit, two rivals to it: more narrative form in general, and the realization of intentional action. To the former, he ascribes merely 'anthropological' value (sections 2.1 and 4.1), in that it accounts for the coherence and attraction of a certain *post-hoc* selection of events in the narrative, but contributes nothing to the logical force of any causal explanation which the narrative may contain. The realization of intentional action he rejects as 'objective teleology . . . collapsing the distinction between fact and value' (p. 146); that is to say, in them the realization of action is wrongly allowed both to account for events *causally* and to locate them in an 'immanent *goal* of the historical process' (my emphasis).

I have argued above (chapter 5) that there are circumstances where, to justify the validity of various causative mechanisms across periods of time that embrace radically different conditions, we have to frame them in a narrative of transitions. In granting narrative only a presentational role in history, Callinicos reverses this requirement for narrative as a device to sustain a viable overview of history. Callinicos's exclusion of intention from historical process, which is the implication of his exclusive emphasis on causative understanding, would be more blinkering still. His argument is comparable to the structural Marxist reaction to earlier 'humanist' philosophy of history: reverting from 'immanent' goals in the historical process to a wholesale rejection of goals *per se* as explanatory principles in history. Yet, prima facie there is no problem about including goals in historical explanation, just as they figure as explanations in other dimensions of human experience. Some human intentions are realized; and many that are not still play a part in the out-turn of events. The blanket rejection of intentions comes as a reaction to earlier philosophies of history which went further. They over-inflated the consciousness whose intentions may weigh upon events by making it immanent, so that its goals would not be susceptible to counter-intentions or contrary forces and, indeed, would constitute the *final* realization of an end-state for history.

At the end of a survey of what revolutions have meant over some centuries, and mean now at the end of the twentieth century, the claims for great revolutionary intentions have, I hope, been brought down to scale. Revolutionary agency has been persistently overstated by those who accepted that it was present, for reasons which my study has sought to show. But intentions for change on the part of human groups are not nothing. They have simply not had the singular history-reshaping capacity that has been attributed to them on the basis of a misconstrual of revolutions' role in historical change. With our view adjusted by a survey of centuries of experience of revolutions, it should now be possible to admit human intentions into our understanding of history without the fear that some supposedly transcendent group's intentions will take over everything.

To sustain his causative anti-narrativism, Callinicos adduces Donald Davidson's fusion of actions and causes. His aim is to show that intentional actions in history, being causes like any other, do not give rise to any anomaly in the skein of causal explanation he is advocating. Reflection on the Davidsonian approach indicates, conversely, that this line of thought can be read in the other direction.[5] To do as Davidson does, and admit the mental furniture of intentional action in full into the causal structure of the processes of change around human beings, not only widens but also *diversifies* the range of what is embraced by causality. Davidson's primary claim is that reasons are one kind of *cause* for actions (Davidson 1980, Essay 1). This underwrites a comprehensive strategy, to *include* many mental elements as causes of (or as components in) human action: unintentional consequences at later stages of action, for example; but also, at the earlier stages, 'pro attitudes' such as desires, wants for the future and value judgements (Essay 5). Thus 'free' human agents enter the causal scheme, but are distinguished within it by the 'desires and beliefs that rationalize' their actions (Essay 4). Once such elements are part of the structure of causation and of human actions, there is no difficulty about having teleological and non-teleological explanation together in the same system.

> Noting that non-teleological causal explanations do not display the element of justification provided by reasons, some philosophers have concluded that the concept of cause . . . cannot apply to the relation between reasons and actions. . . . But suppose we grant that reasons alone justify actions in the course of explaining them; it *does not follow that the explanation is not also . . . causal.* (Davidson 1980, p. 9 – my emphasis)

Embracing intentional action in causality, then, can perfectly well entitle us to pursue the opposite line to Callinicos: to *include* teleology rather than exclude it. What it does exclude, of course, is any teleology which excludes *rival* causalities. An extreme, immanent teleology, for which the intentions of a transcendent subject are certain to triumph over all other forces, would do precisely that. In rightly wanting to reject such overweening teleologies, Callinicos and structuralist-inclined theorists have needlessly ejected altogether the teleology of intentionality and aspirations. It follows that a qualified version of the old philosophies of history is conceivable and may, under the right conditions, be maintained with regard to historical change. Intentions of historical actors, including their 'pro attitudes' and aspirations for the future, *can* 'cause' historical outcomes, even including states of affairs more or less corresponding with those aspired to.[6]

In this sense, future states could be thought to be brought about by the conditions aimed for. The working-out of historical causalities can thus be teleological, and a historical overview is conceivable in which teleological causation through human aspirations holds a place. This is a substantially slimmed down teleology. It is slimmed down by four major qualifications to the earlier, more metaphysical philosophies of history. First, it does not suppose that the *later* state *produces* the earlier; instead the later state is the effect of, *inter alia*, the earlier *intention* to produce it. Secondly, it does not suppose that the realization of the intended state could be guaranteed against the intervention of rival intentions and other causal processes. Thirdly, it does not suppose that the future will be ontologically distinct from the present, an end-state with a special resistance to further change. Finally, it does not suppose that an exact correspondence is ever likely to be achieved, or demonstrated, between intentions and realized outcomes. What stands in the way of achievement is the multiple contingency weighing upon human life, intentional action included: what prevents easy confirmation of the correspondence is the shifting and unfixable character of intentions in any given consciousness. A teleological narrative of history is, then, never incontrovertible.

Group action in history

Having arrived at the possibility of a qualified finalism about intentions in the perceptions of history, and given the earlier arguments of the priorities of groups, we can now move back to the question of how group intentions may be aligned with mechanisms objective to them. I earlier argued that such alignment had to be a logically conceivable, but not a logically necessary link. This is the question of how a group's 'works' (in Aron's terms) may be inserted into history – or of how the actions and intentions of a group may relate to structures objective to them.

The terms of this issue were tirelessly pursued in Jean-Paul Sartre's analyses of the meaning of social structure, historical change and human action – found primarily in the two volumes of the *Critique of Dialectical Reason*. Despite the incompleteness of the texts – and the difficulties of comprehension – Sartre is a good place to find guidance. He approached the problem of human beings' place in relation to structures from a peculiarly demanding position as regards both the perverse outcomes of group action in history and humans' existential relationship to all that lies outside their freedom to determine themselves. For he had embraced Marxism as *the* theory of the modern world at a time when Marxism's most forcefully canvassed outcome, the Soviet system, epitomized precisely the twentieth-century *suppression* of human creativity by the structures of industrialized society. So Sartre had to confront, at its most dramatic, the problem of collective human action versus objective forces. The concept of 'totalization-of-envelopment', the running theme of the second volume of the *Critique* (1991), is intended to account dialectically for this contradiction between the group, with its particular identity and will, and the objective world in which any action takes place. Totalization-of-envelopment highlights the way that shared human activity is articulated in the objective world so as to take possession of that which is objective, or 'exterior' (in Sartre's terminology), to the group, making it an expression of the group's own autonomy (or, in Sartre's terminology, 'interiorizing' it as the group's own).

The *Critique* overall confronts analytically the twentieth century's most prominent, and sharpest, lesson on the ambivalence of revolutionary group action in history. Sartre reflects at length on how active groups are formed and how the outcomes of their action may then reverse intentions to become a manifestation of the objective system *against* human freedom. What he refers to as the 'group-in-fusion' emerged from the first volume as the epitome of active collective identity finding itself in human action. The group-in-fusion is united by resistance, implying organization at least in that it shares a minimum common project to *impose* some change in the given circumstances. The group's activity, in imposing on what is given, manifests power over objective conditions and produces effects which the group must consider in some sense as 'its own'. In other words, the group-in-fusion exhibits the 'power' and 'ownership' I introduced earlier in the collective perception of history. This combination of common aim and effect on the given makes Sartre's discussion an analysis of *praxis*.[7]

Under the circumstances of the day, Sartre's discussion of the question 'Are Social Struggles Intelligible?' takes the form of 'A Historical Study of Soviet Society' (1991, pp. 118–83). The conclusion is a highly ambivalent view of the perverse, not to say cruel, outcomes of 1917. '[I]n a society whose sovereign is a dictator [such as the Soviet Union],' Sartre concludes, internal dissension within the group reinforces an *imposed* unification. But he feels unable to see this effect as confined to societies with dictatorial political systems. Rather, disunity within the group, and reaction against it, are the very dynamics of group formation and action: 'rifts, conflicts and disharmonies – far from breaking the unit of praxis-process – are at once the consequences of that unification and the means it chooses in order to tighten up still further' (p. 183). We are, it seems, confronted in the Soviet Union with an extreme case of how groups form up, generate division and (re-)impose unity: 'The historian *must be able* to comprehend . . . – in the very unity of the sovereign praxis with the process that constantly overflows it and that it constantly reintegrates into itself – the vast histori-cal upheaval which . . . has produced Soviet society as we see it' (p. 183).

The fuller exposition of 'totalization-of-envelopment' (pp. 281–336) shows why this is so. The group's action in coming together around an aspiration to change things constitutes an expression of power over the objective world which will *re*constitute the group itself. The group's very identity as an agent in a partly objective world imposes recognition of, and hence some accommodation to, the product of what *it itself* intentionally produces. That is 'action paying its own expenses' as Sartre incisively puts it (p. 283). This is an account of something I discussed in chapter 5: the way in which humans recognize their own intentions in the *un*intentional outcomes of their own actions.[8] For both 'pure', unqualified intention and the contingent structures in which it must be exercised belong to the field of intentional action:

> Like the Devil according to the Church Fathers, the exteriority of praxis is parasitic, borrowing its efficacy and its being . . . from interiority. . . . Praxis, as it approaches its goal, in practice constitutes *an outside* for itself and, precisely in this, reveals itself as human praxis; for only human society can establish synthetic relation of such a kind. . . . Praxis-process thus appears as a human process, without ceasing to be human *action*. (p.283 – my emphasis)

In short, the unity of the group may be formed in action but cannot, and should not, be stabilized around a predetermined result of action. That view is a far cry from the overweening finalism considered, and criticized, earlier: as soon as intentional results are recognized as 'achieved', conflict with them must ensue. In fact, Sartre feels happy to admit *division* also at every level of the active group: 'the living rift constituted by conflict seems the insurmountable limit of the totalizing effort' (p. 50). Sartre recommends us to understand human intentional action as an open web of meaning: 'signification overwhelmed by counter-finalities [which] loses its logical rigour' (p. 291).

> Will it be said that there are *several meanings* of the synchronic totalization rather than *just one*? That is as you like. Or, if you prefer, there are indeed *several* meanings – very different from each other, too – for the various levels and sectors; but in each . . . the unity of the total meaning is to be found as its foundation and its product. (p. 297)

What emerges from Sartre's discussion, then, is that a group united in historical action is not – indeed, philosophically speaking *ought* not to be – some seamless, stable entity contemplating its own success as it arrives at its final goal. Rather, the identity and the intentionality of the group are – like those of individual human beings – marked by internal hesitation and a contestation with what has already been put into practice. Sartre's 'totalization-of-envelopment' is ever incomplete: human projects write their meaning into the objective world, but never envelop the totality of history itself.[9]

This has consequences, of course, for the meaning of 'progress' and 'history' as ideas guiding action in history. In order to undertake action, it is necessary to have some expectation of improvement; that is, 'progress'. Yet any prediction would have to be reformulated in the context of actual outcomes (Sartre 1991, p. 408). So their validity as predictions is not enough to explain their role.[10] Rather, the prediction of progress *shapes* action: 'it is *lived* in interiority, a practical organization of totalization. It is an *act*' (p. 402). And, just as progress is not a prediction, so history does not have to be one story with one ending. Sartre's surviving notes[11] promise only disappointment for expectations of final ends to history.

> Totalization-in-envelopment . . . does not exist in transcendence.
> A. For the transcendent totality of all History, who will do it? . . .
> B. For a partial transcendent totalization. Interiority does not resemble exteriority. (p. 447)

These philosophical discussions certainly do not indicate that 'works' by the social group cannot intrude into given history. The human group's intentionality can perfectly well be seen to operate alongside – indeed in relation to, or even *through* – the patterns of causality. Ideas of group intentions and their effects make perfectly good sense in themselves. But they have not to be thought of in overweening terms: capable of suppressing differences at all levels or of achieving final, ineluctable goals. Sartre's somewhat tragic reflection on how human action meets human society does point the way to an analysis of the formation of active groups in *any* society, therefore: in terms of the *confrontation* between the given, imposed social system and that which clashes with it.

It is no accident that that vision of human groups confronting the impositions of the given structure has produced an equivalent in sociological analysis: Alain Touraine's 'actionalist' sociology, which (whilst distancing itself explicitly from Sartre's tendency to decompose society into individual experiences – Touraine 1965, pp. 52–3) nonetheless adopts the strategy of examining particular contexts as, at one and the same time, *structures* in which human historical action takes place and arenas for *the subject* (individual, or collective) to define itself. From a phenomenological vision of the human subject's perpetual struggle to take back control of the social world, can be generated, that is to say, a mode of analysis which attends to the conflict between social wholes and human desire for change. The above argument tends to show that the narrative perception of history which the revolutionary experience bequeathed to us (including historical progress and collective human agency in historical progress) remains feasible and logically coherent – the more so if its claims are carefully qualified.

Notes

Introduction: Meanings of Revolution in Time and Place

1 Thus, in Goran Therborn's classification of 'routes to and through modernity' (1995, pp. 5ff), only Europe modernizes as a result of internal forces and endogenous processes. The routes of the extra-European world lie through 'migrations'.

2 Though Dunn himself amended the received field by including, for largely intuitive reasons, Mexico and Turkey. Kumar was likewise sensitive to developments which suggested that, since the historical core of revolutions as a group had moved out of the West, one had to look for the possibility of revolutions not of 'the classic type' (Kumar 1976).

3 One commentator concerned to delineate revolutions for study distinguishes four characteristics of revolution: a process, a change of power, a programme, and *a myth* (Calvert 1996, p. 3). Each of these exists on a different level of analysis, interfering with the others.

4 That point is, essentially, the Tilly thesis, though the associated classification is my own.

Chapter 1   Revolutions in Past History

1 This political form is also the seat of what Hans Baron (1955) and Quentin Skinner (1978) and his followers have studied as civic humanist republicanism.

2 As G. Parker (1985, p. 286) puts it, at the time, 'The Dutch practice of trading openly in wartime, even allowing money for the army of Flanders (the very troops that were trying to attack them!) to be sent from Spain through the banks of Amsterdam, baffled almost everyone.'

3 From the early nineteenth century, peasant rebellion chipped away at imperial authority in the mountains above the Yellow River basin: from the Triads, to the 'Taipeng' rebellion of the 1840s, to the Nien in the 1850s, to the Boxer rebellion at the turn of the twentieth century. Peasant disturbances were still

going on in Hunan and Wuchang when the Manchu dynasty finally abdicated in favour of a republic in 1911.

4   E.g. Thompson (1971) defines these same values in the eighteenth century; Calhoun (1982) finds in their survival in artisan society his explanation for the riots of the 1820s. Tilly (1995, Tilly et al. 1975) locates the demise of such values in the national consciousness developed during the nineteenth century. Wolf (1969) returns with a concept of 'twentieth-century' peasant wars.

5   I.e. that all persons who were not in a state of sin could, regardless of status, partake of the communion in both 'kinds', bread and wine.

6   As the current Spanish governor observed, 'the Spanish mutinies would be enough to make us loathed' (quoted G. Parker 1985, p. 172).

7   'Those whom we call Puritans and many other strongly committed Protestants were so obsessed by fear of an international papist conspiracy . . . that their otherwise instinctively moderate and intellectually conservative political preferences were compelled into an altogether more radical direction' (Aylmer 1987, pp. 30–1). The fear of Catholic oppression held its force even though, as Steinberg (1966, pp. 91ff) demonstrated, it was partly an invention of Protestant, Swedish power during the Thirty Years War.

8   Lucas (1973) gives a classic account for the French Revolution in terms of the whittling away of the *ancien régime* status structure.

9   This line of analysis discounts the facts that the British state itself: (i) was far less than absolutist, as a result of the impact of the earlier Revolution, which I have also classed on the margin as a Reformation revolt; and (ii) underwent a late-eighteenth-century restructuring of its military and popular basis, which *did* take place as an effect of revolutions, but at a distance: *both* the American *and* the French Revolutions (Colley 1996, Tilly 1995). This restructuring was necessitated, of course, by the felt need to *fight* those post-revolutionary regimes.

10 The very term suggests the hold of the idea that a French-style revolution is the probable direction of historical change, and its obverse a mere 'reaction' against it.

11 Galili (1992) describes how industrialists in 1917 harboured progressive hopes but, uncertain of their ground and disappointed by the workers' reaction, turned rapidly away from the revolution.

12 Koekner and Rosenberg (1992), for example, describe how liberal and Bolshevik press vied over the interpretation of strikes whilst workers themselves were doubtful about their legitimacy.

13 South Africa is a rather peculiar case of this: its forced *re*-ruralization under apartheid tended to encourage the revival of 'peasant' resistance (Mbeki 1964).

14 This gave rise to a literature of 'Eastern' revolutions, notably Johnson (1964 and 1966) and Huntington (1968).

15 By 1989, 48 per cent of South Africa's white population believed it sensible to seek compromise with the promoters of sanctions (Schutz and Slater 1990, p. 206).

Chapter 2   Why Revolutions Have Occurred

1   Baechler's debt to Durkheim is evident in this approach to analysis.

2   See Kimmel (1990, ch. 6).

3 Rule (1989, chs. 3 and 5) summarizes the developments of this approach up to the time (the 1970s) when, in his view, it went out of fashion.

4 See *Wirtschaft und Gesellschaft*, part III, ch. 6, pp. 650–78, translated in Gerth and Mills (1991, pp. 196–244).

5 Russian Social Revolutionaries made 'a pragmatic defence of the all-powerful state: a worrying foretaste of the *centralist-bureaucratic* path which Russia could all too easily take, under the influence of radical theoreticians' (Weber, 1995, p.89).

6 Jack Lively captures de Tocqueville's posture nicely: 'A reluctant democrat perhaps, certainly not a republican in the French style, he could nevertheless have stated as his view what was said at a different time in different circumstances – "the only cure for the ills of democracy is more democracy" ' (Lively 1965, p. 120).

7 Chateaubriand's *Essai historique, politique et morale sur les révolutions anciennes et modernes* (1799) stands as a striking counter-example.

8 Written in 1794, but not widely known until decades later. Since it was written in prison, it is not perhaps surprising that Condorcet's progressive version of history finds little place for an active human role.

9 Edward Said (1978, 1993) is the point of reference for analysis of the way that Europeans projected this historical experience of their own on to the globe as a whole.

10 More than the logical character of Moore's account, it is the conservative role he assigns to the peasantry which still provokes dispute (Paige 1990).

11 As Michael Kimmel commented at the time of publication: 'even if Skocpol is correct about the relationships between structural conditions and revolutionary outcomes, her analysis is incomplete. She ignores the mediating factors – human consciousness and action – that are always part of the story and sometimes crucial to it' (review in *American Journal of Sociology*, vol. 86, no. 5, 1981, p. 1153). The debate between William Sewell and Skocpol herself (considered in chapter 6) turns on that question.

12 Classically, Lefebvre (1962) and Soboul (1974), but also, more interestingly, Mazauric (1984).

13 As Tilly (1978, p. 177) puts it, 'most collective violence . . . grows out of actions that are not inherently violent'.

14 Rod Aya (1990) criticizes Tilly for an ontological preference for structures and relationships over individuals (pp. 114–22). He accordingly prefers to stress the 'tactical power' of the oppressed, a concept adopted from Eric Wolf (pp. 106–13).

15 See D. Smith (1991) for a historical sociology of the responses to the political conjuncture in historical sociology from Parsons to Giddens.

Chapter 3   The Trend in Revolutions

1 Pieterse (1990, ch. 2). Wallerstein (1991) gives a quite different picture of the creative possibilities offered by World System Theory. Another common criticism of Wallerstein's account, which need not detract from its usefulness in the present argument, is that it lacks an understanding of how differently the various versions of capitalist accumulation may transfer surplus wealth

around the system. To take a recent example, Peter Hugill has applied what is basically a technological determinist framework (in which the long-term evolution of the technology of transport modulates costs and savings) to undermine the Wallerstein account of how different geographical zones come to be favoured one after another (Hugill 1993, esp. pp. 38–41). Whilst Hugill's views alter the dynamics, and possibly the justice, of the global patterns of accumulation of wealth, they do not affect the core of my present argument: the need of the different centres to reach out in turn towards global expansion. See also Rosecrance (1986).

2 Trade helped the rebels both in attack and in defence: as Braudel remarks (1984, p. 208), the Spanish knew perfectly well that to put a stop to the commerce that was sustaining the rebel effort would ruin *their own* exchequer as well.

3 Others could have been used, since they also can produce insights into the state–society relationship. Manicas (1989), for example, demonstrates a marked interrelationship between war-making and the possibility of democratic political forms.

4 I take the difference between ideological and political to be that the latter works on the articulated interests of different groups to elicit acquiescence or support. Hence calculations of interest are primary. Ideological power works through beliefs – though, of course, beliefs do temper calculations of self-interest.

5 Spence (1996, chs. 19–20) relates the isolation of Hong's final years, when on one occasion he proposed that his people should eat grass sweetened by the falling dew, which would come as manna from heaven. By this period of the Taipeng 'kingdom', Hong Xiuquan was also rejecting the modernizing proposals that his brother, Hong Rengan, brought from his observations of life in the British colony at Hong Kong.

6 Conversely, one could point out that these economic and financial pressures *were* well developed and felt in the Habsburgs' northern European territories, the Netherlands and North Germany. But these pressures do not impinge upon the centre of the system, all the same, since Habsburg-Spanish authority had the option of ceding those areas and sustaining itself in its old form within the Iberian Peninsula and the Americas.

7 D. D. Aldridge (1993) demonstrates the scope for individual choice followed by *mis*understood action in this case. He convincingly argues that the King was not intending to 'escape' at all; rather, Louis's position in the politics of the revolution was being undermined by the activities of his self-proclaimed allies to the north of the country and he wished to bring them to heel. Unfortunately, his ignominious return lent credence to the suspicions of his political adversaries, who easily persuaded others that the 'disloyal' King had been trying to 'escape' and take the head of the enemies of the republic.

8 As Arghiri Emmanuel (1973) pointed out, a version of external dependency in which formal colonization is only a sub-category has to be adopted in order to see the full range of modern imperialism.

9 I postpone to chapter 7 a fuller consideration of both this and the other most recent Latin American revolutionary confrontations: Nicaragua.

10 As Jorge Castañeda (1993, p. 74) puts it: 'in the eyes of many Latin Americans and Cubans, at the outset the island revolution represented a major break

with the Soviet model. It was freer, more democratic, disorderly, tropical, and spontaneous, as well as being intellectually more diverse and politically more liberal.' But he then adds: 'With time, the resemblance between the models would grow, and Cuba come to look much more like the Soviet Union.' The resemblance now extends to the major difficulty of ensuring *any* transfer of power from a single, charismatic leader into the hands of lesser figures schooled in the conformism of bureaucratic party politics.

11 Jorge Dominguez identifies thirty-nine third states that have requested Cuban civilian assistance missions (Bethell 1993, p. 144).

12 'The acceptance of the principle of universal intervention by one power is the end of independence and sovereignty' stated Castro in December 1989. 'If events continue in their present course, . . . the bipolar world we knew will inevitably be transformed into a unipolar world under American hegemony.' ('Discorso ante les restos de los caídas en Angola', 7/12/89, reported in *Proceso*, no. 684, 11/12/89, p. 39; quoted in Castañeda 1993, p. 243.)

13 The 'first guerrilla organization to successfully recruit its social base amongst the urban disenfranchised and destitute' (Castañeda 1993, p. 125). Castañeda attributes this fusion of rural and city resistance to the migration into the towns of Andean, Indian society, with its network structure. The situation bears comparison with the obstinate survival of ETA in the cities of the Basque Country.

Chapter 4   Revolutions and Modernity at the End of the Twentieth Century

1 'The revolutions and ideologies likely to be most important in the second half of the twentieth century are those of the underdeveloped countries. . . . [T]he new revolutions, having altered the terms on which the senior revolutionary ideologies can continue to be influential, may be regarded as the critical new factor in the problems of revolution and ideology of the next several decades' (Macpherson 1966, p. 139). Or see Wertheim (1974), for whom worldwide imperialism must of itself generate contestation by the colonized, who are driven by the very nature of the human condition to self-assertion and 'emancipation'.

2 For example, Ziauddin Sardar, from the Hajj Research Centre of Jeddah University, published such a progressivist defence of Islam in 1979, the very year of Iran's revolution. He advocated an updated version of Muslim society as described in Medina by the *Qu'ran*, which would preserve people's organic awareness of themselves, their family, their community, the *Ummah* (muslim law) and humanity as a whole. At the same time, he sought to bring Islam closer to modern Western values, by showing that the 'principle of social justice in Islam' is based on freedom of conscience, equality of all men, and 'permanent mutual responsibility of society and individuals' (Sardar 1979, p. 222).

3 See chapter 7 for further discussion of the 'progressive' claims of fundamentalisms in general.

4 This is the most obvious reason why a simple restatement of the Marxist scheme of history after the collapse of the Soviet Bloc, in the manner of

McCarney (1991), seems so unsatisfactory.

5   Channon (1992) shows how real was the prospect of a peasant order in 1917.
6   'Can we write a history of the Russian Revolution?', in Hobsbawm (1997). Frankel et al. (1992) offers a contrary assessment of the April 1917 revolution: with different timing and leadership, it might have been sustained by a wide democratic movement (in its introduction – pp. 3–13).
7   'It was a matter of holding out, and at the same time converting socialism *into a reality*' (Serge 1992, p. 374). Serge also quotes Lenin in 1918: 'The proletariat of Russia must bend its every effort to aid the German workers . . . who are called on to wage a most stubborn struggle against their own and British imperialism' (p. 320).
8   Who were just as capable of putting up resistance as the peasantry (Aves 1996, Service 1992).
9   An internal US memorandum of 1955, for example, argued that 'the USSR will, by 1975, have overtaken Western Europe's aggregate GNP' and concluded that this would encourage Third World countries to adopt the Soviet model (quoted by Stirk 1997, p. 136).
10 From her base in the Novosobirsk Institute of Economics, Zaslavskaya had been drawing unpalatable conclusions about the Soviet rural economy since the early 1970s. She rose to the National Academy of Sciences in 1981 and chaired a controversial report on social mechanisms of economic development in the early 1980s, thus attracting the eye of Gorbachev. She was elected, as an unofficial candidate, to the Congress of Soviet Deputies in 1989.
11 Quoted from the playwright Alexander Gelman (Zaslavskaya 1990, p. 129).
12 Romania appears to be the exception; but actually it again proves the rule. The Romanian state's insistence on repaying accumulated debts required such austerity and oppression as to provoke its own revolution. And now that Romania is 'reformed', it finds its difficulties compounded because it commands no interest on the part of Western financial institutions, which alone have the resources to fund industrial reconstruction (East and Pontin 1997, p. 166). In short, the Romanians struggled harder than most against the power of late twentieth-century international financial capital, but still lost.
13 In the summer of 1998, the government of the Russian Federation successfully negotiated an emergency loan of $17 billion, as US domestic opposition was silenced from fear of the knock-on effects of any Russian collapse (Kettle 1998).
14 The army is currently reckoned to own approximately 15,000 businesses with $10 billion of turnover, including an airline and industrial and leisure companies (Pomfret 1998).

Chapter 5   Revolutions and Historical Change: the 'Revolutionary Narrative'

1   The items I list here in the general 'revolutionary narrative' are comparable to, but distinct from, the 'criteria of the concept of revolution' that Reinhart Koselleck extrapolates from the French Revolution: revolution as 'the collective singular'; the acceleration of time; revolution as a 'coefficient of

movement' (i.e. a vector indicating historical direction in itself); the prospects of the future themselves continually altering; etc. (Koselleck 1985, pp. 39–54).

2   It would be fair to say that the earlier, and still more classic, investigation of how the human being can face the passage of time is the work of Heidegger. I use Ricoeur's work, however, because Heidegger addresses the question existentially, rather than with reference to collective action or culture and social existence. Their relationship is further pointed up in note 4 below.

3   This for Ricoeur is the primary ethical impulse. It has been the longest-standing theme of Ricoeur's work, from at least as early as his *Fallible Man* (Chicago: Henry Regnery 1965 – French original published 1960) to his *Oneself as Another* (Chicago: University of Chicago Press, 1994 – French original 1990).

4   Vol. 3, pp. 255–7. Within the intra-subjective context of the human group, Ricoeur's historical narrative – whether lived or retold – explicitly and deliberately addresses each of the powers identified in the existential phenomenology of Being according to Heidegger: a horizon of expectation, the inertia of the past, and the force of the present are all interwoven within the historical narrative. The appendix will take further the question of the relationship between consciousness and the totality of history.

5   See Meschonnic (1988), who also quotes approvingly (p. 21) Aragon's aphorism conveying the absurdity of modernity's address towards the future: 'Modernity is a function of time which expresses the present feeling about certain things whose essential newness does not belong to them, but whose efficacity derives from the recent discovery of what they express' (my translation).

6   The group self-consciously devoted to creating new norms of life in the demise of the old ones can, of course, be found in other revolutionary situations. For the case, for example, of Russia see Stites (1989).

7   Callinicos pursues this general line of thought into a critique of methodological individualism (see 1987, pp. 76–91).

8   I have in mind the debate which ranges from Lukàcs's view of the proletariat in history, to the anti-humanist discussion post-Althusser (where classes may be seen as bearers of assets with an exchange value – e.g. Wright 1997), and the English debates on the relationship between class identity and class-specific attitudes (e.g. Giddens 1973, Giddens and Held 1982). This ambivalence can be seen impinging on the interpretation of revolutionary action and historical change where the specificity of groups' attitudes becomes an issue (e.g. Mann 1995). Among historians, the motivations and self-consciousness of French revolutionary *sans-culottes* has been extensively disputed (Rose 1983). Likewise, E. P. Thompson's account of the specificity of English working-class culture has provoked much dispute (Bush 1992, Calhoun 1982).

9   The logical awkwardness of this solution is explored in Oderberg (1993).

10 Even the highly parsimonious account of individual humans' decisions and their interactions that is given by Jon Elster (1989) appears to be compatible with the idea that expectations of behaviour are assigned to groups in order for individuals' rational calculation to be kept going.

11 Olson's (1965) detailed analysis stresses precisely that kind of development within group resistance: the tendency to reward, or impose, disciplined

participation in order to reduce the problem of free riders – see pp. 105–6.

12   Boudon (1986) develops a comparable intellectual strategy by permitting a variety of uses for 'theories of social change', which do not rely on their strict correspondence with a future reality.

13   Chapter 4 is the first chapter of her Part II: 'Outcomes of Social Revolutions in France, Russia and China'.

14   Hence, a theorist such as John Urry (1973) makes it a starting principle that whatever motivates adherence to revolutionary action, it cannot be expectations of the future.

15   Aya (1990, pp. 67–75) observes that revolutionaries could of course be pursuing power as a *precondition* of realizing any other intentions whatsoever.

16   Unless, that is, Skocpol is referring to the 'real' intentions of the actors. But this position, which runs very much against the spirit of her work, would be, if anything, harder to defend.

17   This emphasis on intention as description and explanation of action is classically explored in Anscombe (1957), which develops the view that intention is the special quality of action one or more descriptions of which makes it comprehensible. Working with this point of view, Anscombe relates intention to future states only in very limited terms: actions arising from intentions as to the future are merely part of a process which produces a future state, without, that is, any especially favoured, determining role in the shape the future takes (see, in particular, sections 18–22).

Chapter 6   The Revolutionary Narrative in History

1   For commentary on the spread and influence of Babeuf's ideology through France in the nineteenth century, see Maillard et al. (1994).

2   As Wandycz (1992, pp. 149–54) observes, after partition Polish nationalists had no political allies, only the sympathy of Western publics, which encouraged a romantic 'all or nothing attitude'. One construction was Polish Christian Messianism, which made 'Poland Christ amongst nations'. Compare also the romantic literary turn of the émigré community (notably Adam Mickiewicz) in exile in Odessa, discussed in Ascherson (1995), pp. 145ff.

3   Quoted, from pp. 486, 489 and 497 of *The Russian People and Socialism*, in Lichtheim (1970), pp. 114–15.

4   Sewell's own thinking about 'social narratives' and how to interpret them has moved on since his drawn match with Skocpol. Introducing a recent group of articles about social narratives, he expressed the hope that 'narratological techniques to take apart a text and show how it works to create specific identities and motivations and to occlude others . . . [will] show that specific text-reading strategies illuminate the meanings and dynamics of social movements and social processes' (Sewell 1992, p. 487).

5   Pataud and Pouget (1990) gives the flavour of this later, turn-of-the-century version.

6   'La Francia nesesitaba une regeneración, La España no nesesitaba más que una renovación', *Obras en prosa*, ed. Fernando Díaz Plaja, Madrid: Alianza Editorial, 1985, p. 163, quoted on p. 31 of D. Jiménez, 'Le Discours

révolutionnaire: analyse d'un exemple espagnol, *A la nación española'*, in Domergue and Lamoine (1991), pp. 24–33.

7 Jiménez, ibid.

8 S. Scandellari, 'La "tesi de complotto" nelle *Causas de la Revolución de Francia en el año 1789* de Lorenzo Hervás y Panduro', in Domergue and Lamoine (1991), pp. 35–48. This is a familiar theme, too, in the black works of Goya, court painter and constitutionalist (see Paulson (1983) or L. Domergue, 'La critique sociale: imagerie révolutionnaire et vision goyesque', in Domergue and Lamoine (1991), pp. 119–30).

9 Calvo de Rozaz, quoted in Lovett (1965), vol. 2, p. 424.

10 Though it may be argued that the 1790s saw the appearance of other, specific types of demand from rural society (Ricuperati 1989).

11 G. Genovesi, 'Illuminismo e Rivoluzione nel pensiero educativo del Risorgimento: il case della *Antologia* di Gian Pietro Vieusseux', in Domergue and Lamoine (1991), pp. 175–98.

12 Schama (1977, p. 68) points out how 'the parochialism of Dutch political preoccupations' meant that though many Enlightenment classics were printed there, they raised almost no interest amongst the Netherlanders themselves.

13 To which Schama (1977) as a whole sought to restore it.

14 Quoted in Clive Brooks, 'John Reeves and his Correspondents: a Contribution to the Study of British Loyalism 1792–1793', in Domergue and Lamoine (1991), pp. 49–76.

15 *The Analytical Review of History and Literature, Domestic and Foreign*, vol. 20, 1794, p. 300, quoted in Rigby (1989), p. 100. Wollstonecraft casts the same supercilious view over other Europeans in her most successful work, *Letters Written during a Short Residence in Sweden, Norway and Denmark* (London, 1796).

16 Marianne Elliott, 'Ireland and the French Revolution', in Dickinson (1989), p. 100.

17 'That is what so quickly gives the Russian revolution of 1917 – February and October mixed together – a universal character, though not its true character.... [T]hat the Russian people demanded peace, that is how it pointed to the way out of the tragic impasse that the governments of the West were locked into, and determined to stay in' (Furet 1995, p. 77 – 'De là vient que ce qui donne si vite à la révolution russe de 1917 – Février et Octobre mêlés – un caractère universel soit moins son caractère propre.... [Q]ue le peuple russe exige la paix, voilà par où il indique une sortie de l'impasse tragique dans laquelle les gouvernements de l'Ouest se sont laissés enfermer et s'obstinent.').

18 I take Iberian experience to be proof of this in spite of itself: for revolutionary successes are quickly neutralized by dominant forces from Europe itself. Spain's 'revolutionary' forces in the 1930s were quickly snuffed out by a combination of domestic counter-violence, counter-revolutionary assistance from other parts of Europe, the connivance of the leading European powers, and Soviet strategic interests. The Portuguese revolution of the 1970s was likewise disciplined from above, as the international community assimilated the new republic through NATO, the European Economic Community (Magone 1997, pp. 161–4 and *passim*) and the community of liberal-democratic states in general.

19 Furet's radical reformulation of French revolutionary history (Furet 1981 etc.)
    consisted in attending to the dynamics of the *political* processes which went
    dramatically wrong in the Revolution. For him, the failure of Marxist histori-
    cal thinking was thus its incapacity to analyse 'the extraordinary diversity of
    forms of state manifested by the French Revolution' (Furet 1988, p. 142).
20 In a very British-sounding response to this, Khilnani puts it down to repub-
    lican, 'Jacobin' power in France always having been fundamentally at odds
    with true democratic processes of civil society: 'Beneath the veneer of a
    Republican political regime, the idea and practices of representative demo-
    cracy in modern France were under continuous threat from the authoritarian-
    ism of both Left and Right' (1993, p. 135).
21 Others at the time (such as Hobsbawm 1970) were critical of such Western
    interpretations of peasant revolutionary activity.
22 One of Debray's most personal writings (1976) is the tellingly titled diary
    from the three years he spent in a Bolivian jail after he had followed Che
    Guevara's guerrilla campaign: *Journal of a petit bourgeois caught between
    four walls and two factions.* See N. Parker (1978).
23 The remarks about Indians and 'miraculous punches in the teeth' refer to
    Debray's time in Bolivia and in a Bolivian jail, where he learnt a humility
    about his revolutionary ideas that he could hardly have acquired back in Paris.
24 A more sceptical view of either the prospects or the blessings of nationalism
    was expressed by the older generation of commentators. See Hobsbawm
    (1992) or Gellner (1991).

Chapter 7   The Revolutionary Narrative at the End of the Twentieth Century

1 It should be noted that there were American voices raised against overconfident triumphalism about the liberal future. Ackerman (1992, p. 36)
   spoke for another strand of more interventionist, New Deal liberalism when
   he warned: 'The challenge here is to break the bubble of self-congratulation
   generated in 1989 and grasp the revolutionary possibilities implicit in the
   emerging order.' He looked to Europe for future innovations in the form of
   liberal society.
2 '[W]hile we communists claim the Great October Revolution as the starting
   point leading to the new world society . . . the socialists of today would find it
   hard to claim and take to themselves the past of social democracy, if they want
   really to be *socialists*' (Carrillo 1977, p. 140).
3 Though the impact on France of its troubles in South-East Asia was, of
   course, dwarfed by the seismic shocks of Algeria, which brought de Gaulle to
   power and the Fourth Republic to an end.
4 Sullivan was US ambassador in Iran at the time of the revolution.
5 Huntington's text, which began life (like Fukuyama 1989, and Johnson 1993)
   in the Washington strategic issues journal *The National Interest*, reads like a
   shrewd adaptation (sad, were it not taken so seriously) of his earlier Cold War
   notions to the *fin-de-siècle* feeling of the post-Cold War, post-Gulf War USA.
   Before, the USA/West could contain the dangers of the transition in modernizing, hence revolution-prone, states by well-judged assistance. Now,

clear-cut 'transition wars' have been replaced by messy 'fault line wars' (1996, pp. 246–98), which merely continue ancient, vicious and fundament-ally irresoluble conflicts between 'civilizations' – defined as totalities founded on culture, religion, ethnicity and even race (p. 42). In this new environment, it appears, the Islamic civilization is globally the most threaten-ing, and the fact that the Gulf War did *not* range Muslims against non-Muslims (and can perfectly well be understood in terms of global power politics) does not prevent Huntington from insisting that there is an 'intercivilizational *quasi* war' (p. 216 – my italics) now going on. Negotiat-ing/imposing truces upon conflicting 'civilizations' to moderate the excesses of the rest – from a position of strength, naturally – emerges as the proper future posture. (See also the critique in Bromley 1997.)

6 Revolutionaries in Latin America key into the global drugs trade by support-ing and 'taxing' peasant cocaine-growing. In 1992 Peru's Sendero Luminoso were reckoned to be making $39 million a year from this source (D. Poole and G. Rénarque,. *Peru: Time of Fear*, London: Latin American Bureau, p. 186 – quoted in Cloonan 1995, p. 18). Conversely, the profits of drugs have also kept local dictators in place, in Mexico (Castells 1997, pp. 283–4) or Panama (e.g. Noriega). It has even fuelled counter-revolution (with Western acquies-cence) in Afghanistan and South-East Asia.

7 This connection is explained in the appendix.

8 A key claim of Fukuyama's argument – that democracies do not go to war against one another – is effectively disputed by Forsythe (1992).

9 Cf. Duprat (1995), for whom democracy has to be the continual *rejection* of any authoritative, single truth.

10 The failure of Nicos Poulantzas's account of fascism was precisely that it did not envisage how ideology could be detached from class (Laclau 1979, ch. 3).

Appendix: Revolutions and the Understanding of History

1 By formulating the question of historical perception in this way, I am will-ingly skirting around the formulation of questions of historical *knowledge* as pursued in the debate that follows in the Anglo-Saxon tradition from the logical positivism of Carl Hempel and others. The question discussed there is how does the form of historical investigation compare with other forms of scientific investigating practice. Some of the parties to that Anglo-Saxon debate (R. G. Collingwood, Michael Oakeshott) do also consider history as a specific form of culture, but the debate's centre of gravity is with knowledge.

2 In this Aron differs from contemporaneous reactions to the same mix of world events, such as that of Karl Popper, whose *The Poverty of Historicism* (1957) inclines to blanket condemnation of total views of history, which are pre-sented as radically unscientific and viscerally drawn to the oppressive pursuit of their overall goals. This is in spite of the anxieties about gullibility and aggressiveness in mass democracy which Aron reveals in, notably, *Les guerres en chaîne* [*The Century of Total War*] of 1951.

3 Written just before Benjamin, on the run from Nazism, committed suicide, the aphoristic text carries an interrelated, political attack on historicism and on the effect of the German Social Democratic Party's overconfident trust in indus-

trial progress on the working class's will to stop fascism. Nonetheless, since its publication, it has been the basis of many reflections on the possible meanings of history: see, e.g., Habermas (1987), pp. 10–15.

4 ... 'l'analyse de ce que le réel contient de virtualités, pour les soumettre à l'épreuve de la réalisation dans la perspective, toujour à redessiner, d'une idée du Bien commun.'

5 Donald Davidson (1980) *Essays on Actions and Intentions* – essays published between 1963 and 1976. My elaboration of the implications of Davidson brings them more into line with the thinking in Callinicos (1987) (considered in ch. 5), which defended the integrity of agents, especially social classes, in the making of history.

6 I argued these points in chapter 5, in the context of revolutionary narratives of historical change.

7 That term is nicely defined in the editor's notes to the second volume (p. 458) as 'an organizing project which transcends material conditions towards an end and inscribes itself, through labour, in inorganic matter as a rearrangement of the practical field and a reunification of means in the light of the end'.

8 Similarly, Sartre's discussion also lays emphasis on the dynamic that is common to both group and individual action (1991, pp. 287ff).

9 Dobson (1993) draws a contrary conclusion from reasoning of this kind on Sartre's part. He concludes that history *is* a single totality for Sartre: 'I have already pointed out how productive it is to read volume two [of the *Critique*] as an investigation into the intelligibility of struggles at increasing levels of complexity. The successful resolution of this investigation inevitably lends weight to the suggestion that History is indeed a seamless web, constituting, as Sartre points out "an intelligible totalisation from which there is no appeal" (vol. 2, p. 817). In this respect no more needs to be said about intelligibility except to underscore the fact that its availability means that human history is not "decomposed into a plurality of individual histories" (p. 16), and that therefore the oneness of History is implied, if not proved, by everything that is said in volume two of the Critique' (p. 109). What Sartre actually intended to conclude is not central to my attempt to explicate in his texts the possibility of a modified philosophy of history. On the other hand, the claims made by Dobson do seem to rely heavily on what Sartre said he wished to achieve in the *Critique*, rather than the evidence of what he actually did achieve.

10 I argued this point, in connection with Skocpol, in chapter 5.

11 Reproduced in the Appendix of volume 2.

References

Abrahamian, E. (1982) *Iran: Between Two Revolutions*, Princeton: Princeton University Press.

Abuza, Z. (1996) 'International Relations Theory and Vietnam', *Contemporary Southeast Asia* 17, no. 4, 406–19.

Ackerman, B. (1992) *The Future of the Liberal Revolution*, Yale: Yale University Press.

Adam, B. (1990) *Time and Social Theory*, Cambridge: Polity.

Ajami, F. (1992) *The Arab Predicament: Arab Political Thought and Practice Since 1967*, Cambridge: Cambridge University Press.

Al-Azmeh, A. (1993) *Islams and Modernities*, London: Verso.

Albrow, M. (1996) *The Global Age: State and Society Beyond Modernity*, Cambridge: Polity.

Aldridge, D. D. (1993) 'A Traveller by His Own Courtesy', paper presented at conference of British Society for Eighteenth Century Studies, Ilkley, Yorkshire.

Alexander, J. C. (1995) *Fin de Siècle Social Theory*, London: Verso.

Anderson, L. (1990) 'Post-materialism from a peasant perspective. Political motivation in Costa Rica and Nicaragua', *Comparative Political Studies* 23, no. 1, 80–113.

Anderson, P. (1974) *Lineages of the Absolutist State*, London: Verso.

Anderson, P. (1992) *A Zone of Engagement*, London: Verso.

Andrieu, J. (1971) *Notes Pour Servir à l'Histoire de la Commune de Paris en 1871*, eds M. Rubel and L. Janover, Paris: Payot.

Anscombe, G. (1957) *Intention*, Oxford: Blackwell.

Arendt, Hannah (1965) *On Revolution*, New York: Viking.

Armstrong, D. (1993) *Revolution and the World Order: The Revolutionary State in International Society*, Oxford: Clarendon.

Aron, R. (1985) 'Three Forms of Historical Intelligibility', in F. Draus (ed.), *History, Truth, Liberty: Selected Writings of Raymond Aron*, Chicago: University of Chicago Press, 37–53.

Arrighi, G. (1994) *The Long Twentieth Century*, London: Verso.

Ascherson, N. (1995) *Black Sea*, London: Jonathan Cape.

Aves, Jonathan (1996) *Workers against :Lenin: Labour Protest against the Bolshevik Dictatorship*, London: Tauris.

Aya, R. (1990) *Rethinking Revolutions and Collective Violence. Studies on Concept, Theory and Method*, Amsterdam: Het Spinhuis.

Aylmer, G. (1987) *Rebellion or Revolution? England 1640–1660*, Oxford: Oxford University Press.

Baechler, J. (1975) *Revolution*, Oxford: Blackwell.

Baker, K. (1990) *Inventing the French Revolution: Essays on French Political Culture in the Eighteenth Century*, Cambridge: Cambridge University Press.

Baron, H. (1955) *The Crisis of the Early Italian Renaissance: Civic Humanism and Republican Liberty in an Age of Classicism and Tyranny*, Princeton, NJ: Princeton University Press.

Baudrillard, J. (1994) *The Illusion of the End*, Chris Turner, tr., Cambridge: Polity.

Bauman, Z. (1992) *Intimations of Postmodernity*, London: Routledge.

Bauman, Z. (1994) 'A Revolution in the Theory of Revolutions?', *International Political Science Review* 15, no. 1, 15–24.

Bello, W. (1994) *Dark Victory: The United States, Structural Adjustment, and Global Poverty*, London: Pluto.

Benjamin, W. (1973) 'Theses on the Philosophy of History', in Hannah Arendt (ed.), *Illuminations*, London: Collins/Fontana, 255–66.

Bercé, Y.-M. (1990) *History of Peasant Revolts: The Social Origins of Rebellion in Early Modern France*, A. Whitmore, tr., Cambridge/Ithaca, NY: Polity/Cornell University Press.

Berman, M. (1983) *All That Is Solid Melts Into Air*, New York/London: Verso.

Bethell, L. (ed.) (1993) *Cuba: A Short History*, Cambridge: Cambridge University Press.

Bhabha, H. (1990) 'Dissemination: time, narrative, and the margins of the modern nation', in *Nation and Narration*, London: Routledge, 291–322.

Bloomfield, J. (1989) *The Soviet Revolution: Perestroika and the Remaking of Socialism*, London: Lawrence and Wishart.

Boudon, Raymond (1986) *Theories of Social Change: A Critical Appraisal*, Cambridge: Polity.

Braudel, F. (1981–4) *Civilization and Capitalism, 15th–18th Century*, Sian Reynolds, tr., New York: Harper & Row.

Braudel, F. (1984) *The Perspective of the World*. Vol. III of *Civilization and Capitalism, 15th–18th Century*, New York/London: Harper & Row/Collins.

Bremmer, I. and Taras, R. (eds) (1993) *Nations and Politics in the Soviet Successor States*, Cambridge: Cambridge University Press.

Brenner, R. (1993) *Merchants and Revolution: Commercial Change, Political Conflict and London's Overseas Traders, 1550–1653*, Cambridge: Cambridge University Press.

Brewer, J. (1989) *The Sinews of Power: War, Money and the English State, 1688–1783*, London: Routledge.

Brinton, Crane (1965) *The Anatomy of Revolution*, 3rd edn, New York: Prentice-Hall.

Broers, M. (1989) 'Revolution and Risorgimento: the Heritage of the French Revolution in 19th Century Italy', in H. Mason and W. Doyle (eds), *The Impact of the French Revolution on European Consciousness*, Gloucester/Wolfeboro, N. Hampshire: Alan Sutton, 81–90.

Bromley, S. (1997) 'Culture Clash', *Radical Philosophy*, no. 85, 2–4.

Brown, D. (1990) 'Sandinisto and the problem of democratic hegemony', *Latin Ameri-*

can Perspectives 17, no. 2, 39–61.

Brown, J. (1991) *Surge to Freedom: The End of Communist Rule in Eastern Europe*, Durham, NC/Twickenham: Duke University Press/Adamantine Press.

Buonarroti, Philippe (1957) *Conspiration pour l'égalité, dite de Babeuf*, ed. G. Lefebvre, Paris: Editions Sociales.

Burke, P. (1992) 'We, the people', in S. Lash and J. Friedman (eds), *Modernity and Identity*, Oxford: Blackwell, 293–308.

Bush, M. (ed.) (1992) *Social Orders and Social Class*, London: Longman.

Calhoun, C. (1982) *The Question of Class Struggle: Social Foundations of Popular Radicalism During the Industrial Revolution*, Oxford: Blackwell.

Callinicos, A. (1987) *Making History*, Cambridge: Polity.

Callinicos, A. (1991) *The Revenge of History: Marxism and Eastern European Revolutions*, Cambridge: Polity.

Callinicos, A. (1994) *Theories and Narratives*, Cambridge: Polity.

Calvert, P. (1996) *Revolutions and International Politics*, London: Pinter.

Camilleri, J. and Falk, J. (1992) *The End of Sovereignty? The Politics of a Shrinking and Fragmenting World*, Aldershot: Edward Elgar.

Canovan, M. (1996) *Nationalism and Political Theory*, Cheltenham: Edward Elgar.

Cardoso, Ferdinando E. and Faletto, C. (1979) *Dependency and Development in Latin America*, Berkeley, CA: University of California Press.

Carrillo, S. (1977) *Eurocommunism and the State*, London: Lawrence and Wishart.

Castañeda, J. G. (1993) *Utopia Unarmed: The Latin American Left After the Cold War*, New York: Alfred A. Knopf.

Castells, M. (1997) *The Power of Identity*. Vol. II of *The Information Age: Economy, Society and Culture*, Cambridge: Polity.

Castells, M. (1998) *End of Millennium*. Vol. III of *The Information Age: Economy, Society and Culture*, Cambridge: Polity.

Caute, D. (1973) *The Fellow-Travellers: A Postscript to the Enlightenment*, London: Weidenfeld and Nicolson.

Chaliand, G. (1977) *Revolution in the Third World: Myths and Prospects*, Hassocks: Harvester.

Chaliand, G. (1990) 'Historical Precedents', in B. M. Schutz and R. O. Slater (eds), *Revolution and Political Change in the Third World*, Boulder, Colorado/London: Lynne Reinner/Adamantine Press, 19–28.

Chan, S. and Williams, A. (eds) (1994) *Renegade States: The Evolution of Revolutionary Foreign Policy*, Manchester: Manchester University Press.

Channon, J. (1992) 'The peasantry in the revolutions of 1917', in E. Frankel, J. Frankel and B. Knei-Paz (eds), *Revolution in Russia: Reassessments of 1917*, Cambridge: Cambridge University Press, 105–30.

Churchill, J. (1995) 'Mayan rebellion? Guatemala and Chiapas', *Small Wars and Insurgencies* 6, no. 3, 357–74.

Clark, J. (1986) *Revolution and Rebellion: State and Society in the Seventeenth and Eighteenth Centuries*, Cambridge: Cambridge University Press.

Cleaver, H. (1994) 'The Chiapas Uprising', *Studies in Political Economy* 44, 141–57.

Cloonan, M. (1995) *Revolution in the Third World? The Case of the Sendero Luminoso (Shining Path)*. York Case Studies for Politics, no. 14, York: Department of Politics, University of York.

Cobban, A. (1974) *The Social Interpretation of the French Revolution*, Oxford: Oxford University Press.

Cockburn, A. (1994) 'A fistful of promises', *New Statesman*, 18 March, 20–2.

Cohen, G. A. (1978) *Karl Marx's Theory of History: a Defence*, Oxford: Clarendon.

Cohn, Norman (1962) *The Pursuit of the Millennium*, London: Heinemann.

Cohn-Bendit, Daniel (1968) *Le Gauchisme: Remède à la Maladie Sénile du Communisme*, Paris: Seuil.

Colburn, F. D. (1994) *The Vogue for Revolution in Poor Countries*, Princeton: Princeton University Press.

Colley, L. (1996) *Britons: Forging the Nation 1707–1837*, London: Vintage.

Comninel, G. C. (1987) *Rethinking the French Revolution: Marxism and the Revisionist Challenge*, London: Verso.

Coser, L. (1956) *The Functions of Social Conflict*, Glencoe, Ill.: Free Press.

Coward, B. (1986) 'Was there an English Revolution in the Middle of the Seventeenth Century?', in C. Jones, M. Newitt, and S. Roberts (eds), *Politics and People in Revolutionary England*, Oxford: Blackwell, 9–39.

Crosland, A. (1956) *The Future of Socialism*, London: Cape.

Csaba, L. (1994) *The Capitalist Revolution in Eastern Europe*, Cheltenham: Edward Elgar.

Davidson, D. (1980) *Essays on Actions and Intentions*, Oxford: Clarendon.

Debray, R. (1967) *Revolution in the Revolution*, Harmondsworth: Penguin.

Debray, R. (1976) *Journal d'un Petit-Bourgeois Entre Deux Feux et Quatre Murs*, Paris: Seuil.

Debray, R. (1977) *A Critique of Arms*, Rosemary Sheed, tr., Harmondsworth: Penguin.

Debray, R. (1981) *Teachers, Writers, Celebrities: The Intellectuals of Modern France*, London: Verso.

Debray, R. (1994) *Charles De Gaulle: Futurist of the Nation*, London: Verso.

DeFronzo, J. (1991) *Revolution and Revolutionary Movements*, Boulder, Colorado/London: Westview.

Dickinson, H. (ed.) (1989) *Britain and the French Revolution 1789–1815*, London: Macmillan.

Ding, X. (1994) *The Decline of Communism in China: Legitimacy Crisis, 1977–1989*, Cambridge: Cambridge University Press.

Dobson, Andrew (1993) *Jean-Paul Sartre and the Politics of Reason: A Theory of History*, Cambridge: Cambridge University Press.

Domergue, L. and Lamoine, G. (1991) *Après 89: La Révolution modèle ou repoussoir*, Toulouse: Presses Universitaire du Mirail.

Dorman, W. and Farhang, M. (1986) 'Reporting Iran the Shah's way', *Journal of Third World Studies* 3, no. 2, 80–94.

Drew, A. (1992) *What Makes Peasants Revolutionary? The Case of South Africa*, occasional paper from Manchester Univ. Dept of Government, Manchester: University of Manchester.

Dunn, J. (1989) *Modern Revolutions: An Introduction to the Analysis of a Political Phenomenon*, 2nd edn, Cambridge: Cambridge University Press.

Dunn, J. (ed.) (1995) *The Contemporary Crisis of the Nation State?* Oxford: Blackwell.

Dunn, J. (1996) 'The heritage and future of the European left', in J. Dunn (ed.), *The History of Political Theory and Other Essays*, Cambridge: Cambridge University Press, 219–28.

Duprat, G. (1995) 'Democracy as a Critique of Politics', in A.-M. Rieu, G. Duprat and N. Parker (eds), *European Democratic Culture*, London: Routledge, 175–205.

East, R. (1992) *Revolutions in Eastern Europe*, London: Pinter.

East, R. and Pontin, J. (1997) *Revolutions and Change in Central and Eastern Europe*, London: Pinter.

El-Affendi, A. (1991) *Who Needs an Islamic State?* London: Grey Seal.

Elster, J. (1989) *The Cement of Society: A Study of the Social Order*, Cambridge: Cambridge University Press.

Emmanuel, A. (1973) 'White Settler Colonialism and the Myth of Investment Capitalism', *New Left Review*, no. 73, 35–57.

Entessar, N. (1984) 'Changing Patterns of Iranian–Arab Relations', *Journal of Social, Political and Economic Studies* 9, no. 3, 341–58.

Feierabend, I. K., Feierabend, R. L. and Gurr, T. R. (eds) (1972) *Anger, Violence and Politics: Theories and Research*, Englewood Cliffs, NJ: Prentice-Hall.

Figes, O. (1996) *A People's Tragedy: The Russian Revolution 1891–1924*, London: Jonathan Cape.

Fish, Steven M. (1995) *Democracy from Scratch: Opposition and Regime in the New Russian Revolution*, Princeton, NJ: Princeton University Press.

Flaherty, P. (1991) 'Perestroika and the Neo-Liberal Project', in R. Miliband and L. Panitch (eds), *Socialist Register 1991*, London: Merlin, 128–68.

Flockton, C. (forthcoming) 'Multi-national Investment on the Periphery of the EU', in N. Parker and B. Armstrong (eds), *Margins in European Integration*, Basingstoke: Macmillan.

Foltz, W. T. (1990) 'Indigenous Factors', in B. M. Schutz and R. O. Slater (eds), *Revolution and Political Change in the Third World*, Boulder, Colorado/London: Lynne Reinner/Adamantine Press, 54–68.

Foran, J. (1992) *Fragile Resistance: Social Transformation in Iran from 1500 to the Revolution*, Boulder, Colorado/Oxford: Westview.

Foran, J. (ed.) (1997) *Theorizing Revolution*, London/New York: Routledge.

Foran, J. and Goodwin, J. (1993) 'Revolutionary outcomes in Iran and Nicaragua: coalition fragmentation, war, and the limits of social transformation', *Theory and Society* 22, no. 2, 209–47.

Forsythe, D. (1992) 'Democracy, war and covert action', *Journal of Peace Research* 29, no. 4, 385–95.

Frankel, E., Frankel, J. and Knei-Paz, B. (1992) *Revolution in Russia: Reassessments of 1917*, Cambridge: Cambridge University Press.

Fukuyama, F. (1989) 'The end of history?', *The National Interest*, no.16, Summer, 3–18.

Fukuyama, F. (1992) *The End of History and the Last Man*, London: Hamish Hamilton/Penguin.

Fukuyama, F. (1995) *Trust: The Social Virtues and the Creation of Prosperity*, London: Hamish Hamilton.

Furet, F. (1981) *Interpreting the French Revolution*, Cambridge: Cambridge University Press.

Furet, F. (1988) *Marx and the French Revolution*, Chicago: Chicago University Press.

Furet, F. (1995) *Le Passé d'un Illusion: Essai sur l'Idée Communiste au XXe Siècle*, Paris: Laffont/Calmann-Lévy.

Furet, F. (1996) *The French Revolution 1770–1814*, Oxford: Blackwell.

Galili, Z. A. (1992) 'Commercial-industrial circles in the revolution: the failure of "industrial progressivism"', in E. Frankel, J. Frankel and B. Knei-Paz (eds), *Revolution in Russia: Reassessments of 1917*, Cambridge: Cambridge University Press, 188–216.

Galtung, Johan (1974) *A Structural Theory of Revolutions*, Rotterdam: Rotterdam University Press.

Garretón, M. A. (1995) 'Transformations sociopolitiques en Amérique: Postautoritarisme, modernité et acteurs sociaux', in F. Dubet and M.Wierviorka (eds), *Penser le Sujet: Autour d'Alain Touraine*, Paris: Fayard, 461–75.

Garton Ash, Timothy (1990) *We The People: The Revolution of '89 Witnessed in Warsaw, Budapest, Berlin & Prague*, Cambridge: Granta.

Gaunt, Peter (1986) 'Law-Making in the First Protectorate Government', in C. Jones, M. Newitt and S. Roberts (eds), *Politics and People in Revolutionary England*, Oxford: Blackwell, 163–86.

Gellner, Ernest (1964) *Thought and Change*, London: Weidenfeld & Nicolson.

Gellner, E. (1991) 'Nationalism and Politics in Eastern Europe', *New Left Review*, no. 189, 127–34.

Gerth, E. and Mills, C. Wright (eds) (1991) *From Max Weber: Essays in Sociology*, London: Routledge.

Ghods, M. R. (1989) *Iran in the Twentieth Century: A Political History*, Boulder, Colorado/London: Lynne Reinner/Adamantine Press.

Giddens, A. (1973) *The Class Structure of the Advanced Societies*, London: Hutchinson.

Giddens, A. (1984) *The Constitution of Society: Outline of a Theory of Structuration*, Cambridge: Polity.

Giddens, A. (1985) *The Nation-State and Violence*. Vol. II of *A Contemporary Critique of Historical Materialism*, London: Macmillan.

Giddens, A. (1990) *The Consequences of Modernity*, Cambridge: Polity.

Giddens, A. (1993) *Modernity and Identity: Self and Society in the Late Modern Age*, Cambridge: Polity.

Giddens, A. and Held, D. (1982) *Classes, Power and Conflict: Classical and Contemporary Debates*, London: Macmillan.

Glenny, M. (1993) *The Revolt of History*, London: Penguin.

Glover, Jonathan (1988) *I: The Philosophy and Psychology of Personal Identity*, London: Penguin.

Godechot, J. (1965) *France and the Atlantic Revolution of the Eighteenth Century, 1770–1799*, New York: Free Press.

Goldstone, J. (ed.) (1986) *Revolutions: Theoretical, Comparative, and Historical Studies*, New York/London: Harcourt Brace Jovanovich.

Goldstone, J. (1991) *Revolution and Rebellion in the Early Modern World*, Berkeley, CA: University of California Press.

Goldstone, J., Gurr, T. and Moshiri, F. (eds) (1991) *Revolutions of the Late Twentieth Century*, Boulder: Westview.

Goldthorpe, J. H. (1996) 'The uses of history in sociology: reflections on some recent tendencies', in M. Bulmer and A. M. Ree (eds), *Citizenship Today: The Contemporary Relevance of T. H. Marshall*, London: UCL Press, 101–23.

Gowan, P. (1995) 'Neo-Liberal Theory and Practice for Eastern Europe', *New Left Review*, no. 213, 3–95.

Gray, J. (1995) *Enlightenment's Wake: Politics and Culture at the Close of the Modern Age*, London: Routledge.

Greene, Thomas H. (1974) *Comparative Revolutionary Movements: Search for Theory and Justice*, Englewood Cliffs, NJ/London: Prentice-Hall.

Gurr, Ted Robert (1970) *Why Men Rebel*, Princeton: Princeton University Press.

Habermas, J. (1987) *The Philosophical Discourse of Modernity*, F. Lawrence, tr., Cambridge: Polity.

Habermas, J. (1990) 'What Does Socialism Mean Today? The Rectifying Revolution and the Need for New Thinking on the Left', *New Left Review*, no. 183,
3–21.

Habermas, J. (1996) 'The European Nation-state – Its Achievements and its Limits.
On the Past and Future of Sovereignty and Citizenship', in G. Balakrishnan (ed.),
Mapping the Nation, London: Verso, 281–94.

Halliday, F. (1988) 'The Iranian Revolution: Uneven Development and Religious
Populism', in F. Halliday and H. Alavi (eds), *State and Ideology in the Middle East
and Pakistan*, London: Macmillan, 31–63.

Halliday, F. (1994) *Rethinking International Relations*, London: Macmillan.

Hamnett, B. R. (1989) 'Spanish Constitutionalism and the Impact of the French Re-
volution, 1808–1814', in H. Mason and W. Doyle (eds), *The Impact of the French
Revolution on European Consciousness*, Gloucester/Wolfeboro, N. Hampshire: Alan
Sutton, 64–80.

Hartnell, H. 'European integration through the kaleidoscope: the view from the Central and Eastern European margins', in N. Parker and B. Armstrong (eds), *Margins
in European Integration*, Basingstoke: MacMillan.

Hawthorn, G. (1991) *Plausible Worlds: Possibility and Understanding in History and
the Social Sciences*, Cambridge: Cambridge University Press.

Haynes, M. (1992) 'State and Market and the "Transition" Crisis in Eastern Europe',
Realism and Human Sciences, St Catherine's College, Oxford.

Hayward, J. (1986) *The State and the Market Economy: Industrial Patriotism and
Economic Intervention in France*, Hemel Hempstead: Harvester.

Hayward, J. (1991) *After the French Revolution: Six Critics of Democracy and
Nationalism*, London: Harvester-Wheatsheaf.

Heale, M. J. (1986) *The American Revolution*, London: Routledge.

Held, D. (1995) *Democracy and the Global Order: From the Modern State to Cosmopolitan Governance*, Cambridge: Polity.

Heller, A. (1993) *A Philosophy of History in Fragments*, Oxford: Blackwell.

Heurlin, B. (1997) *Trends and Structure in the New International System*, DUPI
Working Papers, vol. 1997/20, Copenhagen: Danske Udenrigspolitisk Institut.

Heymann, F. (1955) *John Zizka and the Hussite Revolution*, New York: Russell and
Russell.

Heymann, F. (1965) *George of Bohemia, King of Heretics*, Princeton: Princeton University Press.

Hibben, C. (1983) *Gouda in Revolt: Particularism and Pacifism in the Revolt of the
Netherlands 1572–1588*, Utrecht: H.E.S.

Higgins, A. (1998) 'Long View that leaves the businessman short', *Guardian Weekly*,
week ending 26 April, 14.

Hill, C. (1958) *Puritanism and Revolution*, London: Secker & Warburg.

Hill, C. (1964) *Society and Puritanism in Pre-Revolutionary England*, London: Secker
& Warburg.

Hill, C. (1965) *The Intellectual Origins of the English Revolution*, Oxford: Clarendon.

Hill, C. (1986) 'Political Discourse in Early Seventeenth-Century England', in C. Jones,
M. Newitt and S. Roberts (eds), *Politics and People in Revolutionary England*,
Oxford: Blackwell, 41–64.

Hill, C. (1990) 'The word "revolution"', in C. Hill (ed.), *A Nation of Change and
Novelty*, London: Bookmarks, 100–20.

Hirst, P. and Thompson, G. (1995) *Globalisation in Question: The International
Economy and the Possibilities of Governance*, Cambridge: Polity.

Hobsbawm, E. (1970) 'Guerillas in Latin America', in R. Miliband and J. Saville (eds), *Socialist Register 1970*, London: Merlin, 51–61.

Hobsbawm, E. (1990) *Echoes of the Marseillaise: Two Centuries Look Back on the French Revolution*, London: Verso.

Hobsbawm, E. (1992) *Nations and Nationalism Since 1780*, Cambridge: Cambridge University Press.

Hobsbawm, E. (1994) *Age of Extremes: The Short Twentieth Century, 1914–1991*, London: Michael Joseph.

Hobsbawm, E. (1997) *On History*, London: Weidenfeld & Nicolson.

Hollis, M. (1987) *Cunning of Reason*, Cambridge: Cambridge University Press.

Holmes, L. (1997) *Post-Communism: An Introduction*, Cambridge: Polity.

Holsti, O. and Rosenau, J. (1984) *American Leadership in World Affairs: Vietnam and the Breakdown of Consensus*, Boston/London: Allen and Unwin.

Horvath, Agnes and Arpad, Szakolczai (1992) *The Dissolution of Communist Power*, London: Routledge.

Hroch, M. (1994) *The Social Interpretation of Linguistic Demands in European National Movements*, EUI Working paper No. EUF 94/1, Florence: European University Institute.

Hugill, P. J. (1993) *World Trade Since 1431. Geography, Technology and Capitalism*, Baltimore: Johns Hopkins University Press.

Huntington, S. P. (1968) *Political Order in Changing Societies*, New Haven/London: Yale University Press.

Huntington, S. P. (1996) *The Clash of Civilizations and the Remaking of World Order*, New York: Simon and Schuster.

Ifversen, J. (1996) *Om Magt, Demokrati Og Diskurs. Diskurseret i Lyset Af Den Franske Revolution*, Centre for Cultural Studies Working Papers, Århus: University of Århus.

Ignatieff, M. (1994) *Blood and Belonging*, London: Vintage.

Jaume, L. (1989) *Le Discours Jacobin et la Démocratie*, Paris: Fayard.

Johnson, C. (1964) *Revolution and the Social System*, Stanford, CA: Hoover Institution.

Johnson, C. (1966) *Revolutionary Change*, Boston: Little, Brown.

Johnson, C. (1993) 'Rethinking Asia', *The National Interest*, no. 32, 20–8.

Judt, T. (1986) *Marxism and the French Left: Studies in Labour and Politics in France, 1830–1981*, Oxford: Clarendon.

Kaldor, M. (1993) 'Yugoslavia and the New Nationalism', *New Left Review*, no. 197, 96–112.

Kedourie, E. (1960) *Nationalism*, London: Hutchinson.

Kenworthy, E. (1988) 'Selling Reagan's Nicaraguan Policy in the United States', *Scandinavian Journal of Development Alternatives* 7, no. 2–3, 103–26.

Kettle, M. (1998) 'Right stumps up in face of recession', *Guardian Weekly*, week ending 26 July, 6.

Khilnani, S. (1993) *Arguing Revolution: The Intellectual Left in Postwar France*, New Haven/London: Yale University Press.

Kiernan, V. (1970) 'The Peasant Revolution: some questions', in R. Miliband and J. Saville (eds), *The Socialist Register 1970*, London: Merlin, 9–37.

Kimmel, M. (1988) *Absolutism and Its Discontents: State and Society in Seventeenth-century France and England*, New York/Oxford: Transaction Books.

Kimmel, Michael (1990) *Revolution: A Sociological Interpretation*, Cambridge: Polity.

Koekner, D. and Rosenberg, W. (1992) 'Perceptions and realities of labour protest,

March to October 1917', in E. Frankel, J. Frankel and B. Knei-Baz (eds), *Revolution in Russia: Reassessments of 1917*, Cambridge: Cambridge University Press, 131–56.

Koenigsberger, H. (1971a) 'The States-general of the Netherlands before and during the Revolt', in H. Koenigsberger (ed.), *Estates and Revolutions: Essays in Early Modern European History*, Ithaca, NY: Cornell University Press, 125–43.

Koenigsberger, H. (1971b) 'The organization of revolutionary parties in France and the Netherlands during the sixteenth century', in H. Koenigsberger (ed.), *Estates and Revolutions: Essays in Early Modern European History*, Ithaca, NY: Cornell University Press, 224–53.

Koselleck, R. (1985) *Futures Past: On the Semantics of Historical Time*, K. Tribe, tr., Cambridge, Mass.: MIT Press.

Kotkin, S. (1995) *Magnetic Mountain: Stalinism as a Civilization*, Berkeley, CA: University of California Press.

Krejci, J. (1983) *Great Revolutions Compared: The Search for a Theory*, Brighton: Harvester.

Krueger, K. (1995) 'US military intervention in Third World conflict: the need for integration of total war and LIC doctrine', *Low Intensity Conflict and Law Enforcement* 4, no. 3, 399–428.

Kumar, K. (1971) *Revolution: The Theory and Practice of a European Idea*, London: Weidenfeld and Nicolson.

Kumar, K. (1976) 'Twentieth Century Revolutions in Historical Perspective', in K. Kumar (ed.), *The Rise of Modern Society: Aspects of the Social and Political Development of the West*, Oxford: Blackwell.

Kumar, K. (1986) *Prophecy and Progress*, 2nd edn, Harmondsworth: Penguin.

Kumar, K. (1992) 'The revolutions of 1989: socialism, capitalism and democracy', *Theory and Society* 21, no. 3, 309–56.

Kumar, K. (1996) *From Post-Industrial to Post-Modern Society: New Theories of the Contemporary World*, Oxford: Blackwell.

Laclau, E. (1979) *Politics and Ideology in Marxist Theory: Capitalism, Fascism and Populism*, London: Verso.

Laclau, E. (1990) *New Reflections on The Revolution of Our Time*, London: Verso.

Lane, D. (1996) *The Rise and Fall of State Socialism*, Cambridge: Polity.

Lash, S. (1987) 'Modernity or Modernism? Weber and Contemporary Social Theory', in S. Whimster and S. Lash (eds), *Max Weber, Rationality and Modernity*, London: Allen and Unwin.

Latin American Perspectives (1990) *The Sandinista Legacy: The Construction of Democracy*, vol. 17(3).

Laurell, A. C. (1992) 'Democracy in Mexico: Will the First Be the Last?', *New Left Review*, no. 194, 33–53.

Lebon, G. (1980) *The French Revolution and the Psychology of Revolution*, Robert A. Nye, tr., New Brunswick: Transaction Books; original French edn, Paris 1912.

Lecourt, D. (1997) *L'Avenir Du Progrès: Entretien avec Philippe Petit*, Paris: Les Éditions Textuelles.

Lefebvre, G. (1962) *The Coming of the French Revolution*, London: Routledge and Kegan Paul.

Lefebvre, G. (1973) *The Great Fear*, London: Verso.

Lenin, V. (1902) *What is to Be Done?*; tr. Moscow: Progress Publishers, 1947.

Lenin, V. I. (1918) *State and Revolution*; tr. Moscow: Foreign Languages Publishing Hse, n.d..

Lewis, G. (1993) *The French Revolution: Rethinking the Debate*, London: Routledge.

Lichtheim, G. (1970) *A Short History of Socialism*, London: Weidenfeld and Nicolson.

Lieven, Anatol (1993) *The Baltic Revolution: Estonia, Latvia, Lithuania and the Path to Independence*, London: Yale University Press.

Lipset, S. (1996) *American Exceptionalism: A Double-Edged Sword*, New York: Norton.

Lively, J. (1965) *The Social and Political Thought of Alexis de Tocqueville*, Oxford: Clarendon.

Lovett, G. H. (1965) *Napoleon and the Birth of Modern Spain*, New York: New York University Press.

Lucas, Colin (1973) 'Nobles, Bourgeoisie and the Origins of the French Revolution', *Past and Present*, no. 60, 84–126.

Lukàcs, Georg (1971) *History and Class Consciousness*, London: Merlin.

McCarney, J. (1991) 'The True Realm of Freedom: Marxist Philosophy after Communism', *New Left Review*, no. 189, 19–38.

McCarney, J. (1993) 'Reflections on Fukuyama', *New Left Review*, no. 202, 37–53.

MacKerras, C., Taneja, T. and Young, G. (1994) *China Since 1978: Reform, Modernisation and Socialism with Chinese Characteristics*, Melbourne: Longman Cheshire.

McNamara, R. S. (1995) *In Retrospect: The Tragedy and Lessons of Vietnam*, New York: Random House.

Macpherson, C. (1962) *The Political Theory of Possessive Individualism: Hobbes to Locke*, Oxford: Oxford University Press.

Macpherson, C. (1966) 'Revolutions of the Late Twentieth Century', in C. J. Friedrich (ed.), *Revolutions: Nomos VIII*, New York: Atherton, 139–53.

Magone, J. (1997) *European Portugal: The Difficult Road to Sustainable Democracy*, London: Macmillan.

Maillard, A., Mazauric, C. and Walter, E. (eds) (1994) *Présence Du Babeuf: Lumières, Révolution, Communisme*, Paris: Publications de la Sorbonne.

Manicas, P. T. (1989) *War and Democracy*, Oxford: Blackwell.

Mann, M. (1986) *A History of Power from the Beginning to 1760*. Vol I of *The Sources of Social Power*, Cambridge: Cambridge University Press.

Mann, M. (1995) 'Sources of Variation in Working-Class Movements in Twentieth-Century Europe', *New Left Review*, no. 212, 14–54.

Mann, M. (1996a) 'Nation-states in Europe and Other Continents: Diversifying, Developing, Not Dying', in G. Balakrishnan (ed.), *Mapping the Nation*, London: Verso, 295–316.

Mann, M. (1996b) 'Ruling class strategies and citizenship', in M. Bulmer and A. M. Ree (eds), *Citizenship Today: The Contemporary Relevence of T. H. Marshall*, London: University College Press, 125–44.

Manning, Brian (1991) *The English People and the English Revolution*, 2nd edn, London: Bookmarks.

Manuel, F. (1962) *Prophets of Paris*, Cambridge, Mass.: Harvard University Press.

Mao Zedong (1927) 'Report on an Investigation of the Peasant Movement in Hunan', in *Selected Readings*, Beijing: Foreign Languages Press, 1967, 20–32.

Martinez Torres, M. E. (1996) *Networking Global Civil Society: The Zapatista Movement. the First Informational Guerrilla*, Berkeley, CA: University of California Press (internal research paper).

Mason, D. S. (1992) *Revolution in East-Central Europe: The Rise and Fall of Communism and the Cold War*, Oxford: Westview.

Mason, H. and Doyle, W. (eds) (1989) *The Impact of the French Revolution on European Consciousness*, Gloucester/ Wolfeboro, N. Hampshire: Alan Sutton.

Mason, T. D. (1990) 'Indigenous Factors', in B. M. Schutz and R. O. Slater (eds), *Revolution and Political Change in the Third World*, Boulder, Colorado/London: Lynne Reinner/Adamantine Press, 19–28.

Mazauric, C. (1984) 'Quelques voies nouvelles pour l'histoire politique de la Révolution Française', in C. Mazauric (ed.), *Jacobinisme et Révolution*, Paris: Messidor.

Mbeki, G. (1964) *South Africa: The Peasants' Revolt*, Harmondsworth: Penguin.

Meschonnic, H. (1988) *Modernité Modernité*, Paris: Verdier.

Michelet, J. (1974) *Le Peuple*, ed. P. Viallaneix, Paris: Flammarion.

Mises, L. von. (1947) *Human Action: A Treatise on Economics*, New Haven: Yale University Press.

Molloy, I. (1992) 'The Empire strikes back: the Sandinista defeat in context', *Australian Journal of International Affairs* 46, no. 1, 109–28.

Moore, B. (1967) *The Social Origins of Democracy and Dictatorship*, London: Penguin.

Moore, B. (1978) *Injustice: The Social Bases of Obedience and Revolt*, White Plains, NY: M. E. Sharpe.

Moravcik, A. (1993) 'Introduction', in P. B. Evans, H. Jacobson and R. D. Putnam (eds), *Double-Edged Diplomacy: International Bargaining and Domestic Politics*, Berkeley, CA: University of California Press, 3–42.

Morrill, J. (1976) *The Revolt of the Provinces: Conservatives and Radicals in the English Civil War, 1630–1650*, London: Allen and Unwin.

Mousnier, R. (1970) *Peasant Uprisings in Seventeenth-Century France, Russia and China*, Brian Pearce, tr., New York: Harper & Row.

Nash, J. (1995) 'The reassertion of indigenous identity: Mayan responses to state intervention in Chiapas', *Latin American Research Review* 30, no. 3, 7–41.

Niethammer, L. (1992) *Posthistoire: Has History Come to an End?*, London/New York: Verso.

Nillson, A. (1991) 'Swedish Social Democracy in Central America', *Journal of Interamerican Studies and World Affairs* 33, no. 3, 169–99.

Norval, A. (1996) 'Social Ambiguity and the Crisis of Apartheid', in Ernesto Laclau (ed.), *The Making of Political Identities*, London: Verso, 115–37.

O'Brien, C. C. (1989) 'Nationalism and the French Revolution', in G. Best (ed.), *The Permanent Revolution: The French Revolution and Its Legacy, 1789–1989*, Chicago: Chicago University Press, 17–48.

Oderberg, D. S. (1993) *The Metaphysics of Identity Over Time*, London: St Martin's Press.

Olson, Mancur (1965) *The Logic of Collective Action: Public Goods and the Theory of Groups*, Cambridge, Mass.: Harvard University Press.

Østergård, U. (1990) 'Republican Revolution or Absolutist Reform', session on Reform and Revolution. International Historical Conference, Madrid.

Pagden, A. (1989) 'Old Constitutions and Ancient Indian Empires: Juan Pablo Viscardo and the Languages of Revolution in Spanish America', in L. V. Mannuci (ed.), *The Languages of Revolution*, Milan: Istituto de Studi Storici, 257–71.

Paige, J. M. (1990) 'The social origins of dictatorship, democracy and socialist revolution in Central America', *Journal of Developing Societies*, 6, no. 1, 37–42.

Paige, J. M. (1997) *Coffee and Power: Revolution and the Rise of Democracy in Central America*, Cambridge, Mass.: Harvard University Press.

Palmer, R. (1959) *The Age of Democratic Revolution: Europe and America 1760–1800*, Princeton, NJ: Princeton University Press.

Paquot, T. (1982) 'Présentation: Sorel, retour, détour', in Thierry Paquot (ed.), *Georges*

Sorel: La Décomposition Du Marxisme, Paris: Presses Universitaires de France, 7–35.

Parker, G. (1985) *The Dutch Revolt*, Harmondsworth: Penguin.

Parker, N. (1978) 'Régis Debray in Prison: on Class and Commitment', *Radical Philosophy*, no. 20, 34–41.

Parker, N. (1990) *Portrayals of Revolution: Images, Debates and Patterns of Thought on the French Revolution*, Hemel Hempstead: Harvester.

Parker, N. (1994) 'The World turned right-ways-up: British tv on the Revolutions of 1789 and 1989', *Critical Survey* 6, no. 2, 243–50.

Parry, R. and Kornbluh, P. (1988) 'Iran-contra's untold story', *Foreign Policy*, no. 72, 3–30.

Pataud, E. and Pouget, E. (1990) *How We Shall Bring About the Revolution: Syndicalism and the Co-Operative Commonwealth*, C. Charles and F. Charles, tr., London: Pluto.

Paulson, Ronald (1983) *Representations of Revolution 1792–1820*, New Haven/London: Yale University Press.

Phillips, A. (1995) *The Politics of Presence*, Oxford: Oxford University Press.

Pieterse, J. N. (1990) *Empire and Emancipation: Power and Liberation on a World Scale*, London: Pluto.

Pike, D. (1993) 'Vietnam in 1993: uncertainty closes in', *Asian Survey* 34, no. 1, 64–71.

Pocock, J. G. A. (ed.) (1980) *Three British Revolutions, 1641, 1688, 1776*, Princeton, NJ: Princeton University Press.

Polanyi, K. (1957) *The Great Transformation: The Political and Economic Origins of Our Time*, Boston: Beacon Press.

Pomfret, J. (1998) 'China's Army Told to Give Up Business', *Washington Post* (syndicated to the *Guardian Weekly*, week ending 2 August, 15).

Popkin, Samuel L. (1979) *The Rational Peasant: the Political Economy of Rural Society in Vietnam*, Berkeley/London: University of California Press.

Popper, K. (1957) *The Poverty of Historicism*, 2nd edn, London: Routledge and Kegan Paul.

Pottinger, J. (1989) 'Liberation Theology's critique of capitalism: the argument of Gustavo Gutierrez', *Southeastern Political Review* 17, no. 2, 3–31.

Poulantzas, Nicos (1973) *Political Power and Social Classes*, T. O'Hagan, tr., London: New Left Books.

Poulantzas, Nicos (1978) *State, Power, Socialism*, P. Camiller, tr., London: New Left Books.

Prins, G. (ed.) (1990) *Spring in Winter: The 1989 Revolutions*, Manchester: Manchester University Press.

Read, C. (1986) *Religion, Revolution and the Russian Intelligentsia 1900–1912: The Vekhi Debate and Its Intellectual Background*, London: Macmillan.

Richardson, R. C. (1989) *The Debate on the English Revolution Revisited*, London: Routledge.

Richter, Melvin (1969) 'Tocqueville's Contributions to the Theory of Revolution', in Carl J. Friedrich (ed.), *Nomos VII: Revolution*, New York: Atherton Press.

Ricoeur, Paul (1965) *History and Truth*, C. Kelbley, tr., Evanston Ill.: Northwestern University Press.

Ricoeur, Paul (1984–6) *Time and Narrative*, London/Chicago: Chicago University Press.

Ricoeur, Paul (1994) *Oneself as Another*, K. Blamey, tr., Chicago: University of Chicago Press.

Ricuperati, G. (1989) 'The Changing Image of "The People" in Italian Spaces from the Crisis of the Ancien Régime to the Revolution', in L. V. Mannuci (ed.), *The Languages of Revolution*, Milan: Istituto de Studi Storici, 257–71.

Rigby, B. (1989) 'The French Revolution and English Literary Radicals: the Case of the *Analytical Review*', in H. Mason and W. Doyle (eds), *The Impact of the French Revolution on European Consciousness*, Gloucester/Wolfeboro, N. Hampshire: Alan Sutton, 91–103.

Ritter, J. (1982) *Hegel and the French Revolution: Essays on the 'Philosophy of Right'*, R. D. Winfield, tr., London/Cambridge, MA: MIT Press.

Roberts, M. J. (1996) *Khomeini's Incorporation of the Iranian Military*, McNair Papers, vol. 48, Washington DC: National Defense University.

Roeder, P. G. (1991) 'Soviet Federalism and Ethnic Mobilization', *World Politics*, 43, no. 2, 196–232.

Roemer, J. (1982) *A General Theory of Exploitation and Class*, Cambridge, MA: Harvard University Press.

Rondfeldt, D. (1995) 'The battle for the mind of Mexico', http://www.eco.utexas.edu/homepages/faculty/cleaver/chiapas95/netwars.

Rose, R. (1983) *The Making of the Sans-Culottes: Democratic Ideas and the Institutions of Paris, 1789–92*, Manchester: Manchester University Press.

Rosecrance, R. (1986) *The Rise of the Trading State: Commerce and Conquest in the Modern World*, New York: Basic Books.

Rosenau, J. N. (1988) 'Patterned Chaos in Modern Life: Structure and Process in the Two Worlds of Politics', *International Political Science Review*, 9, no. 4, 327–64.

Rosenberg, J. (1994) *The Empire of Civil Society: A Critique of the Realist Theory of International Relations*, London: Verso.

Rosenstock-Huessy, E. (1993) *Out of Revolution: Autobiography of Western Man*, Providence, RI/Oxford: Berg.

Rubin, B. R. (1995) *The Fragmentation of Afghanistan: State Formation and Collapse in the International System*, New Haven/London: Yale University Press.

Rule, J. B. (1989) *Theories of Civil Violence*, Berkeley: University of California Press.

Russell, B. (1938) *Power: A New Social Analysis*, London: Allen and Unwin.

Russell, C. (1990) *The Causes of the English Civil War*, Oxford: Clarendon.

Ryan, A. (1992) 'Introduction', in *History Today* (ed.), *After the End of History*, London: Collins and Brown, 1–5.

Said, E. (1978) *Orientalism*, New York: Pantheon.

Said, E. (1993) *Culture and Imperialism*, London: Chatto and Windus.

Sampson, R. (1956) *Progress in the Age of Reason*, London: Heinemann.

Samuel, R. (1994) *Theatres of Memory*. Vol.1: *Past and Present in Contemporary Culture*, London: Verso.

Sardar, Z. (1979) *The Future of Muslim Civilization*, London: Croom Helm.

Sartre, J.-P. (1970) 'Masses, Spontaneity, Party', in R. Miliband and J. Saville (eds), *The Socialist Register 1970*, London: Merlin, 233–49.

Sartre, J.-P. (1991) *Critique of Dialectical Reason*. Vol. II: *The Intelligibility of History*, ed. Arlette Elkaïm-Sartre, Quintin Hoare, tr., London: Verso.

Schama, S. (1977) *Patriots and Liberators: Revolution in the Netherlands: 1780–1813*, New York: Random House.

Schama, S. (1987) *The Embarrassment of Riches: An Interpretation of Dutch Culture in the Golden Age*, London: Collins.

Schrag, C. O. (1992) *The Resources of Reason: A Response to the Postmodern Challenge*, Bloomington, Indiana: Indiana University Press.

Schutz, Barry M. and Slater, Robert O. (eds) (1990) *Revolution and Political Change in the Third World*, Boulder, Colorado/London: Lynne Reinner/Adamantine Press.

Scott, James C. (1976) *The Moral Economy of the Peasant: Rebellion and Subsistence in Southeast Asia*, Hew Haven/London: Yale University Press.

Serge, V. (1992) *Year One of the Russian Revolution*, P. Sedgwick, tr., London: Bookmarks.

Service, R. (ed.) (1992) *Society and Politics in the Russian Revolution*, London: Macmillan.

Sewell, W. H. J. (1992) 'Introduction: Narratives and Social Identities', *Social Science History*, 16, no. 3, 479–88.

Shaw, William H. (1978) *Marx's Theory of History*, London: Hutchinson.

Shklar, J. (1976) *Freedom and Independence: A Study of the Political Ideas of Hegel's 'Philosophy of Mind'*, Cambridge: Cambridge University Press.

Skinner, Q. (1978) *The Renaissance*. Vol. 1 of *The Foundations of Modern Political Thought*, Cambridge: Cambridge University Press.

Skocpol, T. (1979) *States and Social Revolution: a comparative analysis of France, Russia and China*, Cambridge: Cambridge University Press.

Skocpol, T. (1994) *Social Revolutions in the Modern World*, Cambridge: Cambridge University Press.

Smith, A. D. (1995) *Nations and Nationalism in a Global Era*, Cambridge: Polity.

Smith, D. (1991) *The Rise of Historical Sociology*, Cambridge: Polity.

Soboul, A. (1974) *The French Revolution 1787–1797*, A. Forrest and C. Jones, tr., London: New Left Books.

Sommerville, J. P. (1986) *Politics and Ideology in England, 1603–1640*, London: Longman.

Sorel, G. (1898) 'La crise du socialisme', in Thierry Paquot (ed.), *Georges Sorel: La Décomposition du Marxisme*, Paris: Presses Universitaires de France, 77–92.

Sorel, G. (1908a) *Réflexions sur la Violence*, Paris: M. Rivière.

Sorel, G. (1908b) 'La Décomposition du Marxisme', in Thierry Paquot (ed.), *Georges Sorel: La Décomposition du Marxisme*, Paris: Presses Universitaires de France, 211–56.

Spence, J. (1996) *God's Chinese Son: The Taipeng Heavenly Kingdom of Hong Xiuquan*, London: HarperCollins.

Sreberny-Mohammadi, A. (1990) 'Small media for a big revolution: Iran', *International Journal of Politics*, 3, no. 3, 341–71.

Starobinski, Jean (1979) *Les Emblèmes de la raison*, Paris: Flammarion.

Steinberg, S. (1966) *The 'Thirty Years War' and the Conflict for European Hegemony 1600–1660*, London: Edward Arnold.

Stirk, P. M. (1997) *A History of European Integration Since 1914*, London: Pinter.

Stites, R. (1989) *Revolutionary Dreams, Utopian Vision and Experimental Life in the Russian Revolution*, Oxford: Oxford University Press.

Stone, Lawrence (1972) *The Causes of the English Revolution*, London: Routledge and Kegan Paul.

Sullivan, W. H. (1980) 'Dateline Iran: the road not taken', *Foreign Policy*, no. 40, 175–86.

Talmon, J. L. (1986) *The Origins of Totalitarian Democracy*, Harmondsworth: Penguin.

Therborn, G. (1995) *European Modernity and Beyond: The Trajectory of European Societies, 1945–2000*, London: Sage.

Thompson, E. P. (1963) *The Making of the English Working Class*, London: Gollancz.
Thompson, E. P. (1971) 'The Moral Economy of the English Crowd in the 18th Century', *Past and Present*, no. 50, 76–136.
Thompson, E. P. (1994) *Customs in Common*, London: Merlin.
Ticktin, H. (1992) *The Origins of the Crisis in the USSR*, London: M. E. Sharpe.
Tilly, C. (1964) *The Vendée: A Sociological Analysis of the Counterrevolution of 1793*, Cambridge, Mass.: Harvard University Press.
Tilly, C. (1978) *From Mobilization to Revolution*, London: Addison-Wesley.
Tilly, C. (1985) 'War making and state making as organized crime', in P. Evans, D. Reuschesmeyer and T. Skocpol (eds), *Bringing the State Back In*, Cambridge, Mass./ Oxford: Blackwell.
Tilly, C. (1986) *The Contentious French*, Cambridge, Mass./London: Belknap.
Tilly, C. (1990) *Coercion, Capital and European States, AD990–1992*, Cambridge, Mass./Oxford: Blackwell.
Tilly, C. (1993) *European Revolutions, 1492–1992*, Oxford: Blackwell.
Tilly, C. (1995) *Popular Contention in Great Britain 1758–1834*, Cambridge, Mass.: Harvard University Press.
Tilly, C., Tilly, L. and Tilly, R. (1975) *The Rebellious Century: 1830–1930*, London: Dent.
Tin, H. (1998) *The Slave, the Native and the Serf: Three Sites of Violence in the South African Ethnic Spaces 1652–1994*, Center for Kulturforskning Arbejderpapirer, vol. 59–98, Århus: University of Århus.
Tiruneh, A. (1993) *The Ethiopian Revolution 1974–87: A Transformation from an Aristocratic to a Totalitarian Autocracy*, Cambridge: Cambridge University Press.
Tocqueville, Alexis de (1856) *L'Ancien régime et la Révolution*, in J. P. Mayer (ed.), *Oeuvres complètes*, Paris: Gallimard, 1953 trans. *The Ancien Régime and the Revolution*, Stuart Gilbert tr. London: Collins (Fontana), 1966.
Tocqueville, Alexis de (1968) *Democracy in America*, eds J. P. Mayer and M. Lerner, London, Collins (first published 1835).
Tønesson, S. (1991) *The Vietnamese Revolution of 1945: Roosevelt, Ho Chi Minh and de Gaulle in a World at War*, London: Sage.
Touraine, A. (1965) *Sociologie de l'Action*, Paris: Seuil.
Trimberger, Ellen Kay (1972) 'A Theory of Elite Revolutions', *Studies in Comparative International Development*, 7, 191–207.
Trimberger, Ellen Kay (1978) *Revolution from Above: Military Bureaucrats and Development in Japan, Turkey, Egypt and Peru*, New Brunswick, NJ: Transaction Books.
Trotsky, Leon (1957a) *The Revolution Betrayed*, New York: Pioneer Publishers.
Trotsky, Leon (1957b) *The Third International after Lenin*, New York: Pioneer Publishers.
Tuck, R. (1993) *Philosophy and Government 1572–1651*, Cambridge: Cambridge University Press.
Urry, J. (1973) *Reference Groups and the Theory of Revolution*, London: Routledge and Kegan Paul.
van Gelderen, M. (1992) *The Political Thought of the Dutch Revolt*, Cambridge: Cambridge University Press.
Vanden, H. and Prevost, G. (1993) *Democracy and Socialism in Nicaragua*, Boulder, Colorado/London: Lynne Reinner.
Vo, V. A. (1990) 'Reform runs aground in Vietnam', *The Journal of Democracy*, 1, no. 3, 81–91.

Waites, B. (ed.) (1995) *Europe and the Wider World*, London: Routledge.

Walker, R. (1993) *Inside/Outside*, Cambridge: Cambridge University Press.

Waller, M. (1993) *The End of the Communist Power Monopoly*, Manchester: Manchester University Press.

Wallerstein, I. (1979) *The Capitalist World Economy*, Cambridge: Cambridge University Press.

Wallerstein, I. (1983) *Historical Capitalism*, London: Verso.

Wallerstein, I. (1984) *The Politics of the World Economy: The States, the Movements and the Civilisations*, Cambridge: Cambridge University Press.

Wallerstein, I. (1991) *Unthinking Social Science: The Limits of Nineteenth-Century Paradigms*, Cambridge: Polity.

Walzer, M. (1966) *The Revolution of the Saints: A Study of the Origins of Radical Politics*, London: Weidenfeld and Nicolson.

Wandycz, P. S. (1992) *The Price of Freedom: A History of East Central Europe from the Middle Ages to the Present*, London: Routledge.

Wang, G. (1993) 'Migration and Its Enemies', in B. Mazlish and R. Buultjens (eds), *Conceptualizing Global History*, Boulder, Colorado/Oxford: Westview, 131–51.

Weber, M. (1995) *The Russian Revolutions*, eds Gordon C. Wells and Peter Baehr, Cambridge: Polity.

Wertheim, W. F. (1974) *Evolution and Revolution: The Rising Waves of Emancipation*, Harmondsworth: Penguin.

Wiener, Antje (1994) 'Institutionalising revolution for reform – Mexican politics from Zapata to the Zapatistas', *Studies in Political Economy*, no. 44, 125–40.

Williams, B. (1996) 'The Impact of the French Revolutionary Tradition on the Propaganda of the Bolshevik Revolution. 1918–1921', paper given at 'Symbols, Myths and Images of the French Revolution' conference held at the University of Regina, Saskatchewan.

Williams, H., Sullivan, D. and Matthews, G. (1997) *Francis Fukuyama and the End of History*, Cardiff: University of Wales Press.

Wolf, Eric R. (1969) *Peasant Wars of the Twentieth Century*, New York/London: Harper and Row.

Wright, E. O. (1978) *Class, Crisis and the State*, London: New Left Books.

Wright, E. O. (1997) *Class Counts: Comparative Studies in Class Analysis*, Cambridge: Cambridge University Press.

Youngs, G. (1996) 'Dangers of Discourse: The Case of Globalization', in E. Kofman and G. Youngs (eds), *Globalization: Theory and Practice*, London: Pinter, 58–71.

Zaslavskaya, T. (1990) *The Second Socialist Revolution: An Alternative Soviet Strategy*, S. M. Davies, tr., London: Tauris.

Zeman, Z. (1991) *The Making and Breaking of Communist Europe*, Cambridge, Mass./Oxford: Blackwell.

Zwerling, P. and Martin, C. (1985) *Nicaragua: A New Kind of Revolution*, Westport, Conn.: Lawrence Hill and Co.

Index